care management series

cms

Diversity and Rights in Care

Spencer-Perkins

www.heinemann.co.uk
✓ Free online support
✓ Useful weblinks
✓ 24 hour online ordering

01865 888058

Heinemann
Inspiring generations

Heinemann Educational Publishers
Halley Court, Jordan Hill, Oxford OX2 8EJ
Part of Harcourt Education

Heinemann is the registered trademark of
Harcourt Education Limited

Text © Neil Moonie, Dee Spencer-Perkins, Anne Bates, 2004

First published 2004

09 08 07 06
10 9 8 7 6 5 4 3 2

British Library Cataloguing in Publication Data is available
from the British Library on request.

10-digit ISBN: 0 435 40126 2
13-digit ISBN: 978 0 435 40126 9

Designed by Lorraine Inglis
Typeset by TechType, Abingdon, Oxon
Original illustrations © Harcourt Education Limited, 2004

Printed in the UK by Bath Press Limited

Cover photo: © Alamy

Acknowledgements
Every effort has been made to contact copyright holders of material reproduced in
this book. Any omissions will be rectified in subsequent printings if notice is given to
the publishers.

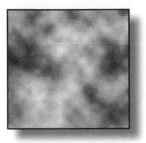

Contents

Preface

Well, it mostly focuses on a self-narrative approach to diversity, identity and human rights.

What?

We believe that we live in an ever-changing world, where a person's identity can no longer be deduced from knowledge of that person's physiology, geographical habitat and circumstances of his or her birth. Identity or self-narrative is a socially negotiated phenomenon that permits a vast range of diverse possibilities. In simple terms, diversity is a critically important but complex issue.

Nowadays, social care is dominated by systems of regulation, measurement and financial constraints. The time available for interaction with service users has almost certainly decreased over the past two decades – but this student book swims against this tide. We believe that social interaction should lie at the heart of care work and is a vital component of human rights.

Naturally, the most important human right is the right to stay alive. But if you stay alive, then your life has to be worth living. If you do not have a viable way of making sense of your life then your life will not mean much to you. We believe that service users have a moral right to develop and/or maintain a sense of personal agency and identity. We argue that a sense of personal agency and identity depends on the ability to formulate and develop a 'self-story'. Services that ignore personal narrative may result in a 're-storying' of the service user in terms of available 'dominant narratives'. This is disempowering. There needs to be an appropriate balance between the need for 'efficiency' and responsiveness to the expression of diversity.

So conversation needs to be about much more than just communicating information. We believe that celebrating diversity should result in service users receiving emotional support in order to control their own story. We would want to promote the idea of a human rights culture that included the right to express diverse self-narratives.

This is not the only story in *Diversity and Rights in Care*. This student book also provides an insight into recent social policy and a review of legal rights. The role of legal knowledge within a narrative approach to practice is explored. There is an overview of ethical theory; an analysis of how language works; an explanation of people in terms of cognitive and emotional functioning; and some philosophy of knowledge. We draw heavily on the emerging field of narrative psychology/therapy.

Some people might look for a simple account that follows a time-honoured format; or perhaps a book with all the answers, maybe defining every category of people and the actions required in order to meet their needs. But the authors of this book do not think it is plausible to reduce diversity to a system of categories. We believe that both people and society are immensely complex. As the old saying goes: 'for every complex problem there is a simple answer – and it's wrong!' Each interaction is unique; care workers have to use skilled judgement in order to work out how best to respond to diverse needs.

Neil Moonie, Dee Spencer-Perkins and Anne Bates

Authors' acknowledgements

We would like to thank the following people who have variously offered time, advice, information and practical or technical support: Sylvia John, Gail Lincoln, Roger Carruthers, Pip Crilley, Alan Finch, Gladys and John Forristal, Liam Forristal, Patricia O'Connor, Walter Reid, Dennis Spencer-Perkins and Joannah Weightman.

Photo acknowledgements

Alamy: pages 74 and 75
Gareth Boden: pages 96, 135, 153, 170 and 213
Corbis: page 39
Photofusion/Ulrike Preuss: page 106
Rex: page 57
SPL: pages 77 and 81

Introduction

National Vocational Qualifications define good care practice in terms of a series of O Units. The O Units are designed to be applicable to all people who work within the health and social care sector. There are different levels of O Unit, ranging from one to three, designed to cover different levels of responsibility. This student book is not designed to be a handbook for supporting the attainment of NVQ qualifications, but is intended to explore some of the key concepts and issues identified by this analysis of good care practice.

O Unit standards

Unit O2 is titled: 'Promote people's equality, diversity and rights' and this unit identifies three Elements of Competence:

- O2.1 Promote people's rights and responsibilities
- O2.2 Promote equality and diversity of people
- O3.3 Promote people's right to the confidentiality of information.

Unit O3 follows a similar structure but is focused on the theme of 'develop, maintain and evaluate systems and structures to promote the rights, responsibilities and diversity of people'.

Diversity

Unit O2.1 performance criteria 1 requires workers to recognise people's right to make their own decisions in the context of their socio-economic and personal lives. Unit O2.2 requires the worker to promote the equality and diversity of people. In order to do this the actions of the worker must be 'consistent with people's expressed beliefs and views and acknowledge the benefits of diversity' (PC 1). The knowledge specification for Unit O2 includes knowledge of 'why the decisions which people make about their lives are complex and the nature of this complexity' (34); 'knowledge of the diverse experiences and perspectives which people bring to any interactions and the benefits of diversity in a multi-cultural society' (36).

The O Units also acknowledge that 'discrimination against people may occur for a wide range of reasons'. These reasons include membership of the groups described in Chapter 1.

Rights

O Unit Standards emphasise the issue of rights, equality and freedom from discrimination. These issues can be argued as being central to the creation of a fair and just society. Human rights, which include equality and freedom from discrimination, are central to care work because carers are working with people who are vulnerable. Care workers are employed in order to protect vulnerable people and to promote their well-being. If care workers fail to work within an established framework of rights, or if they discriminate against certain groups of people, they are not simply behaving unjustly; they would be failing in their core responsibility of a duty of care towards vulnerable people.

The chapters in this book

In terms of practical decision-making the issue of diversity cannot be separated from issues of equality and rights, but within this book we have devoted separate chapters to the issue of diversity because of the complexity we perceive in the issues involved. We argue that on the level of working with individual service users, it would be inappropriate simply to classify people into categories. Chapter 2 explores the social construction of diverse identities and argues that the concept of self-narrative is a useful tool for understanding diversity in care work. This book adopts a model of the person as functioning on both an emotional and a cognitive level. On a cognitive level, language represents a central system for understanding and making life experience meaningful.

Chapters 3 and 4 explore how diversity is expressed through language. We examine cultural and social variations to this expression, and consider how personal narratives vary in their content and telling. We also argue that the telling of narratives is collaborative, and that the social care worker must recognise his or her role in the formation of a personal story. The re-storying of narratives is an inevitable part of human activity, and the practitioner must act responsibly and sensitively in the way a service user's narrative is retold. We also believe that whilst language is central to relationship work within care, it is an under-explored area that has much to contribute to theories of care practice at a more advanced level.

The fifth chapter of this book explores the issue of moral rights and responsibilities. Equality and freedom from discrimination are perceived as central human rights. This chapter explores ethical theory and adopts the view that ultimately ethical codes have to be prescribed. The importance of developing a human rights culture is identified. The sixth and seventh chapters of this book provide an overview of social policy that is relevant to understanding the framework in which care services operate. Legal rights and the duties and responsibilities of care workers are explained with examples of current practice. The link between the individual service user and the implementation of good practice in line with legal and policy requirements is also explored.

Finally, in Chapter 8 we provide an overview of professional development issues associated with self-narrative and other themes in this book. In constructing this chapter we have taken the National Vocational Qualification standards defined in Unit CU 7 as a focus for exploration.

CHAPTER 1

Diverse standpoints

Introduction

This chapter explores a range of categories used to identify diverse groups in society. The concept of social group membership is explored. Statistical data that may identify discrimination and disadvantage is presented, with respect to groups that are identified within NVQ standards as being vulnerable to discrimination.

In this chapter we argue that it is important to gather information on the characteristics of diverse social groups in order to understand the risks of disadvantage and inequality that exist for particular people. It is vital to collect statistical evidence about diverse social groups in order to develop and monitor government policy.

An analysis of the disadvantage and potential risks of discrimination faced by specific groups will not be sufficient to guide care practice. This chapter simply seeks to explore some structural level issues associated with social group membership.

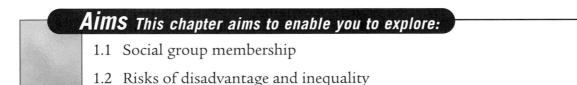

Aims *This chapter aims to enable you to explore:*

1.1   Social group membership

1.2   Risks of disadvantage and inequality

1.1 Social group membership

Try writing any ten things about yourself on a piece of paper. You will probably come up with personal qualities such as caring, friendly, well organised and so on. You may also come up with issues to do with your social identity such as your:

- ethnicity
- gender
- age group
- sexuality
- social class
- religion
- disability
- lifestyle.

One way in which we understand others and ourselves is to identify the social groups that we belong to. Many people identify themselves as having a specific religion, gender, belonging to a specific ethnic and age group. Individuals often think of themselves in terms of work roles and leisure interests. One very important way of understanding diversity is to identify potential beliefs and life experiences associated with different social group membership.

Ethnicity

The National Census in 2001 used the system set out in Table 1.1 in order to identify ethnic group membership.

Table 1.1 Ethnic group membership

ETHNIC GROUP	CATEGORIES INCLUDED	STATISTICS
White	• White • White British • White Irish • Other White background	Statistics can be totalled for all white groups – 92.1% of the United Kingdom population
Mixed	• Mixed White and Black Caribbean • Mixed White and Black African • Mixed White and Asian • Other mixed background	Statistics can be totalled for all mixed groups – 1.2% of the United Kingdom population
Asian or Asian British	• Asian or Asian British • Indian • Pakistani • Bangladeshi • Other Asian background	Statistics can be totalled for all Asian groups – 4% of the United Kingdom population
Black or Black British	• Caribbean • African • Other Black background	Statistics can be totalled for all Black groups – 2% of the United Kingdom population
Chinese or other ethnic group	• Chinese • Other ethnic group	Statistics can be totalled for all Chinese and other groups – 0.8% of the United Kingdom population

Source: National Census 2001

National statistics suggest that there are significant differences in the experience of economic activity, low income and risk of becoming a victim of crime between different ethnic groups.

The 2001 National Census reported that people from minority ethnic groups were more likely than White people to live in low-income households in 2000/2001. Sixty-eight per cent of Pakistani and Bangladeshi respondents were reported as living in low-income households. Forty-nine per cent of Black non-Caribbean households were reported as living on a low income, compared with 21 per cent of White people.

The 2001 National Census reported that 20 per cent of Bangladeshi men were unemployed, compared with 5 per cent of White men (Figure 1.1).

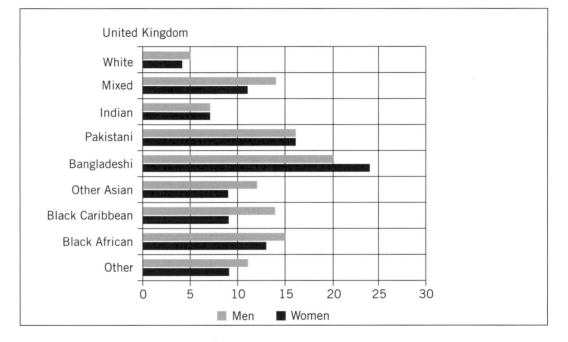

Figure 1.1 Graph to show unemployment rates by ethnic group and sex (per cent)
Source: National Census 2001

Social Trends (2003) reports that more Black and Asian families are likely to have a low income when compared to White families. Table 1.2 shows the proportion of people from different ethnic groups who were in the bottom 20 per cent of the population for the amount of disposable income that they had.

Table 1.2 Families with the lowest 20 per cent of disposable income (per cent)

White	19
Black Caribbean	24
Black non-Caribbean	34
Indian	29
Pakistani/Bangladeshi	64

Source: Social Trends (2003)

Both Black and Asian people are more likely to be victims of crime than White people. The British Crime Survey in 2000 showed that Black and Asian adults in England and Wales were approximately twice as worried as White people about becoming victims of crime. Table 1.3 displays the percentage of people in different ethnic groups who were worried about crime.

Table 1.3 Ethnicity and worry about various crimes (per cent)

CRIME	WHITE	BLACK	ASIAN
Theft of car	20	37	37
Theft from car	15	33	30
Burglary	18	37	41
Mugging	16	32	38
Physical attack	17	35	38
Rape	18	34	34

Source: British Crime Survey (2000)

With respect to racial crime, the 2001 census reports the risk of being a victim of a racially motivated crime as:

- 4.2 per cent for Pakistani and Bangladeshi people
- 3.6 per cent for Indian people
- 2.2 per cent for Black people
- 0.3 per cent for White people.

Classifying people in terms of ethnic group membership enables the gathering of statistical evidence to measure and monitor key issues with respect to equality of opportunity and quality of life. The brief range of statistics presented here provides evidence for the significance of ethnic group membership. It is reasonable to interpret these figures as providing evidence of structural inequalities in the experience of different ethnic groups within the United Kingdom.

Within a care context it will be important to recognise that ethnic group membership may be central to the identity and self-concept of many service users.

Service users may also be at risk of discrimination in terms of the way that services are constructed, as well as the quality of interpersonal behaviour that they may experience. The needs of diverse social groups are likely to be ignored in any system that seeks to 'treat everybody the same'. The term 'colour-blindness' is sometimes used to describe the tendency to ignore ethnic diversity.

Religion

The 2001 National Census analysed religious identity using the categories given in Table 1.4.

Table 1.4 Religious identity in the UK

RELIGION	PERCENTAGE OF THE UNITED KINGDOM POPULATION	RELIGION	PERCENTAGE OF THE UNITED KINGDOM POPULATION
Christian	71.6	Sikh	0.6
Buddhist	0.3	Other religion	0.3
Hindu	1.0	No religion	15.5
Jewish	0.5	Not stated	7.3
Muslim	2.7		

The Department for Trade and Industry (2003) and British Social Attitudes Survey (2001) found that only 2 per cent of the British public believes that employers discriminate against job applicants on the grounds of religion or belief. However, the DTI calculates that 2 per cent could still amount to some 94,000 people who might be vulnerable to discrimination.

The European Union has produced a 'Directive on equal treatment' requiring member states to introduce legislation prohibiting discrimination at work on the grounds of age, sexual orientation, religion and disability. New equality legislation – the Employment Equality (Religion or Belief) Regulations – came into force in December 2003. Details can be found on the DTI website.

Religion may be the single most important aspect of social group membership for some service users. Religion may represent an active set of spiritual beliefs and observances, or a person's religion may simply form part of his or her cultural context. Some service users receive voluntary sector care that is specifically focused on their religious identity. A service that did not acknowledge the diversity of religious belief and associated cultural traditions would be likely to threaten the emotional security of some individuals.

Reflect on practice

National Minimum Standards for Care Homes for Older People, Standard 12.2, states that service users have the opportunity to exercise their choice in relation to:

- leisure and social activities and cultural interests
- food, meals and meal times
- routines of daily living
- personal and social relationships
- religious observance.

Service users' right to have a choice will also be reflected in other national standards.

How far does your own service provide an effective range of choice in relationship to the needs of diverse social groups?

Disability

Social Trends (2001) estimates that there were 6.8 million people of working age with long-term or work-limiting disabilities in the United Kingdom in the spring of 2001. Disabled people were 'much more likely to be economically inactive than non-disabled people'.

The Department of Health quote 157,000 people on the register of blind people in England in March 2003, with 155,000 people on the register of partly sighted people. In March 2001, 50,282 people were registered deaf, with 194,840 people registered as deaf or hard of hearing in England.

A Department of Health survey for England in 2001 found that 18 per cent of people over the age of 16 reported having at least one of the five types of disability used within the survey; 5 per cent of those surveyed reported a serious disability. Table 1.5 shows the classification of disability used within the survey and the numbers of men and women reporting each type.

Table 1.5 Classification of disability and numbers of men and women in each category (per cent)

TYPE OF DISABILITY	MEN	WOMEN
Locomotor disability	12	14
Personal care disability	6	7
Hearing disability	6	4
Sight disability	2	3
Communication disability	1	1

Source: Department of Health Survey for England in 2001

The survey found that 'just over half (55 per cent) of men and women with any disability had one disability, one third had two disabilities and about one tenth had three or more disabilities'. There was also 'a steady increase with age in the prevalence of multiple disabilities'. 'The most commonly occurring combination of disabilities were locomotor with personal care disability.' It may be that severe locomotor disability (the inability to move from place to place) impacts on the ability to perform personal care tasks.

As a generalisation, disabled people may be less exposed to direct prejudice or the risk of being treated as 'the same as everyone else' – compared to ethnic and religious minorities. One of the issues often identified by self-advocacy groups revolves around the 'impairment narrative'; this involves the perception of an individual person as being a defective being. A person's own view of him or herself may be turned into a story of how he or she fails to cope with leading a 'normal' life. Discriminatory behaviour may sometimes be founded on the assumption that people with disabilities are not 'normal' but that they should be made to become 'as normal as possible'. Chapter 2 argues that there can be no general standard of normality across the many diverse social and cultural groups that exist within the UK. Service users need to be in control of their own story if they are to be free of discriminatory assumptions.

Health status

As with disability, health status and mental health status may provide a focus for discriminatory assumptions. A person who is HIV positive, for example, may be associated with a storyline of being at risk. A stereotyped perception of disease may be used to construct a story of the individual as a threat to others who must therefore be excluded. Discrimination may sometimes be founded on storylines or narratives that people are familiar with. People's assumptions may be difficult to challenge with objective information, if that information is inconsistent with pre-existing theories about health, mental illness and disease.

Gender

It was only in 1928 that women were granted equal rights with men to vote in elections. Eighty years ago women were considered to have a lower social status than men. UK society largely adopted the storyline that women should look after children, do housework, cook and generally tidy and do light jobs. Men did the more valuable administrative, management and labouring jobs.

Great changes have come about in the nature of work and the nature of family life since 1928. Women are now generally seen as having equal opportunities in education and employment. The Sex Discrimination Act of 1975 made it illegal to discriminate against women in education and employment.

However, the Government's Women's Unit (2003) reports that 'women who work full-time are paid on average just 81 per cent of men's hourly earnings'. In January 2004 the Equal Opportunities Commission published a paper entitled 'Sex and power: who runs Britain?'. This paper contains a range of statistics with respect to senior appointments. Figure 1.2 illustrates the number of women working in senior posts as a percentage of the total across a range of occupations.

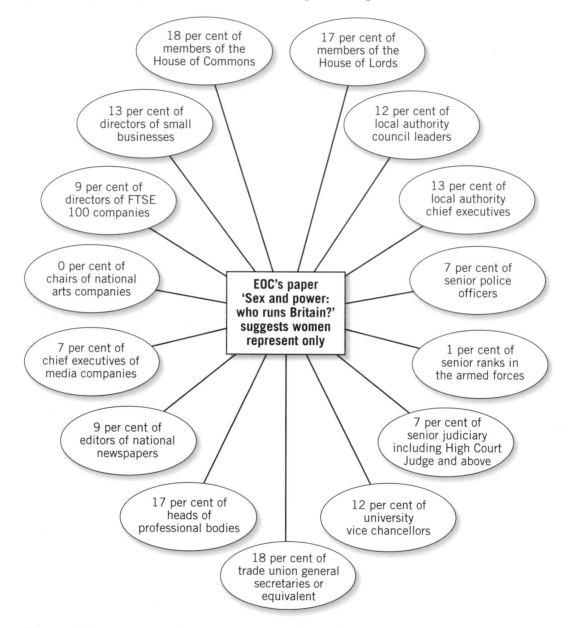

Figure 1.2 Percentage of women employed in senior posts
Source: Equal Opportunities Commission (2004)

In a press release on the paper, Julie Mellor, the chair of the Equal Opportunities Commission, stated 'Almost 30 years since the Sex Discrimination Act was passed, women are still massively under-represented in positions of influence in Britain. No one can argue anymore that it's just a matter of time until more women make it to the top'. 'Women are still often prevented from getting to the top because they take on more caring responsibilities than men. Until every organisation accepts that they can't capitalise on the talent available without taking account of people's caring roles the profile of the people who run Britain will not change.'

There is compelling evidence of structural inequality that results in disadvantage for women. Women still hold fewer top jobs and seem to profit less from promotion. Women far outnumber men in jobs like nursing and primary school teaching. Often these jobs are not highly paid. Men often get the more highly paid jobs such as head teachers, even within areas of work mainly dominated by women. When it comes to domestic work, men still seem to do generally less childcare, washing and cooking duties, although they may do more gardening and maintenance jobs.

Table 1.6 is taken from Social Trends (1997). In general, it would appear that men and women still make assumptions about who should do what within the household.

Table 1.6 Time spent on household tasks during one week

HOUSEHOLD TASK	HOURS AND MINUTES PER WEEK	
	FATHERS	MOTHERS
Cooking/preparing meals	2.50	13.30
Cleaning	2.00	13.15
Washing and ironing clothes	0.55	9.05
Spending time with the children	5.05	8.45
Shopping	2.50	5.50
Washing up	2.00	3.40
Driving children to school	1.45	2.55
Gardening	3.00	2.00
Sewing/mending clothes	0.10	1.20
Other household tasks	2.25	1.40
All household tasks	23.00	62.00

Source: Social Trends (1997)

The lived experience of women is likely to be very different from that of men. It is important to continue to identify the risks of discrimination on a structural and individual level associated with gender roles.

Relationship status and responsibility for dependants

NVQ standards identify relationship status, family role and responsibility for dependants as an area in which discrimination may occur. Once again, the idea that there is one 'normal' or 'right way' to live can provide a basis for assumptions, and for interpreting diversity as deviance from a norm. A snapshot of household composition taken from Social Trends (2004) provides an outline of some of the changes that have taken place over the last 30 years (see Table 1.7).

Table 1.7 Snapshot of household composition in 1971 and 2003 (per cent)

	1971	2003
One person under State pension age	6	15
One person over State pension age	12	14
Two or more unrelated adults	4	8
One family households: no children	27	28
One family households: 1–2 dependent children	26	18
One family households: 3 or more dependent children	9	4
One family households: non-dependent children only	8	6
Lone parent households with dependent children	3	5
Lone parent households non-dependent children only	4	3
Multi-family households	1	1

Source: Social Trends (2004)

Norms have changed. The table above shows a dramatic increase in the number of younger people who live alone and who share their household with other unrelated adults. At the same time, there is a noticeable decline in the number of people living in a 'nuclear family' of two parents and children. Whatever is perceived as normal, it is important to recognise the risks of assumptions such as people with dependants may be either 'more' or 'less reliable' than people in other family situations. Homelessness may represent another facet of diversity with respect to household lifestyle.

A Shelter Fact Sheet (2003) states, 'of those households that approached local authorities in 2002/03, 201,060 households were found to be homeless. Local authorities have a duty to re-house nearly 130,000 of those households who were deemed to be in priority need and unintentionally homeless.' 'Shelter estimates that over 100,000 children lived in households accepted as homeless during 2002/03.'

There may always be the risk of feeling comfortable with people who have led a similar lifestyle, and feeling uncomfortable with people who have different life experiences.

Class

Since the 2001 census, a new system for classifying social class has been used in all official statistics and surveys. This system uses eight classes to classify occupations and is called the National Statistics Socio-economic Classification. The whole system is very complex and can be viewed at www.statistics.gov.uk. The eight 'analytic classes' used in the system are set out in Table 1.8.

Table 1.8 The National Statistics Socio-economic Classification – analytic classes

1	Higher managerial and professional occupations. This class is split into: **1.1** Large employers and higher managerial occupations **1.2** Higher professional occupations
2	Lower managerial and professional occupations
3	Intermediate occupations
4	Small employers and own account workers
5	Lower supervisory and technical occupations
6	Semi-routine occupations
7	Routine occupations
8	Never worked and long-term unemployed

1.2 Risks of disadvantage and inequality

A person's occupation may have a major impact on the expectations and assumptions that he or she may make about him or herself and his or her economic opportunities. Self-employed people may make different demands on themselves from individuals who report to a 'boss'. There is evidence (Argyle, 1993) that people in professional roles often experience their work as more enjoyable and more productive of self-esteem than people who work in routine occupations.

Whilst the analytic classes of the socio-economic classification system above do not simply reflect income levels, people who work in routine occupations are generally less well paid than people in the higher classes. General income level is likely to be a major factor in influencing a person's expectations and assumptions about life.

Just under one fifth of Britain's population (18 per cent) were considered to be living on a low income in 2000 (Social Trends, 2002). People who receive less than 60 per cent of the income that an average person expects may be considered to be at risk of poverty and 'social exclusion'.

Key groups of people who have to live on very little money include:

- one-parent families
- people who are unemployed
- elderly people
- people who are sick or disabled
- single earners
- unskilled couples (where only one person works in an unskilled job).

In 2001 an estimated 10.7 million people (18 per cent of the population) in Britain lived on/or below the 60 per cent of average earnings poverty line; in 1979 only 4.4 million people were estimated to live in poverty. The number of people who may be considered to be poor increased dramatically between 1985 and the early 1990s. The proportion of people with low income (18 per cent of the population) has remained the same for the last few years.

People on low income may have enough money for food, for some clothes and for heating, but poverty means that there is little money for the interesting purchases that buy into exciting lifestyles. People who depend on benefits have limited life choices.

The latest clothes, nice cars, latest electronic equipment, digital TV and so on, may not be choices for people on low income. People with little money have to restrict what they can buy when they visit a supermarket or shopping centre.

Many lifestyles are not possible for people in poverty. Belonging to a sports club is not possible if you can't afford the membership fees, the equipment and so on. Even jogging isn't possible if you feel your neighbourhood isn't safe to go out in.

The Government's 'Opportunity for all' (1999) publication makes the following statements.

- People living in households with low incomes have more than doubled since the late 1970s.
- One in three children live in households with below half the average income.
- Nearly one in five working-age households have no one in work.
- The poorest communities have much more unemployment, poor housing, vandalism and crime than richer areas.

The problems that prevent people from making the most of their lives include the following characteristics.

- **Lack of opportunities to work** – work is the most important route out of low income by the current government. But the consequences of being unemployed go wider than lack of money. It can contribute to ill health and can deny future employment opportunities.
- **Lack of opportunities to acquire education and skills** – adults without basic skills are much more likely to spend long periods out of work.
- **Childhood deprivation** – with its linked problems of low income, poor health, poor housing and unsafe environments.
- **Disrupted families** – the evidence shows that children in lone-parent families are particularly likely to suffer the effects of persistently low household incomes. Stresses within families can lead to exclusion: in extreme cases to homelessness.
- **Barriers to older people living active, fulfilling and healthy lives** – too many older people have low incomes, lack of independence and poor health. Lack of access to good-quality services is a key barrier to social inclusion.
- **Inequalities in health** – health can be affected by low income and a range of socio-economic factors, such as access to good-quality health services and shops selling good-quality food at affordable prices.

- **Poor housing** – directly diminishes people's quality of life and leads to a range of physical and mental health problems, and can cause difficulties for children trying to do homework.
- **Poor neighbourhoods** – the most deprived areas suffer from a combination of poor housing, high rates of crime, unemployment, poor health and family disruption.
- **Fear of crime** – crime and fear of crime can effectively exclude people within their own communities, especially older people.
- **Disadvantaged groups** – some people experience disadvantage or discrimination, for example, on the grounds of age, ethnicity, gender or disability. This makes them particularly vulnerable to social exclusion.

Source: 'Opportunity for all' (1999)

Reflect on practice

Reflecting on the problems listed above suggests that living on a low income might lead to a whole range of other problems that are not specifically about cash flow or debt. For example, if you have a low income, you might live in a poor neighbourhood; if you live in a poor neighbourhood, you may experience more fear of crime. Disadvantage and an unsatisfactory quality of life will involve interaction between a range of factors.

Assumptions based on class and lifestyle provide an obvious basis for discrimination. One storyline associates victims of disadvantage with the idea that some moral or biological defect must be responsible for their situation. Blaming the victim provides an effective emotional defence in a world of structural inequalities.

In your own experience, how far can you identify interactions between various sources of disadvantage? Can you think of an instance where the complexity of all this has created an emotion that could be summarised as 'These people are just bad people'?

Caste

Diversity in terms of caste is in issue identified within the NVQ standards. The term caste implies a rigid social division between social classes. People are born into a caste and their social status is not open to review. Within a class system your status can change if you can manage to change your type of employment – there is 'mobility' between class groups. Like social class, a person's caste might become a basis for discrimination.

Diversity in lifestyle and geographical location

People who feel confident about their future income and finances can choose their lifestyle. They can also choose where they would like to live. People in the higher social classes tend to live in more expensive housing areas, with good facilities for travel and education. People with lower incomes tend to live in housing areas that are more densely occupied. People on lower incomes are often forced to rent rather than buy their homes.

Different social class groups often live in different neighbourhoods. Marketing companies often use post codes to work out which adverts to send to different areas.

There can be disadvantages to living in poor quality or high-density housing. These can include noise, pollution, overcrowding, access to shops and other facilities, and stress from petty crime. When people receive a low income, household maintenance can become a problem. Poorly maintained housing can create health hazards. If you live on a low income in a crowded block of flats or high-density housing, you may experience:

- noise from neighbours
- difficulties in maintaining an appropriate sleep pattern
- disputes with neighbours
- pollution from traffic on busy roads near to housing
- overcrowded accommodation
- more crime or fear of crime including burglary, car crime and personal assault
- increased difficulty with car parking and travel
- emotional stress resulting from the above problems.

Low income and poor housing are a source of stress to many people. Table 1.9 lists the percentages of householders who said they had problems with the issues listed in the left-hand column. In general people who have money appear to experience fewer problems when compared with people who live in low-income areas. Living in the suburbs or in the country may also cause less stress than living 'in town'.

Table 1.9 Problems with geographical locations (per cent)

	PEOPLE IN WEALTHY SUBURBAN OR RURAL AREAS	PEOPLE IN COUNCIL OR LOW INCOME AREAS	PEOPLE IN WEALTHY URBAN AREAS	PERCENTAGES IN GENERAL
Crime	49	66	59	56
Litter and rubbish	26	58	49	42
Vandalism and hooliganism	25	58	42	40
Dogs	22	37	25	29
Noise	16	31	35	23
Graffiti	11	36	32	22
Neighbours	7	18	17	13
Racial harassment	1	8	9	4

Adapted from Social Trends (2002)

Geographical communities can provide a powerful base for the construction of individual identity. Many people understand themselves in the context of social relationships with neighbours and community groups. Many individuals can experience unease when meeting with people from different community groups. Like all perceived differences, locality may provide a basis for assumptions.

Offending background

NVQ standards identify offending background as a focus for discrimination. As with health status, it is possible to be influenced by storylines. In the case of offending background storylines, these may include explanations of crime as resulting from a biological basis, a basis that cannot be altered. Whilst it is important to protect vulnerable children and adults from individuals who might reasonably be assessed as presenting a risk, it is also important to arrive at appropriate decisions that are not derived from stereotypes.

Political beliefs

NVQ standards identify political beliefs as an area of diversity and potential discrimination. It is a central assumption of democracy that individuals should be 'free' to argue and support diverse political policies and viewpoints. The right to freedom of expression formed part of the European Convention on Human Rights and is now part of the Human Rights Act 1998. The right to maintain a political viewpoint has to be balanced with responsibilities towards others. A human rights perspective would grant individuals the right to argue for humanistic ethical interpretations, and the right to argue for radical approaches to the redistribution of wealth. Political viewpoints may not embrace criminal acts such as advocating 'hate crimes' against diverse groups. Political viewpoints might include a vast range of different standpoints on geopolitical, economic and social issues. There must always be the risk of assuming that there can be only one truth and that by happy chance our own beliefs happen to represent that truth. People who adopt different views must, therefore, be morally or intellectually deficient – see the theory on worldviews in Chapter 2.

Reflect on practice

Freedom to express political views is a human right

continued

A human rights culture has to ensure that people are not discriminated against because of political beliefs. A workplace culture that adopted a unitary political belief system might violate this principle. For example, the belief that 'you can't be a social worker unless you are a socialist', 'or you can't work in a private home unless you are committed to free-market enterprise' could create a workplace culture that would be likely to discriminate against members of specific political communities.

If staff in your own work setting held different political viewpoints, where might the boundaries be drawn between the freedom to hold your own viewpoint and the risks of creating a discriminatory culture through an over-emphasis on a specific standpoint?

Age

More than 40 per cent of the adult population are over 50 years of age, according to Age Positive (2004). In 1900 the average life expectancy of a newborn boy was 55; the average life expectancy of a newborn girl was 57. In 2003, a newly born boy might expect to live to 76 and a girl to 81. It is frequently argued that current social institutions such as compulsory retirement are based on outdated assumptions about the health and ability of older people.

According to Age Positive (2004) 69 per cent of people between age 50 and State pension age are in employment. Older workers are more likely to work part-time or to be self-employed. The European Union is concerned that older workers may face discrimination and has produced a directive that requires member states to implement legislation to prevent discrimination against older people in the field of training and employment. The current government has declared an intention to introduce legislation to prevent discrimination against older workers by 2006.

Discriminatory assumptions about older people are not restricted to employment. The 'Ageing as decline' – 'What do you expect at your age?' – narrative represents a way of explaining neglect and exclusion of older people. Discriminatory attitudes towards older people are often perceived as deriving from a stereotype of ageing.

Sexuality

In the past, lesbian, gay and bisexual people have not had access to the same property and pension rights associated with marriage that the heterosexual community has enjoyed. In the past, there have been assumptions that lesbian, gay or bisexual relationships were deviant and something that the State should suppress.

Currently the Department for Trade and Industry in its study of the 'Regulatory Impact Assessment for Sexual Orientation' estimates that between 5 and 7 per cent of the UK population may benefit from new anti-discriminatory legislation, to be implemented in accordance with the European Directive. The DTI assumes that about 20 per cent of lesbian and gay and bisexual employees have suffered discrimination at work. In addition, other employees may be afraid to disclose their sexual orientation because of fear of discrimination. New equality legislation – the Employment Equality (Sexual Orientation) Regulations – came into force in December 2003. Details can be found at the DTI website.

Homophobic storylines interpret gay and lesbian relationships as deviant from the norm and usually as being a 'defective' form of sexuality. Damaging and discriminatory clinical practices in the not-too-distant past have focused on attempting to change gay men's sexuality to 'normal heterosexual' sexual practice and identity. A human rights approach provides a basis for going beyond the idea of one 'normal' lifestyle.

Culture

The culture of an individual may incorporate a range of other standpoints such as the person's ethnicity, social class, religion, sexuality and local geographic community. A way of perceiving the influences of culture on the individual is set out in Chapter 2. Culture may be perceived as an area where diverse influences interact. Diverse cultures may maintain a range of different assumptions, expectations, beliefs and attitudes about daily living and what is desirable in life.

The term culture can also be used to describe the assumptions and expectations that surround people in a specific group context such as a work setting. Care managers may perceive themselves to have a leadership role involving the establishment of a 'human rights culture' within the service that they manage.

Reflect on practice

How far can knowledge of diverse social groups and the risks of discrimination and disadvantage that they face be sufficient to establish a 'human rights culture'? What else is needed?

Summary

- ○ There are a number of categories that are used to classify diverse groups of people. There are a number of categories such as, for example, ethnic group membership, gender, sexuality and religion that are used in order to classify diverse groups of people.
- ○ Where people identify with a specific social group, we refer to this identification as social group membership.
- ○ Social group membership can be a focus for disadvantage and discrimination.
- ○ A classification of social groups is necessary for the development and monitoring of social policy.

CHAPTER 2

Diversity as narrative

Introduction

This chapter argues that diversity cannot be reduced to the collection of factual information about different communities. When working with individual people it may be important to understand how each person has built up his or her understanding of self.

This chapter introduces a theory of 'self-narrative'. Self-narrative provides a way of understanding diversity at an individual level.

One hundred years ago most people lived in a world of straightforward 'common-sense truths' about social class, gender role, ethnic group membership, the significance of age, and so on. This chapter does not say 'things have changed and now there is a new truth!' It argues that we live in a new 'post-modernist' era, with a whole new way of thinking. Social and economic principles are fluid and ever changing – there are few common-sense certainties that we can cling to. We do not have a simple set of correct beliefs (i.e., new stereotypes) to substitute for the old stereotypes! The story in this chapter is much more scary. The story is that we live in a world of infinite possibilities and multiple 'knowledge communities' – diversity that cannot be classified into neat little tick boxes.

This chapter presents a social-constructivist model of the way in which meaning is processed in people. This model represents a synthesis of some recent theory about the nature of self. An understanding of this theory is not

Aims *This chapter aims to enable you to explore:*

2.1   Theory of self-narrative

2.2   Three worldviews

2.3   The concept of self

2.4   The importance of self-narrative

vital for understanding diversity, but we have chosen to provide a context for narrative theory.

We argue that each person needs a self-narrative in order to maintain a sense of individuality, purpose and control in his or her life. However, a person is more than his or her self-narrative. People have an emotional and symbolic level of functioning as well as an intellectual level. We present a theory of self in order to provide an appropriate context for interpreting the significance of self-narrative.

This chapter presents a theory of diverse assumptions about knowledge – 'worldviews'. It explores the idea of dominant narratives that exist within culture and that may result in oppression. Many service users and care workers may lack a coherent sense of identity. The significance of self-narrative and identity is explored and the critical importance of conversational work and listening skills is advocated.

2.1 Theory of self-narrative

The significance of narrative theory is that it explains the relevance of listening and conversation skills for the maintenance of fundamental human rights. The right to develop and maintain a personal identity has to be central to the establishment and maintenance of a human rights culture. Communication in care is not significant because there is a need for information to be transmitted between people. Communication in care is central to respect for persons. The maintenance of individual dignity, the ability to exercise choice and emotional safety, depend, at least in part, on the development and/or maintenance of a viable self-narrative.

Individuals, social groups and diversity

Gathering information on social group characteristics is vital in order to understand the risks of disadvantage and inequality that exist for particular groups of people. Many people would argue that the government has a moral and elected responsibility to develop economic and social policies aimed at preventing disadvantage and inequality. The government-sponsored report 'Opportunity for All' (1999) states 'Our aim is to end the injustice which holds people back and prevents them from making the most of themselves'. The goal of government policy is 'that everyone should have the opportunity to achieve his or her potential. But too many people are denied that opportunity. It is wrong and economically inefficient to waste the talents of even one single person'.

People may experience discrimination because of their membership of a specific social group. Understanding people in terms of their social group membership is necessary in order to understand how discrimination works within social and economic contexts. Many people construct a sense of self that is built on their social identity and where issues such as religion or ethnicity are absolutely central to their understanding of who they are. At the very least, social group membership is likely to provide a standpoint that an individual might use in order to narrate an understanding of himself or herself.

It is possible to understand diversity simply in terms of identifying social group membership. When exploring issues of social justice at a structural or government policy level, it might not be appropriate to explore the lived experience of specific individual people. A statistical analysis and categorisation of people is vital for formulating social policy. But when working face to face with real people, we argue that the concept of diversity needs to be understood in terms of individual experience and not solely in terms of the classification systems useful for statistical analysis.

A model for interpreting diversity

The model we propose for understanding the diversity of people is set out on page 21. We believe that each person develops an interpretation of his or her life within a social and cultural context. Individuals are specifically influenced by the assumptions and conventions involved in the speech and language systems that they are exposed to. However, we do not believe that an individual person's identity is somehow given to that individual by his or her culture, or by the language that a person uses. The way in which we interpret human diversity is based on the perspective of social constructivism. Our explanation of individual identity includes the idea that each person actively interprets and builds his or her own idea of who he or she is using culturally available ideas. Culture and social context provide the building materials from which an individual creates his or her own theory of a 'self'.

We argue that when working face to face with another person, respecting and understanding diversity must involve a successful interpretation of that individual's identity or sense of self. We believe that understanding diversity is necessary in order to work closely with a service user. We believe that understanding diversity is more complex than simply locating an individual person within a social group membership category.

Our model or interpretation of individuality can be expressed dramatically as shown in Figures 2.1, 2.2 and 2.3.

Each person develops a sense of who he or she is within a cultural context and within a framework of meaning provided by our language system.

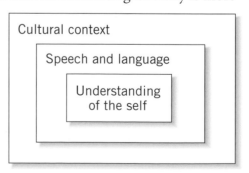

Figure 2.1 The major systems involved in the creation of human diversity

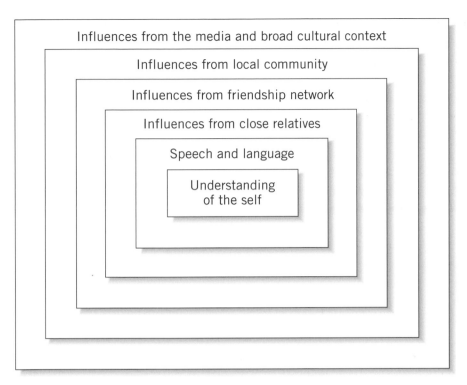

Figure 2.2 The cultural context

The cultural context in which a person's sense of him or herself develops is always relative to a given individual. Individuals will experience the assumptions of other people in a given geographical location, or perhaps in a diverse range of geographical locations. Influences can be construed as originating from different layers of intimacy. The most external level of influence, i.e., that of the media and broad culture, can itself be understood as existing within a historical context.

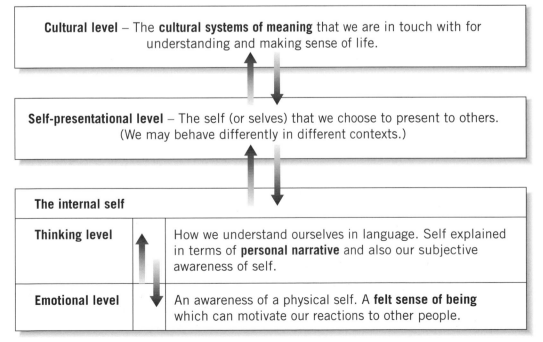

Figure 2.3 Systems involved in the self

Our understanding of what it is to be a person involves more than an individual's cognitive or thinking ability. Following a model proposed by Greenberg and Pascual-Leone (2001), we suggest that it is important to include the idea that each person works on an emotional level as well as an intellectual level. People have a 'felt sense of being' as well as a sense of self that can be represented in linguistic form.

Social constructivism

The view that people actively develop their own idea of identity and self is associated with the social constructivist perspective. Constructivism is a perspective that emphasises the role of the individual in building, or constructing, his or her own interpretation of what is real and what it is to be a person. Social constructivism emphasises the importance of culture and social context in influencing what an individual can build. Social constructivism is sometimes distinguished from cognitive constructivism. Cognitive constructivism emphasises the thought processes involved in building an interpretation of reality, but places less emphasis on the importance of social context.

Our model of diversity takes the view that people are almost infinitely complex and diverse. Not only is human nature immensely complex, but also it is continually open to change. Individual identity is a story that is constantly being adapted and developed by the individual. People are not mechanisms, which technicians may seek to adjust, nor should we try to understand people as simply being members of a social group. Personal identity cannot be reduced to family history, ethnic identity, social-class group identity, or age-group identity – unless an individual chooses to construct his or her sense of who he or she is in terms of a single category. Each person will actively build a 'self-story' using both personal experience and culturally available storylines.

People will explain themselves by referring to culturally available stories. Freedman and Combs (1996: 16) state ' societies construct the "lenses" through which their members interpret the world. The realities that each of us takes for granted are the realities that our societies have surrounded us with since birth. These realities provide the beliefs, practices, words, and experiences from which we make up our lives.'

The way an individual service user understands his or her own needs can only be understood by getting to know that person and learning about his or her construction of self. Reducing diversity to a study of social group membership will only provide limited understanding of lived experience.

2.2 Three worldviews

Freedman and Combs (1996) quote a theory originated by David Pare. This theory describes three 'worldviews' of reality. Worldviews are frameworks of assumption that influence an individual's understanding of how the world works and, therefore, what it is to be a person. We have adapted this idea as a way of understanding different assumptions about what it is to be human.

Worldview one: reality is obvious – there is nothing to discuss

Worldview one is a 'a common-sense' view that makes the assumption that we live in a straightforward world. What we see and hear are accurate representations of what exists in reality. There is only one truth about the way the world works and about the way people function. Any dispute or discussion is caused because we have not learned enough, or because somebody is wrong. Objects and people can be described, measured and understood without the need for inquiry about the nature of knowledge.

Worldview one can be traced to the philosophical assumptions made by John Locke (1632–1704) in his 'Essay Concerning Human Understanding'. Locke argued that human knowledge was directly caused by the world around us. Our minds can remember a red object because a red object in our environment directly causes this sensation in our minds. What we think is a direct representation of what is out there.

The assumption that people experience 'raw reality' was adopted by many scientists before the second half of the last century. Donald Schön (1983) referred to a 'technical rationality' model of assumptions about professional skilled performance. The technical rationality model is often referred to as a technical-rational model nowadays. This technical-rational approach interprets problem solving as simply involving logical reasoning and an internalised collection of facts that directly represent reality. Schön contrasted the technical-rational approach with a more effective reflective model of thinking. The technical-rational model shares the assumptions of worldview one.

Within the technical-rational viewpoint reality is not problematic. What we see and hear is accurately represented in our thoughts. Disputes and discussions are caused by inaccuracy and not because there is anything inherently difficult about interpreting the physical or social world. Within this 'worldview', understanding diversity is simply a matter of collecting data on the different behaviours and customs associated with different social groups. The technical-rational approach would emphasise the importance of understanding issues such as Jewish people do not eat pork and Hindus do not eat meat. These issues can be viewed as straightforward facts that can be stored for use in an appropriate context. Celebrating diversity might reduce to learning hundreds of useful pieces of information. These pieces of information might need to be built into organisational policy considerations, or into prescriptions for individual conduct towards members of diverse groups.

SOME PROBLEMATIC CONSEQUENCES OF WORLDVIEW ONE

Worldview one may result in some problematic consequences for understanding human diversity. If what each person thinks is a direct representation of reality, then how do we make sense of people who hold different or opposing views? If people or cultures come to different conclusions about the correct way to live, then they cannot all be right. One individual may hold the view that the only correct lifestyle for adults is to live within a family unit sanctioned by the institution of marriage. Another individual may disagree and choose a contrary lifestyle. Within the assumptions embodied in worldview one, at least one of these choices must surely be inferior. There must be a logical solution to the best way to live a life. Within worldview one it must always be tempting to make the assumption that your own choices are, indeed technically, the best ones.

Celebrating diversity may be difficult within the assumptions embodied in worldview one. In order to make sense of diversity, it may be easiest to handle it by reducing it to a list of facts about specific groups – facts such as many black African people adopt different styles of hair care when compared to white people. Hindus, Buddhists and Muslims may have different dietary requirements from Christians. There are different religious rituals and symbols associated with different religions. Knowledge of diversity can then be safely compartmentalised. We know that everybody does things differently and we can suspend judgement and logical analysis in this area of diversity and rights.

Reflect on practice

It is important that care workers know the fact that Islamic practice is not to eat or drink during the daylight hours of Ramadan. But then how do you make sense of a colleague who says, 'Yes it is Ramadan and I do consider myself to be a devout Muslim. But I would like to be offered a sandwich. I hate it when other people make assumptions about my religion, my religion is a matter for me to interpret.'

Simply applying information we have learned about groups to individual people may result in oppressive or discriminatory practice. Care workers must find a way to avoid making assumptions. Narrative theory may provide a framework to help with this.

TRYING TO CLASSIFY PEOPLE IS NOT PRACTICAL WHEN WORKING WITH INDIVIDUALS

Within worldview one the encounter above is difficult to make sense of. How can an individual be a true member of a classification system if he or she does not conform to all the expected characteristics of that system? Do we need ever-more complex sub-categories in order to capture the nature of diversity? An alternative way of understanding diversity is to accept that classification systems can never be straightforward, that understanding human diversity is not unproblematic.

Whilst it may be useful to be able to access a range of general knowledge about diverse social groups, a technical-rational approach to understanding individuals may limit our ability to value and understand people. Assumptions embodied within the technical-rational way of thinking may make it difficult to establish psychological contact with others.

Worldview two: what is real depends on how you look at it – different people see things differently

Worldview two starts from the assumption that we are 'prisoners of our perceptions'. There is a reality out there, but all we can know is our perception of it. Different people can draw different conclusions from witnessing the same event. Social group membership such as membership of a specific ethnic, gender, age, or social class group may influence how we structure our interpretation of events. Worldview two accepts that different perceptions are equally valid. It is impossible to establish a bedrock of reality that is independent of personal interpretation. All interpretations of physical and social reality are influenced by perception.

Worldview two might be associated with the philosophical interpretation of knowledge put forward by Immanuel Kant (1724–1804). Kant argued that it was not possible for human beings to directly experience 'raw reality'. Kant used the term 'noumena' to describe the external world or what we have called 'raw reality'. Kant argued that people could only ever experience their own sensory perception of reality or phenomena. Humans experience, think and talk about phenomena, but knowledge can be limited and distorted by the nature of sensory perception. People cannot experience pure external reality or 'noumena'. Kant's philosophy has had a major impact within social science at least during the last half-century. Humanistic psychology and counselling have adopted a phenomenological model, where helpers try to understand an individual's internal system of thinking and perception, rather than look for external causes of psychological states, such as explaining depression purely in terms of biochemistry, or the influence of an early experience.

People who think using the assumptions involved in worldview two are unlikely to expect there to be any one single best way of living. Coming to terms with reality is not simply a matter of being 'logical'. What we think of as being real is strongly influenced by the way we have learned to use language to perceive the world around us. Phenomenological theory teaches that each person only ever develops an approximate understanding of the social and indeed the physical world that he or she lives in. The life experience of affluent people will be different from people who live in poverty. Assumptions about morality may differ within different cultures and religious contexts. Naturally, people with different life experiences are likely to perceive things differently. The assumptions that a person makes may be logical for that person. A person with different life experience will be expected to make different choices and see things differently.

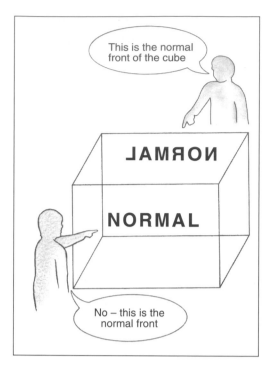

Figure 2.4 Within worldview two people are expected to develop different understandings of life because they will perceive the world differently

Within worldview two, diverse lifestyles, cultures and personal choices are an inevitable part of human perception. Whilst it is possible for a particular social group to impose its assumptions and customs on others, there can be no appeal to logic to justify the idea of one lifestyle or set of customs as superior.

Worldview two emphasises the importance of perception. The way one person understands physical and social reality may be quite different from the way another person understands reality. Celebrating diversity cannot simply be a matter of collecting information or adapting policies or systems. Within a viewpoint that sees knowledge as something which is invented by each individual person, it is vital to attempt to understand the way each individual person interprets his or her own life story.

Reflect on practice

In January 2004, National Statistics reported research on national identity. The report stated, 'In most non-white ethnic groups in Britain, the majority of people describe their National Identity as either British, English, Scottish, Welsh, or Irish. This included 87 per cent of people from the mixed group, 81 percent of the Other Black group, 80 per cent of the Black Caribbean group, and 75 per cent of the Indian, Pakistani and Bangladeshi groups.' The key issue is that national identity is a matter of perception and choice. The ethnic categories provided in the census are not the only ways in which people perceive and understand themselves.

How far is your own identity associated with a national or regional group?

HOW REAL IS SELF?

Both worldview one and worldview two assume that a person's understanding of him or herself is real. In worldview one a person's self-concept might be understood as being caused by the environment that he or she has lived in. A person's socialisation might be argued to cause him or her to believe in a particular religion or set of customs. In worldview two, a person might discover his or her 'inner self'. This discovery might result from learning to discard the false perceptions and assumptions associated with past learning and seeing things differently. Whether your self-concept or identity has been given to you, or whether it has been discovered, or even created by you, it is still nevertheless quite real.

The third worldview described by Freedman and Combs (1996) may be quite startling for many people.

Worldview three: what we think of as being real is an invention – different people live within different negotiated realities

Worldview three takes a radical view, that is, knowledge is not only influenced by perception, but it is basically invented or constructed within communities. The realities that we inhabit are those we negotiate with one another. In worldview three, individuals make sense of their daily experience not because they experience objective reality, and not through a distorted perception of reality, but within a socially constructed system of meaning, which has to be 'plausible' rather than 'real' as such.

Worldview three is associated with the perspective known as 'post-modernism'. 'Modernism' might be described as a view of Science, Art and Literature that was prevalent between the 1920s and 1950s. 'Modernism' is essentially the 'technical-rational model': the idea that we can advance human understanding through careful analysis and measurement, because knowledge is straightforward and only needs to be measured. Post-modernism rejects the assumptions of modernism and argues that there is no bedrock of truth common to every one. Knowledge is essentially socially invented, rather than simply being discovered through observation and experiment.

Within worldview three, human diversity is an inevitable result of the way people have to make sense of lived experience. Each person will build an idea of who he or she is using the conventions available to him or her within the communities of people that he or she mixes with.

Freedman and Combs (1996: 22) describe four ideas that are central to worldview three. See Figure 2.5.

Within worldview three, understanding human diversity involves understanding the narrative that each person might use to express his or her individuality. Working with people in a care environment might also require some understanding of the vast range of narratives that people tap into in order to build an understanding of who they are.

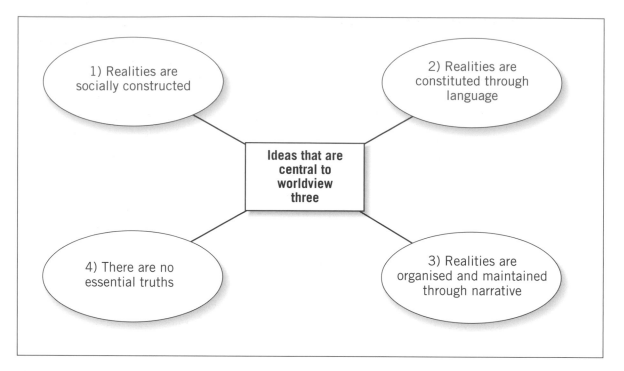

Figure 2.5 Worldview three: Freedman and Combs' ideas (1996: 22)

CASE STUDY – Fantasy group membership

In the 2001 census, 390,000 people (0.7 per cent of the population of England and Wales) gave their religion as 'Jedi' – a fictional group that exists within the Star Wars series of films. In part, this may have been due to an Internet and word-of-mouth campaign. One email, quoted by National Statistics, urged people to do it 'because you love Star Wars... or just to annoy people'.

But why would so many people choose to do this?

From the standpoint of worldview three, this behaviour is easy to interpret. Reality is not defined by authorities, reality is socially constructed – it has to be 'plausible' rather than 'real'. Narratives, including obviously fictitious ones, are part of how we come to understand our world. In a post-modern world, groups of people can negotiate their own identity. Why not upset authority and assert your right to a non-plausible fantasy group membership?

Do you associate yourself with any fictitious groups or characters – or do you live in a purely objective world?

Narrative theory is concerned with exploring how assumed reality has been negotiated and constructed by individuals and social groups. The metaphor of a story – that is being developed by a storyteller – is a useful tool for exploring the diverse perceived realities in which people live.

SOCIALLY CONSTRUCTED UNDERSTANDING

The idea that our understanding of self is an 'invention of the mind' can easily be misunderstood. If 'self' is just a story and not 'real' in any ultimate sense, then perhaps everyone just lives in isolated bubbles of reality – and anything goes when it comes to social behaviour or morality? This is not what worldview three is arguing. Take the idea of 'money'. The concept of money was invented about two-and-a-half-thousand years ago and it has since proved very popular. The paper money that you own has no ultimate reality; no reality that is guaranteed by the physical nature of the universe in which we live. The value of the pieces of paper we call 'money' depends on a socially negotiated system of meaning. The value of a given note changes with time – inflation and deflation take their effects. You would not regard your money as irrelevant just because its value depends on a system of social meaning. Socially negotiated systems often feel very 'real'!

Equally, our understanding of self can only be understood in the context of a social system. A person's identity is meaningful; money is meaningful – even if this meaning cannot be traced back to some physical location in the body or in the laws of nature.

WHAT IS WRONG WITH COMMON SENSE?

The common-sense view of worldview one is all most people usually need to get them through the day. You don't need to understand the physics of aviation in order to catch a holiday flight; you don't need to understand how your car works if you can afford to take it to a garage for repair. A simple set of assumptions might be all you need to be able to function with a group of similar people. The more you can simplify the world, the easier it is to handle it. But if you do design and build aircraft it is useful to know some physics; if you work with people and contribute to the design and delivery of care services, then it is important to question assumptions about the diversity of human need.

There are so many conventions that we all agree with. We don't need to explore the views of different knowledge communities if we discuss which side of the road to drive on! Worldview one works for much of what we encounter in our lives.

Once we move on from discussing everyday conventions, common sense becomes a problem. The problem with common sense is that it is only 'common' within specific knowledge communities. At least this is the view taken within worldview three. Worldview two would also emphasise that diverse perceptions are likely to limit how 'common', common sense can be. Care workers will find themselves working with a great range of people with diverse social and language group memberships. Worldview three enables a different standpoint on diversity from that which is possible within the assumptions of the technical-rational view of knowledge.

PEOPLE ARE NOT STATIC OBJECTS

We argue that understanding diversity involves coming to understand the identity narrative that an individual person will develop in the context of his or her life experience. This narrative will be an ongoing process. A person's explanation of his or her life will change as his or her life does. A person's identity will not reduce to a simple set of factual information. Worldview three entails a complicated way of looking at life, holding out the possibility that carers may take a positive role in assisting others to maintain and develop a sense of identity that may be needed to take control of personal life.

A more common-sense view of difference might result in people being seen as static objects that require some different 'treatments', depending on how they have been categorised.

Worldview three emphasises that we each live with in a socially constructed system of meaning. Each individual has to construct a plausible interpretation of his or her experience. Whether we work within a radical social constructivist viewpoint or simply accept the importance of perception, we need to understand diversity as involving more than the collection of information associated with various identifiable social groups.

2.3 The concept of self

How self comes about – a life story

George Mead (1934) believed that self-awareness developed from children's ability to imitate adult behaviour and to imagine characters. When children play, they can copy actions that they have seen. They do not need to understand fully – they just do the action. For example, a young child might pretend to be a dog, just because the child had watched the family's pet dog.

By 4 or 5 years of age, children might start to act out adult behaviour patterns. Again, children don't really need to understand adult behaviour; they just copy what they think they see. In this way, children can start to copy, or assimilate, adult roles involving culturally available scripts. For example, children might imagine that they are working together in a kitchen, cooking something for some imaginary children. As they play, they may copy behaviour that they have seen adults perform. As well as imitating adults, children will imitate stories they have seen on TV. This might involve dramatic scenes like rescuing people, nursing people in hospital and, of course, car chases and fights. When children play, they are using imagination – involving concepts, scripts and stories – in order to take on the roles of other people.

Mead believed that children might start to create a character for themselves – the child would start to invent a 'me'. The 'I' creates a 'me' because children can imagine appropriate scripts and narratives and put themselves in the place of other people.

As children develop self-awareness, their idea of a 'me' will be strongly influenced by the culture that they grow up in. Culture includes the concepts, scripts and narratives often identified as 'beliefs, norms and values' belonging to a cultural group.

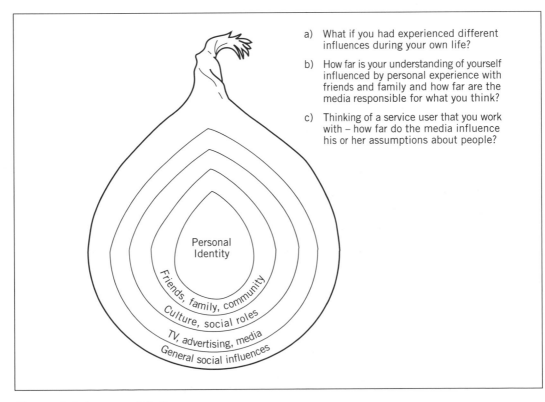

a) What if you had experienced different influences during your own life?

b) How far is your understanding of yourself influenced by personal experience with friends and family and how far are the media responsible for what you think?

c) Thinking of a service user that you work with – how far do the media influence his or her assumptions about people?

Figure 2.6 Layers of influence

Self-concept – creating a plausible self-story

Within Mead's explanation, children will come to be socialised into the beliefs, values and norms of their initial family or care-giving group. Later, children will be influenced by the beliefs, values and norms of the friends with whom they mix and play. Children adopt others' values and norms in order to be accepted into social groups. To be liked and to be popular, they have to show that they fit in with others. Mead (1934) believed that children come to learn general social rules and values at this stage. They might be able to imagine 'generalised others' and general social scripts and stories which they need to live up to.

Children do not simply do what others teach them to do, however. They internalise concepts, scripts and storylines that are built into a sense of self. This sense of self determines behaviour.

Narratives – or 'constructed stories' – become part of the child's self-concept and social identity. This sense of self will influence how a person interprets the events that he or she encounters. A narrative that involves the concept of honour might encourage a person to engage in experiences that would achieve honour and avoid shame. A narrative that involves the accumulation of wealth might influence an individual to evaluate him or herself in terms of material possessions.

Mead's theory provides an explanation of how social influences work on an individual. It is the idea of a self, a 'me' that explains how social values influence individual behaviour. Nowadays, the development of self also needs to take account of the influence of the media. People may develop their ideas of social norms

Anil has a learning difficulty. He used to feel safe and secure with his parents, but he relied on them to tell him what to do

Anil began to explain the things he liked and disliked during life story work

Today Anil chooses his own music. Anil is able to make choices and is more self-confident because of the life story work

A story of self may help people to 'take control' of their life through experience of broadcast material as well as through first-hand experience of other people. Narrative psychology would argue that each person builds his or her own interpretation of self, using the concepts, scripts and narratives available to him or her.

The benefits of a secure sense of self are shown in Figure 2.7.

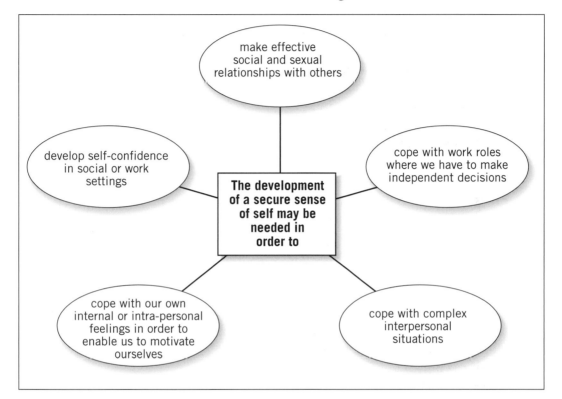

Figure 2.7 Benefits of a secure sense of self

Making sense of 'I' – an emotional/cognitive model

If 'I' creates 'Me', then how can we make sense of the mechanisms involved? One way of thinking about people is to try to understand the physical systems that might be involved in perceiving the world. A widely accepted interpretation of the human nervous system is that we have an emotional response system located in our mid-brain and a system that enables us to think and reason located in the cortex or outer part of our brain. Daniel Goleman (1996) argues that successful living, interaction with others and performance at work depend on the interaction of both thinking and emotional systems.

Goleman (1996: 28) states: 'In the dance of feeling and thought the emotional faculty guides our moment-to-moment decisions, working hand-in-hand with the rational mind, enabling – or disabling – thought itself. Likewise, the thinking brain plays an executive [controlling] role in our emotions – except in those moments when emotions surge out of control and the emotional brain runs rampant.' 'In a sense we have two brains, two minds – and in two different kinds of intelligence rational and emotional. How we do in life is determined by both.'

In the field of counselling, Whelton and Greenberg (2002) have developed a model to explain interaction in terms of systems of emotion and thinking. At the emotional level, we process information in a way that is 'rapid, automatic, affective and out of awareness' (2002: 103). This level of processing allows us to instantly recognise and categorise experiences, enabling us to make rapid responses. Emotion enables us to instantly identify a threat and to take rapid action to escape from the threat. Emotional processing also enables us to rapidly identify positive situations. Emotion may, therefore, lead us to experience fear or anger, attraction or pleasure: a desire to become involved with, or a desire to avoid a particular person.

A second level of processing is the slow, conscious, deliberate act of thinking where we reflect on and conceptualise a situation. At the thinking level, we are capable of the following.

- We can reason things out.
- We can analyse assumptions that we might be making.
- We can try to solve problems.
- We can compare a current situation with past experiences we have had.

Whelton and Greenberg (2002) argue that both the emotional and thinking levels can be influenced by past experience. The way we find ourselves responding to others will be influenced by an interaction of our emotions and thoughts. Our own narrative of a self will also be created from the interplay of emotion and thought.

Greenberg and Pascual-Leone (2001) identify five steps, which may be expected when a person makes sense of an experience – such as meeting someone new.

Firstly, there will be a physiological process responding to new sensory information. The way a person looks and sounds will be interpreted. Secondly, there will be an emotional response – a set of feelings – associated with the first perception. Thirdly, the emotional response will trigger built-in action responses such as the desire to approach a person or to withdraw from him or her.

These first three steps might be felt 'just to happen' and be 'experienced as an entirely automatic process'. However, this emotional level of response contains and expresses the fundamental meaning of a situation for an individual (Whelton and Greenberg, 2002: 106).

At the fourth and fifth steps the individual will use his or her thinking skills to make final sense of the situation and to plan a response. It is at this level that a person's understanding of his or her own self-narrative and understanding of the narrative world of another come into play.

An outline of Greenberg and Pascual-Leone's (2001) model of how thought and emotion interact in the creation of meaning is set out in Figure 2.8.

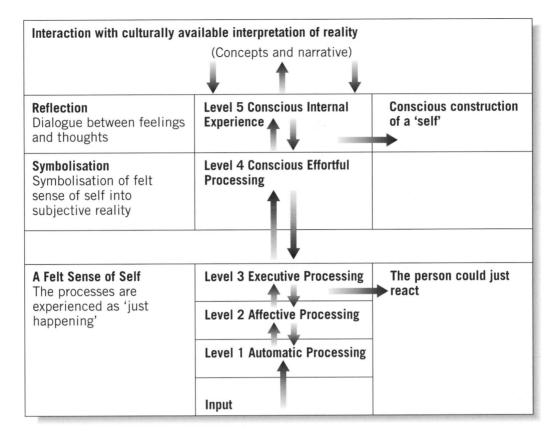

Figure 2.8 An outline of Greenberg and Pascual-Leone's (2001) model of how thought and emotion interact in the creation of meaning

Whelton and Greenberg (2002) argue that an individual's interpretation of experience 'emerges from an awareness of the complex internal world of feeling and sensation that blended with out-of-awareness learning and cognition, forms our emotional experience. Only a portion of this internal world is ever attended to and brought into conscious awareness and symbolised with words, that portion which tends to have the best fit with one's preferred conscious view of self' (2002: 106). Our emotional level of perception provides a basic 'felt sense of self'. Our cognitive and thinking level of perception enables us to invent a narrative self, using the building materials available to us within our culture.

Our perception of other people will be influenced by assumptions that operate at an emotional level. We can use our cognitive ability and thinking skills to make sense of this emotional level. We can also use our intellectual power of analysis to interpret cultural systems of meaning that may influence our conscious judgement.

Toukmanian (2002) argues that it is useful to understand perception as involving a network of complex schemata or meaning structures that the person uses to interpret reality. Toukmanian (2002) also identifies an automated, very rapid mode of processing similar to the emotional system described above. Alternatively, people can use a controlled, slow, deliberate and reflective method of processing, similar to the cognitive level described above. When people rely on 'automatic processing' they are unlikely to change their assumptions about themselves or their world. The ability to change may be dependent on mere use of cognitive, reflective systems.

Emotion and diversity

Diversity is a challenge. Many people feel a mild sense of threat when they encounter someone that is different. On an emotional level, we know what to expect when we mix with people who are similar to ourselves. Difference may often lead to an automatic reaction of wanting to withdraw – the 'I hope that person doesn't sit next to me' response. Prejudice and discrimination are partly founded within our emotional levels of responding. But we can use our thinking abilities to override automatic emotional reactions. The ability to enjoy diverse narratives can change threat to excitement. Learning new ideas can make meeting new people interesting and enjoyable – rather than stressful. A potential source of joy associated with working in a caring role is the joy of involvement with so many different life stories. Perhaps involvement with other people's life stories may help to enrich our own.

Building a self

The model that we are advancing in this book is that each person has real emotional and cognitive systems for processing information. The emotional system can be physically located in the mid-brain; the cognitive system can be physically located in the cortex of the brain. What these 'real systems' do is to interpret our experience in order to invent an interpretation of what we are – the 'self'. This 'self' is a construction built from socially available concepts, ideas and narratives. Self is socially negotiated, or in other words, your idea of who you are has to be accepted by other people around you. Each person needs a sense of himself or herself in order to meet the demands of society. Self has to 'have meaning' or be 'plausible' but self has no physical location within a person's nervous system.

For many people the idea of 'me' will start with scraps of memory. These memories may include images or snatches of dialogue associated with birthdays, holidays, family gatherings, games and other social activities. Many people will also associate emotions, visual symbols and metaphors with their idea of a self or 'me'. Some adolescents maintain a diary. This diary may read like a logbook of events that have occurred day by day. For many people, a cognitive interpretation of self may simply revolve round the events that have occurred within that person's life. At some stage, experience needs to be turned into a plausible life story if an individual is to be able to cope effectively with the challenges that the modern world will present.

Age 8   Age 12

Age 15   Now

Life stories are built up from 'scraps' of life experience

Agency and empowerment

Why is it necessary to develop lived experience into a story of 'who I am'? We argue that a plausible sense of self is needed in order to motivate a person to cope with interpersonal relationships and with work within Western society. A cognitive sense of self is needed in order to believe that you can take control of your life and solve problems that affect you. The ability to narrate an explanation of who you are confers a sense of agency. Assisting a service user to develop or maintain a sense of self may result in empowerment.

The notion that a self-narrative is critical for social functioning is not new. Erik Erikson originated the idea that each person had to develop a clear sense of 'ego identity' in order to cope successfully with the demands of Western society. In 1963 Erikson wrote, 'in the social jungle of human existence, there is no feeling of being alive without a sense of ego identity' (page 240).

Erikson argued that developing a sense of identity would result in:

- a sense of individuality – a sense of being special
- a sense of wholeness – different aspects of life experience could be brought together to create a unified sense of self
- a sense of continuity – of knowing where you have come from, a sense of having 'roots'
- a sense of social solidarity or social meaningfulness – identity had to be socially plausible.

The notion of identity was developed by Glynis Breakwell (1986). Breakwell argued that an identity was necessary in order to take responsibility for self and make appropriate choices within the demands of Western culture. The ability to construct an identity was argued to result in a sense of distinctiveness, continuity, and self-esteem. When the plausibility of an individual's identity is threatened, people will use a range of defence mechanisms in order to protect their working sense of self. Without a functioning interpretation of self, individuals may fail to cope with the demands of relationships or employment.

More recently, narrative psychology seeks to interpret self as being a kind of story, constantly modified and updated by a narrator. The narrator can be considered to be the 'me' that creates the self-story or 'me'. A sense of self or identity is still implied by this narrative; Crossley (2000: 41) writes: 'It is the central premise of this book that when we actually turn to examine the full range of experiences, knowledge and understandings of self that people live and struggle with, therein resides a sense of unity, continuity and coherence.'

Once lived experience is turned into a narrative it has the power to organise a person's behaviour and to create a motivational basis for action. As a person develops his or her narrative so he or she will potentially develop his or her capacity for autonomy and taking control of his or her own life.

Valuing diversity should involve:

- identifying an individual's standpoint (such as ethnicity, gender, and age group)
- demonstrating value for diversity by listening to sections of an individual's narrative.

Narrative work

A practical outcome of valuing diversity is assisting people to maintain or develop their narrative. Sometimes this may form the focus of social work intervention, or of practical projects within care settings as detailed below. It is noteworthy, however, that the significance of personal narrative is not limited to these systematic forms of intervention. Every conversation between carers and service users needs to take into account the issue of personal narrative.

Examples of large-scale projects are described below.

REMINISCENCE WITH OLDER PEOPLE

Reminiscence work is often intended to assist older people to maintain a sense of worth and value and in some circumstances the development of a sense of self with which to face death. Jeffrey Garland (1993) defines life review therapy as 'a process of systematic reflection in later life, with a therapist and client trying to understand a life history's implications for current coping strategies. Outcome is assessed in terms of resolution of conflicts and improved well-being based on self-acceptance and having come to terms with life.'

Reminiscence work can help older people maintain a sense of worth and value

LIFE STORY RESEARCH WITH PEOPLE WHO HAVE LEARNING DIFFICULTY

Dorothy Atkinson (2000) describes a real-life story research project to recover the 'lost voices' of people with learning difficulty. Life stories matter because they express the identity of individuals. Atkinson sought to collect the life stories of people who had been socially excluded and argued that life story books 'have the power to transform lives – as well as maintain them if they are given due time and space (2001: 172). Helen Sanderson et al. (1997) describe a life map approach to designing care for people with learning difficulty. In part, this approach involves enabling service users to explain the key issues including dreams, hopes and fears that exist within their life story.

NARRATIVE THERAPY

In his introduction to a textbook on narrative and psychotherapy John McLeod (1997: x) explains that 'all therapies are narrative therapies. Whatever you are doing, or think you are doing, as a therapist or client can be understood in terms of telling and retelling stories.' McLeod points out that 'Stories are co-constructed. Even when a teller is recounting a unique set of individual, personal events, he or she can only do so by drawing upon story structures and genres drawn from the narrative resources of a culture' (1997: 94). New meanings and understanding can come about when a life story is narrated to an actively involved listener.

CASE STUDY – 'Whose fridge is it anyway?'

A home care worker might be working in the home of an older woman who can no longer manage to maintain a clean and tidy kitchen. The agreed care plan involves the home care worker to clean and prepare food in this kitchen. The narrative or storyline of the service user is that she has always been a competent cook and always been able to manage her own kitchen. The service user's fridge is a significant area of territory within this story. The service user, therefore, asks the home care worker not to look into the fridge. From a food safety point of view the home care worker needs to check that there is no out-of-date food in the fridge. But if we are to respect the personal narrative of the service user, then the fridge must not be looked at.

A skilled carer may be able to resolve this dilemma through conversational work. By listening to the service user it may be possible to validate the person's sense of self as a competent cook. If the carer can remove the threat to the service user's self-esteem, then they may be able to get permission to clear the fridge.

What impact would ignoring the service user's own self-narrative be likely to have? Why is respect for the service user's dignity, privacy and choice so important?

2.4 The importance of self-narrative

Respect, dignity, privacy and choice

The GSCC Code of Practice identifies key rights such as dignity, respect, privacy and choice. Practical work to show respect, maintain dignity and enable choice cannot be reduced to a context-free repertoire of behavioural responses. Working within the code of practice will require carers to develop some understanding of service users' self-narrative.

Some service users will have established a plausible and effective self-narrative or identity. Individual service users may be secure and proud in their explanations of their own ethnic, religious or sexual identity. Where this is the case, the carer's duty to protect the vulnerable might be met by showing respect and value for that person's self-narrative. Many vulnerable service users do not possess a safe, secure and plausible identity. The essence of vulnerability is often a threat to a person's interpretation of self or self-esteem, or self-worth.

When carers work with threatened individuals, 'valuing diversity' might require positive approaches aimed at assisting service users to re-construct a plausible sense of self.

CASE STUDY – The protective power of narrative

Compare these two accounts – one person enjoys a good degree of emotional well-being, whereas the other person does not.

Bill Solomon

Bill Solomon lost his partner 2 years ago and states that he often feels very lonely now in the evenings. He experiences painful arthritis and shortness of breath. He belongs to a religious community and he receives assistance to attend religious services and meetings. Mr Solomon receives frequent visits and practical help with daily living activities from friends and members of the religious group to which he belongs. Bill explains that he has a strong sense of purpose in life, and this enables him to cope with poor health. He says, 'Well, everything happens for a reason you know; sometimes I feel I'm being tested, but you know what – I know that with God's help I'm going to pass that test. Yes, the last few years of my life have not been good – but there is no point becoming bitter and twisted about it. I think about all the good friends I have – they keep me strong you know, strong on the inside. I know that God watches over me, and when the time comes – well, I'll meet everyone again on the other side. If things seem a bit puzzling now – well, they are all going to be explained later. I'm not worried or afraid about anything – I have my Faith.'

Bill enjoys a clear religious identity. Within his religion, Bill can narrate a coherent and plausible interpretation of self and life. Bill not only has the ability to narrate his story, but he also has a community of friends with whom he can rehearse and explain his story. Although Bill has to work through a grieving process, and although he experiences pain, his self-narrative provides a sense of meaning and purpose.

Bill might have had a similar sense of purpose if he had belonged to a professional or trades union group that met with him. A narrative and a social context to support that narrative are likely to protect a person's emotional well-being.

Reg Morrison

Reg Morrison was referred for assessment a year ago. Reg has great difficulty coping alone and complains of loneliness and isolation. Reg's wife died five years ago of cancer. 'She suffered and I couldn't help her.' Reg feels that health services did not do enough to support her. Reg feels that 'No one cares about the old people now – when I was young we used to look after our own and yet we had nothing. Nowadays, people have got everything, but I'm just left on my own. No one cares if I live or die.'

A major event in Reg's life was the Second World War. Reg was called up to serve in the desert war in North Africa, where he was seriously wounded. This event dominates much of his conversation, and he says that his 'young life was taken from him' by the war. 'People today have it so easy. I had to struggle to survive before the war, and in the war I nearly died – no one understands what I went through. Now life is even worse than it was then – at least I had pals around me. We thought we were fighting for something, but it was all a waste of time. If I had known what I know now – how bad things would be – I wouldn't have done it. What's the point of living? It's just an existence – and nobody cares. I just think my life has been a waste of time.'

Reg experienced life in terms of a narrative of fighting for a cause and then in terms of partnership with his wife. Reg can no longer interpret his experience in terms of these narratives. Reg has not developed a new self-narrative to make life meaningful and Reg does not live within a family, friendship group, or community setting that might provide the audience that he needs to construct a working narrative. Reg might be understood as vulnerable because he does not have the social support of an 'audience' to listen to him.

What could be done to support Reg?

Vulnerability and motivation

Care settings could – theoretically at least – provide a setting where individuals might find themselves with an audience of other service users. Managers might wish to establish reminiscence or discussion groups in order to provide this vital facility.

Imagine the situation when an older person, perhaps like Reg (above), goes into respite care, maybe just for a couple of weeks. The person will have a life story perhaps of being successful at work and having led an enjoyable life with a partner. But now the person is unable to cope alone. The dominant narrative of 'ageing' might suggest that the person has little to look forward to. Many people believe that the final years of life might be expected to involve mental and physical decline, resulting in the need to be cared for by others. Care workers could exert a major influence in assisting the individual to maintain his or her story of a worthwhile life with a sense of purpose. On the other hand, care workers could regard the person as simply being a defective body – a body that needs a range of inputs in order to keep it ticking over for two weeks. The older person could find that he or she loses control of his or her narrative. Care workers might re-story the person in terms of a stereotype of ageing.

The key question is 'Who is narrating the life story?' Is the service user in charge of the story of who they are? Or does the worker have a different narrative to explain the service user's needs? Empowerment means that service users stay in control of their identity and life story.

It needs to be emphasised that a self-narrative is rarely just an old story, or a set of assumptions about self. A person's self-narrative, or identity, can be the driving force that motivates the individual in everything he or she does. Some individuals associate the development of self-narrative with personal creativity; there is a feeling of security and satisfaction that is associated with being able to confidently explain your role in life.

One source of vulnerability that service users may experience stems from cultural storylines that they may encounter. Some explanations for difference are loaded with interpretations of social worth. Some explanations are accepted uncritically by a majority of people as being common sense. Such explanations can be referred to as dominant narratives, i.e., narratives that dominate a culture.

From childhood on we are exposed to stories that depict heroic struggles; romantic engagements; views of what is right or good; and ideas of what is socially unacceptable or bad. We will also be exposed to a vast range of characters and storylines, which help us to build expectations about our lives. Individuals will attend to and choose stories that help them to represent a plausible interpretation of their own situation and identity.

One way of interpreting the concepts of power and oppression is that the powerful choose their own story, whereas the oppressed have their story told for them by others.

The diversity of culturally available narratives has dramatically increased

One hundred years ago, many children would have first imagined a 'me' based on circles of influence, where the experience of interaction with their own family would have been at the heart of the influences on them. Experiences of interaction with friends and relatives might have formed the next circle of influence, and interaction with members of the wider community that they lived in would have formed a more distant circle of influence. Naturally, ideas broadcast in newspapers and books would have influenced the community.

Most people's sense of self would be developed from real-life experience within a local community. It would be possible for a local community, perhaps say, of middle-class people to hold completely different images of what was important in life compared with a different community living a few hundred yards away, perhaps say, of working-class people. The family, friends, and community network that individuals grow up with could explain the influences that shaped their sense of who they were.

Today, authors who write about the construction of the self – for example, Crossley (2000), Freedman and Combs (1996), Holstein and Gubrium (2000) – argue that influences on the development of self are now rather different from what they were one hundred years ago. Nowadays, children and adults are bombarded with second-hand experience and storylines through the media. The broadcast media – including TV, films, music video and the Internet – represents a major socialising influence. Many people's development of a 'me' – of a self-concept – may be strongly influenced by experience of the media, and not just through interpersonal experience. It is no longer safe to assume that knowledge of a person's social context as indicated by his or her ethnicity, religion, gender and social class will provide us with the major framework we need to interpret the individual's sense of who he or she is. Naturally, ethnicity, gender and social class are still important variables that describe diverse influences on self-concept. But people now live in a world that is saturated with diverse stories, metaphors, theories and explanations of what life is about. Experience within a given family or community may influence the stories and images that we attend to, but it is still possible to 'tune into' an almost infinite range of 'secondary experience'.

Power

Because we live in a world saturated with media influences, many vulnerable people may fail to develop a plausible, working sense of who they are. Some people may come to explain their sense of self in terms of the stories that they hear. Such people may not develop their own 'self story' in a satisfying and fulfilling way; they would rather buy a 'ready-made' story off the shelf of the dominant narratives available to them.

The personal identity of many people may be based on the 'dominant explanations' or 'dominant narratives' that they come in contact with. These dominant explanations may be accepted as truths against which people evaluate themselves.

Dominant narratives

Some examples of narratives that may have distorted many people's interpretation of themselves are described below.

THE IMPAIRMENT NARRATIVE USED TO EXPLAIN DISABILITY

A simple 'common sense' explanation of disability is that a disabled person is a defective, damaged or impaired version of a normal person. The focus of care must be to correct or repair the defect. If the defect cannot be repaired then the victim is to be pitied, and perhaps separated from 'normal' people.

THE INTELLIGENCE NARRATIVE USED TO EXPLAIN LEARNING DIFFICULTY

In the last century many people employed the concept of 'intelligence' to interpret the social worth of people. The dominant narrative was that people were born with lesser or greater degrees of this quality. People who were intelligent were more socially valued because of their special skills with language and reasoning. People with learning difficulties were assumed to be born with an insufficient quantity of intelligence.

Nowadays the concept of intelligence is a contested area. Modern theorists argue that there are multiple intelligences rather than a single, simple, quality which everyone has a lesser or greater degree of. The story has moved on.

THE AGEING AS DECLINE NARRATIVE

This narrative interprets people's interests and ability in terms of a process of biological maturation and decline. Human life is split into stages, which include childhood, adolescence, adulthood and old age. Interest in reproduction may be restricted to adolescence and early adulthood within this narrative. Old age is constructed as a time of loss and decline. 'It's your age' is offered as an obvious explanation for ill-health and disability with the inference that little can be done, or should be attempted, once we interpret need in terms of the life cycle narrative.

THE TARGETS/OUTCOMES AS THE PURPOSE OF WORK NARRATIVE

In an immensely diverse society – where individuals adopt many varied perspectives – how can we make sense of the purpose of an organisation and quality of work? The 'targets and outcomes narrative' offers a solution. Define targets for every service and for every worker; define criteria to measure success and quality. The system of targets and definition becomes the purpose of work. Perhaps any outcomes or targets will do – the important thing is to have them in order to create a structure. Each worker will evaluate his or her worth in terms of performance to meet targets. 'Targets culture' becomes a narrative that compels workers to monitor and control their own behaviour. If individuals apply this narrative uncritically to their own sense of self-worth then their self-esteem may be a hostage to this story.

THE MATERIAL POSSESSIONS IS THE PURPOSE OF LIFE NARRATIVE

You are what you own. Your social worth is measured in terms of financial worth and perhaps particularly by the nature of your dwelling/car/fashionable status of clothing. Your social group membership (including age and ethnicity) will influence which specific possessions you most need to display in order to establish status.

Prejudice

Some familiar discriminatory prejudices can also be understood as once dominant narratives. Examples include racist theories of cultural superiority; homophobic interpretations of gay and lesbian behaviour in terms of defective sexuality; and the sexist narrative of a weaker sex whose place is in the home.

Part of anti-discriminatory practice is to identify and challenge the role of dominant narratives in distorting an individual's assumptions about him or herself. A starting point for empowerment is for people to be able to narrate their own story – to be able to control the explanation of their own diversity. As McLeod states, 'there is implicit power in authoring, in having a voice. Being powerful requires a willingness of other people to listen, to hear, to be influenced by what that voice has to say. There are many people in the world who possess little power of this kind, who are effectively silenced' (96). Within a narrative model, valuing diversity involves listening to and giving a voice to each person's interpretation of difference, whilst challenging assumptions that may restrict or diminish members of different communities.

It can be argued that in a care context all service users have a moral right to a 'voice'; this voice should not be restricted to making complaints about mundane service delivery issues. Having a voice means being able to influence other people's perception of you. It entails having an audience.

Does the service user have a voice – or does the standard narrative become a story he or she has to live in?

Reflect on practice

Within the care setting that you work in, what opportunities exist for service users to discuss their lives with friends, relatives, other service users, or care workers?

CASE STUDY – An example of the discriminatory power of 'dominant narrative'

A male service user with learning difficulty in the 1970s understood himself in terms of the impairment narrative; he said, 'I know I can't live the same as you do – I'm not "high grade" enough'. Today, it would be nice to imagine that this person was a member of a self-advocacy group, who had developed his own life map and voiced his own wishes. A human rights culture might immediately identify the issue that a person with learning difficulty has the same human rights as anyone else.

Using the concept of narrative helps to identify an issue that is central to human rights and equality. The service user explained his understanding of self in terms of what we might regard to be a discriminatory narrative. By adopting the impairment narrative he was able to make sense of the things that had happened to him. The impairment narrative explained his place in the social order. Because the impairment narrative was the main culturally available system of explanation, the service user used it in order to create a sense of self. Naturally, this narrative limited the chances of the service user 'fulfilling his potential'.

What if...

What might have happened if a care worker had offered false reassurance and said 'of course you are not "low-grade" – you are very clever'?

In this situation the service user would have maintained his way of thinking, but might be tempted to swap categories within the narrative. This swap might be short lived, however, because a self-evaluation has to be plausible. You cannot maintain that you are clever if few people support you in your belief.

Reassurance would have been damaging and inappropriate in this context. What is needed is the possibility of a new way of thinking about self.

Empowerment involves narrating your own story – not having to live within other people's story

The dominant narrative as a means of understanding power and oppression

White and Epston (1990) provide an extensive account of the role of dominant narrative as a way of understanding power relationships and oppression within society. White and Epston draw heavily on the work of the French philosopher Foucault, whose theory of social power might be superficially summarised as follows. Historically, in feudal times Kings and Lords controlled the populace through coercion and threat. Subjects of a kingdom might suffer physical harm if they disobeyed commands. Nowadays, power is exercised through the construction of dominant narratives. Nowadays, people subjugate themselves. People evaluate themselves and monitor and control their own behaviour in terms of socially constructed systems of knowledge. According to Foucault, concepts of power cannot be usefully separated out from knowledge. Knowledge (in the sense of dominant narratives) is power. The majority of people in society make assumptions about themselves and their potential. People label and stereotype themselves.

An analysis of discrimination, and the role of stereotyping and labelling, should not be restricted to an analysis of what care workers might do to service users. White and Epston (1990) write: 'since we are all caught up in a net or web of power/knowledge, it is not possible to act apart from this domain, and we are simultaneously undergoing the effects of power and exercising this power in relation to others' (22). An analysis of human rights and the risk of discrimination should explore the network of assumptions which surround relationships. The concept of dominant narrative may provide a useful tool to assist in this analysis.

Reflect on practice

The notion of a 'reflective practitioner' is central to care work. One focus for professional development might be to analyse and explore the role of dominant narrative in creating assumptions that lead to oppression.

Thinking about your own service users, what are some of the dominant narratives that led them to make assumptions about their own potential? How far do dominant narratives constrain the lives of the service users that you work with?

Some service users interpret themselves in terms of oppressive assumptions: 'Well, I've had my life', 'I'm only a woman', and so on. The role of care workers operating within a human rights culture will involve identifying dominant narratives, and providing a social context that might enable the service user to re-story his or her life using different narratives. This new story might involve narratives that do not place the same limits on human potential.

But another issue is that some people might not be used to being an active participant in their own story. Some people simply accept the labels and classifications that other people provide for them. Many people acquiesce in having their story told for them. In Foucault's terms the ability to narrate your own story represents power.

McLeod (1997) writes, 'the culture in which we live has closed down many of the possibilities for telling personal stories. We inhabit a densely storied world, but in the main find ourselves acting as the passive recipients of waves of stories transmitted by television, newspapers and novels. Perhaps one of the central forms of social control in modern times has been achieved through the massive expansion in non-participant narrative.'

One interpretation of the concept of empowerment is that it involves enabling others to identify and narrate their own identity, rather than having to live with an identity that is specified for them.

Reflect on practice

How 'empowering' is the culture of a care setting that you are familiar with? How far do service users have the power to 'tell their own story'? How far are service users 're-storied' so that needs might be easily catalogued, or so that service users' situations can be explained using dominant narratives – such as the ageing and impairment narratives?

Diversity is dynamic

Historically, a person's identity was sometimes understood in terms of a 'social determinism' narrative. Social determinism involves the assumption that the environment makes us who we are. Social determinism argued that a person who was socialised into middle-class values would become permanently 'middle class'. Identity was created by social group membership and there was the assumption of adult-self being fixed for life, within what – for a time – might be perceived as a dominant narrative.

Breakwell (1986) defined identity as a 'dynamic social product', residing in psychological processes. Identity was explained as developing out of the interactive learning process between an individual and his or her social context. Social constructivism takes a similar view. A person's self-narrative is a process. Self-narrative can constantly change. Diverse interpretations of self not only exist between individuals, but diverse interpretations of self are possible within an individual person. For most people, the story of self is never complete. Even facing your own death might involve re-storying life in order to maintain what Erik Erikson explained as 'ego integrity'. But as well as never being complete, self is rarely 'set in stone' at any given time.

Rom Harre (1998) argues that there are three different ways in which we can understand the concept of self. Firstly, self can be understood as a construction that is 'a unique, embodied centre of consciousness with a history' (1998: 91). Secondly, self can be understood as a series of potentials and aspects – a wider range of attributes that we might take as a central self. Thirdly, self can be understood as the 'presented self' – presentation of self will depend on the social context that an individual experiences at any given time.

The significance of Harre's analysis is that for most people the interpretation of self or of identity is fluid and evolving. The way we describe who we are will vary according to who our audience is. We are likely to present our self differently to close family members or friends than we do to service users. Traditionally, the concept of role has been used to explain different behaviours. Harre's analysis puts forward the possibility that some people can happily maintain different 'presented selves' for different social contexts. There is diversity between an individual's 'embodied centre of consciousness' and the 'self', which individuals present to certain people. Sometimes presented self might feel like a mask, which is worn in order to conform to the perceived norms of a social group.

An example of such behaviour might be a care worker who is deeply committed to a human rights perspective while at work, but who can become abusive and aggressive when out for an evening's entertainment with friends. Ideas that are central to the construction of self might not always be incorporated in the self that we present.

Using narrative

We might not only present different selves, our own construction of self might vary from time to time, depending on what attributes of self are in focus. Narrative is a critical issue in enabling a person's construction of self to progress. For example, imagine you had to engage with the conversation in the case study below.

CASE STUDY — A depressing conversation

Depressed woman: I can't go on. I just don't want to live any more. You won't understand, but it is just no good. I have lost everything.

Carer: But would you like to tell me? I would like to try to understand.

Depressed woman: But you can't know what it feels like. I mean you've got everything – everything has gone wrong for me. I've got no job, no money, no partner, and no one cares. I've got nothing to live for. I would be better off dead, wouldn't I?

Carer: I can understand that you feel very bad. But are things really as hopeless as they feel?

Depressed woman: Yes they are! You might think I could get a 'menial' job down the road, but I can't live with that. I used to be important. I can't give that up. I don't want to live in some awful flat somewhere, with social services telling me how to budget. No I'd be better off dead. I just want to get it over with!

Question: From the care perspective what help can you provide?

Issues: It's no use arguing with this depressed service user; a rational step-by-step task-centred plan will be rejected. Ideas that seem plausible to care professionals are not plausible within the depressed woman's construction of this situation. Just listen to the woman's tale of despair. You might start to become engulfed in despair yourself. Reassurance – 'Oh, it's not that bad' – might be understood as patronising and uncaring. Refer the problem on? But surely there is something positive you could do now?

A narrative approach might involve keeping the depressed woman talking. The carer might then be able to steer the conversation into other aspects of a person's life and experience. The depressed woman is presenting a narrative of a 'lost self'; she can no longer be the person that she used to be, so death would be preferable to accepting this situation. But self-narrative is constructed from many different fragments of life experience. It might be possible to engage the woman in reflection and review of many positive or happy memories. These memories might provide a basis for re-storying self-narrative. Only the service user can narrate or tell his or her story. Only the service user can adapt and develop his or her story. If the carer attempted to impose a story on the woman, the carer might infringe her rights, be perceived as not understanding, or not respecting the service user. A carer who tries to take over a service user's story might be perceived as attempting to control the service user. By enabling the depressed woman to explore memories of past selves, or to explore diverse attributes, it is possible that the woman might find a basis for revising her self-narrative.

Carer: So when you were in charge of your own company you enjoyed challenges. You didn't let anything get you down?

Depressed woman: Yes but that was then. It's all different now. I've lost it all.

Carer: But you've been a very successful person, who could cope with so much. Why is it that you have to change now, and give up now?

Depressed woman: Don't know, it just feels so bad.

Carer: Well, tell me how it felt when you got that special deal through, the one you told me about. I would like to imagine how that must have felt.

In some ways the carer is just talking. But this kind of conversation is aimed at enabling the service user to develop her own narrative and perhaps adjust her construction of self. A service user may need an appropriate audience in order to adapt and develop his or her own self-narrative. As McLeod (1997) points out, telling a story is a shared activity. According to McLeod, 'stories are co-constructed' (1997: 94). The way an individual or group responds will influence how a story is organised and presented. (See Chapter 4 for further details of how narratives are co-constructed.)

Listening provides a method that might enable carers to cope with their own emotional reactions. Encountering service users with challenging behaviour will naturally create emotions, annoyance or anger or threat. Rather than concentrate on the emotion of 'Why do I have to listen to this?', the ability to take a narrative approach might enable a feeling of 'I know how to respond to this person'.

The great privilege and power of being a carer is the privilege and power of being a listener. Listening should never be construed as a passive, detached activity that is somehow an inefficient waste of time for carers. The potential to act as an audience represents a potential to understand and respect diversity. Acting as an audience also provides a critical context for empowering a service user to control and develop his or her own self-narrative.

The implications of narrative theory for care work

Narrative theory suggests that care managers should aim to create a culture in which all care workers can:

- interpret and manage their own emotions without adopting discriminatory assumptions. The 'people who are different make us feel uneasy' reaction
- identify and explore their own assumptions about people
- identify the risk of intentionally, or unintentionally, imposing their own assumptions and narratives on other people
- show respect for service users by not imposing their own narratives and interpretations on them
- listen to service users and at least provide an audience for service users' self-narrative
- identify and reflect on the dominant narratives or assumptions that surround different service user groups.

Some 'key worker' roles or senior caring roles may include a responsibility to:

- analyse service delivery to ensure that the service is not 're-storying' service users in terms of dominant narratives such as the impairment narrative
- analyse literature about the service such as homes' brochures, in order to ensure that these documents do not 're-story' individuals
- establish self-advocacy groups that have the purpose of facilitating service users to establish control of their own self-narrative or identity
- establish activities such as discussion groups that have the purpose of facilitating service users' ability to maintain their own self-narrative
- establish staff development activities that promote listening skills and conversation
- refer service users to counselling services that can assist individuals to explore new possibilities for the development of self-narrative

- establish an organisational culture that celebrates the diversity of individual narrative together with established narratives associated with specific religious or cultural groups.

The central issue is that conversation represents a major way for understanding and celebrating diversity. Showing respect to service users involves listening and communication skills. The maintenance of individual dignity and the ability to exercise choice and emotional safety depend at least in part on the development and/or maintenance of a viable self-narrative.

Summary

○ Gathering information on social groups may provide a useful starting point for valuing diversity, but a more in-depth way of understanding diversity is necessary for interpersonal work.

○ Diversity can be understood on a personal level as involving the construction of self.

○ The construction of self can be understand in terms of social context influences, the role of language and intra-personal emotional and cognitive systems for interpreting experience.

○ There are different assumptions (or worldviews) about the nature of knowledge. Social constructivism adopts the view that knowledge is constructed within 'knowledge communities'. Diverse communities will interpret life experience differently.

○ Diversity cannot be reduced to a collection of facts about different communities, and any attempt to do this would ignore the constructed nature of knowledge.

○ People cannot be understood purely in terms of self-narrative. Self-narrative exists only at an advanced level of cognitive mental processing. However, a self-narrative or identity is necessary in order to create a sense of 'agency' and purpose in life.

○ 'Dominant narratives' provide a theoretical 'tool of analysis' for interpreting oppression and disempowerment.

○ Some people do not have access to a plausible personal narrative.

○ Care workers have a vital role to play in assisting service users to take control of and narrate their own self-narrative or identity. The ability to listen and reflect issues back is central to valuing diversity and supporting service users.

Expressing diversity: culture and conversation

Introduction

In this chapter and Chapter 4 we will focus on how diversity is expressed through language. Effective use of language is a key tool for the social care worker, not least when establishing, sustaining and disengaging from relationships with service users. The way language is used at work can also make the difference between good and poor relationships with colleagues. It is hoped that some of the information presented here will challenge you to reflect upon how you (and your service users) use language, and will ultimately empower you to work more sensitively and effectively.

If you are going to establish a productive dialogue (either with your service users or with your colleagues) you will need to be aware that there is a cultural aspect to discourse, and that speech and language practices are deeply embedded in the cultures which give rise to them. You will need to be sensitive to the nuances and subtleties of holding a conversation, and also to the fact that if a conversation goes wrong, for whatever reason, a negative emotional response may be the result (either in yourself or the person to whom you are speaking). This chapter presents information to illustrate these points,

Aims *This chapter aims to enable you to explore:*

3.1   Terminology

3.2   Language and worldviews

3.3   Variety in language: speech communities and discourse practices

3.4   The everyday expression of diversity: conversations and scripts

3.5   The expression of power through language

3.6   Deafness and discourse: disability or difference?

together with some terminology from the study of linguistics, which helps when talking about language.

We also hope to challenge the common view that between individuals and in groups, the spoken word is the only key language device for communication. Writers on both psychology and language have tended to ignore issues raised by the language practices of people with disabilities, and in the worlds of medicine, education and social work there has been a tendency to assume that there is something called 'normal', to which everyone automatically aspires. As Chapter 2 illustrates, this is an idea that buys into the 'impairment' narrative, presupposing that there is something inherently superior in being 'non-disabled'. However, this chapter considers how the assertion of some Deaf people to the right to be seen as forming a distinct language community challenges the impairment grand narrative. It also challenges all of us to examine our own value systems.

Chapters 3 and 4 demonstrate how insights drawn from both the social and postmodern models of language study can inform social work practice. We will explore how language practices cannot be separated from their cultural context (a social view of language), and also consider how power relationships affect the way in which language is used. Finally, in looking at the way in which deaf people regard sign as a first language, we will be drawing on the postmodern view that language is not limited to words, and also that 'reality' is created as a result of individual interpretation.

3.1 Terminology

Before delving deeper into how diversity is expressed in language, and how an awareness of the way that language works can help you in working with diversity, it is necessary to clarify some of the terminology you will encounter in Chapters 3 and 4.

In these chapters you will find the terms **text** and **discourse** are used frequently. These terms were at one time used to distinguish written and spoken forms of communication ('text' signifying the written word, as in a play text, and 'discourse' meaning spoken language). Traditionally, a reader was seen as not interacting with a written text in contrast to a listener, who is at liberty to respond to, or interrupt, a speaker during the flow of the spoken discourse. Written and spoken communication were seen as having very distinct characteristics (broadly speaking, written language was seen as more formal and neatly expressed, in contrast to the informality and untidiness of the spoken word). This is no longer the case, and in

Chapters 3 and 4 you will find that the word 'text' is used to refer to examples of both spoken and written communication.

One or two examples will serve to demonstrate why the old division between speech and writing (when analysing language) is not helpful. A politician may deliver a carefully prepared speech. The speech has been written down, but its delivery is oral, and the speaker may very well extemporise at certain points, adding off-the-cuff remarks, jokes and even responses to heckling from the floor. The end result thus has aspects of both written and spoken communication. Conversely, a radio broadcast is made through the spoken medium, but with the exception of phone-in programmes, where callers interact with the broadcaster, the conversational nature of communication is lacking. Even when a listener does call in to chat to the presenter, the rest of the listening audience is denied this opportunity of interaction. The increasing use of electronic communication is also breaking down some of the old distinctions between written and spoken communication. Emails, for example, often combine aspects of speech with more formal written communication devices. Such a message is just as likely to open with a friendly 'Hi Sanjit!', rather than with a more formal opening, even if the rest of the message is concerned with aspects of business.

Although there remain some differences between written and spoken language, the old rigid distinction between 'text' and 'discourse' is no longer helpful. Language scholars are now more likely to use the term 'text' to mean an actual language event, and 'discourse' to signify the complex interactions taking place around that event, between the people involved, the text itself and the context for that text (Graddol, Cheshire and Swann, 1994).

CASE STUDY – What is a text?

Jas works in a day centre for older people. Several of the day centre users are from the local Bangladeshi community, and languages spoken there include both Bengali and Sylheti, as well as English.

Jas switches into both these language easily, and can communicate with service users well. If Jas is working on a one-to-one basis she is very likely to switch to the preferred language of the person she is talking to.

If a linguist were to visit the centre and make a tape recording of Jas talking to service users, that tape recording would constitute a text, as would the written transcript made from it. The linguist would also regard the original conversation as a text. If Jas were to make a written assessment based on a conversation she has had with a service user that would also be described as a text.

Do you tend to think of a text exclusively as something that is written down?

Using the concept of a text to mean speech or sign as well as writing allows us to talk about language more precisely.

Thus, the words spoken between yourself and a service user can be described as a text, as can your written report of the event. The context for this language event may be a formal interview, which constitutes the 'discourse' within which the text is located. It is important to bear in mind that the discourse of a formal interview, perhaps taking place in an office in the Town Hall, may have very different characteristics from that which takes place on an outing for day centre users. In the former, only yourself and your client are present, the surroundings may be intimidating for your service user and you may follow a formal process to obtain information from him or her. However, in the case of the outing, participants and context will have changed. It is likely that there will be more people present, and the atmosphere will certainly be different if you are at the seaside or in a pub. These factors will change the nature of the text — the speech events which take place between you. The discourse of an outing is thus likely to be very different from the discourse of an interview.

CASE STUDY – What is 'discourse'?

All languages have certain rules and practices associated with them. The sum total of these rules and behaviours constitutes the 'discourse', and the majority of languages have different rules for different situations.

At the day centre we encountered in the case study above, when Jas switches into Sylheti or Bangladeshi, she will observe the special ways of speaking and behaving that go with these languages, such as ways of greeting people, or marks of respect. Each language has its own discourse practices.

Also, the day centre as a whole might be said to have its own discourse, as there will be special words for events that happen there, and terms which derive from local authority jargon, and so on. Although English is officially the main language of the day centre, it is both multicultural and multilingual in character. People may use elements of more than one language to describe ways of working which are unique to the way things are done in the centre. The discourse of the centre as a whole is therefore quite distinctive.

Is there a distinctive discourse in your place of work?

The discourse at a day centre can be quite distinctive

3.2 Language and worldviews

How would you feel if someone greeted you by saying 'Hello there! I think you've put on weight'? Many people might take this as an insult, particularly those living in countries where obesity is a problem, and the slender, catwalk-worthy figure is an ideal promoted by the media and aspired to by many. However, in Zambia, this same opening remark would be received positively. It would be taken to mean something like 'You're looking well!' in the context of local systems of meaning and language use (Berns, 1990). This very simple example alerts us to the potential complexity of meaningful communication, which involves more than the literal meaning of the words chosen by the speaker. It also demonstrates that even when speakers are using the same language (in this case, obviously, English is used) social and cultural factors can completely change the perceived meaning of the words. As a social care worker, whilst you cannot be expected to become an expert in all the many ways in which people speak, you will at least need to become sensitive to the fact that language practices vary considerably between communities. It is how you respond to these variations that will empower you to work sensitively with service users, and to genuinely demonstrate that you value and respect diversity.

Models of language description

Interestingly, just as Freedman and Coombs have identified three distinct philosophical worldviews, those who study language may also be broadly grouped into three similar camps. Graddol (1994) refers to these as three models of language description.

The first model, **Structuralism**, is concerned mainly to analyse the structure of texts, and to determine the 'ideal' form of a language. This way of looking at language tends to treat it as something mechanical – a system of signs to be decoded by the listener or reader. As long as the speaker or writer chooses the right words and puts them in the right order (according to the grammatical rules of whatever language is being used), then there should be no problem in decoding the message. This way is also known as the 'transmission' model, and is very close to Freedman and Coombs' worldview one (see Chapter 2). According to this view of language, there is a 'correct' way to speak and write, and as long as people follow the rules (by using approved grammatical practices), then meaning will be transparent.

However, as our Zambian greeting example suggests, there is more to it than simply getting the grammar right, and the second model of language description (which Graddol calls the **Social Model**) is very similar to Freedman and Coombs' worldview two. Just as this perspective emphasises how social group membership influences our perception and interpretation of events, so the Social Model of language description focuses on social and cultural aspects of language use.

Freedman and Coombs' worldview three is an extreme development of the idea that everything is socially determined, taken to the conclusion that 'reality' is socially negotiated. Under this view, social systems of meaning are constructed which are 'plausible' rather than 'real'. Graddol also refers to parallel developments in language studies as the **Postmodern Model**. For postmodernists, 'signs' are not limited to words but can include any language-like 'signifying practices'. Thus the use of music, visual material, and so on, is considered to be part of the communication process. Scholars who fall within the scope of language model 3 are often concerned with issues of power and social role. They also emphasise the joint nature of the production of texts. For postmodernists, 'meaning' is an elusive and fragile thing.

3.3 Variety in language: speech communities and discourse practices

Ethnography: the work of Malinowski

Just as a text is set within discourse, so discourses may be set within cultural contexts. The close interaction between language and societal contexts was first put forward in the late nineteenth century, but was significantly developed by Malinowski in the 1920s. Malinowski worked extensively among the Melanesian tribespeople in Eastern New Guinea, collecting a wide range of texts including magical formulae, narratives, conversations and statements (research reprinted as Malinowski 1994, but first published in 1923). Take a look at the section of text in the box below.

TEXT 1: TROBRIAND ISLANDS (NARRATIVE)

we run	front-wood	ourselves;	
we paddle	in place;	we turn	we see
companion ours;	he runs	rear-wood	
behind	their sea-arm	Pilolu	

Abstracted from Bronislaw Malinowski, 'The Problem of Meaning in Primitive Languages' in Janet Maybin (ed.) *Language and Literacy in Social Practice* (Clevedon: Multicultural Matters and The Open University, 1994), p.1–10 (p.2).

What did you make of Text 1? It obviously has something to do with boats because of the references to 'paddle' and 'sea-arm', but is Pilolu a person? Some languages tend to place the subject of a sentence at the end, rather than at the beginning as English does. We really need to have more information in order to make sense of this piece of narrative.

In fact, the immediate context for Text 1 is a conversation between a group of Trobriand islanders. One of them has just come back from a trip across the sea, and at this point he is telling them about the return journey. An essential piece of local geographical information is that Pilolu is actually a stretch of water a little distance from the shore where the village is situated. Wood is a metaphor for canoe and, therefore, front-wood and rear-wood are the leading and trailing canoes in the flotilla. The verb, which Malinowski has had to translate as 'paddle', has no exact equivalent in English, and actually refers to the spatial and temporal location of the leading canoe. The explanation for this is that when the islanders approach the shore in their boats they take down the sails and use the paddles; at this particular point the water is too deep for punting, so the act of paddling locates them in a particular stretch of water.

Beyond a description of the return journey, this narrative is also a boast, which Malinowski observed to be a significant characteristic of Trobriand Island culture. The narrator is exulting over the fact that he was nearly home when the last canoe was still on the stretch of water named Pilolu.

You may be wondering at this point what possible relevance this data can have for social work practice in twenty first century Leeds, Cardiff, Edinburgh or Belfast. In our view, the great thing about Malinowski's material is that in its original form it is almost impenetrable to anyone who doesn't belong to this particular community. It thus demonstrates very starkly that we need to know the context of a situation if we are to understand the words. If we had started with a language and a context that were more familiar to British degree students, the impact of cultural subtleties may not have been immediately obvious. This approach to studying language, setting it in its cultural context, is referred to as **ethnography**.

Speech communities and the creation of meaning: the work of Hymes

Malinowski's ethnographical approach was subsequently developed by other scholars, and the contribution of Dell Hymes to this process is particularly useful to social care workers. In the 1970s, Hymes suggested that an integrated, ethnographic approach to the study of society and language would be more meaningful than a fragmentary method in which disciplines such as linguistics and sociology were rigidly and separately defined. This method, said Hymes, would 'approach language ... as situated in the flux and pattern of communicative events' (Hymes, 1994: 12). Within his framework for an ethnography of communication, Hymes distinguished the concepts of speech act, speech event, speech situation and speech community. Figure 3.1 shows this diagrammatically.

In this example, the speech act is a joke, which takes place during a conversation (the speech event), at a party (the speech situation). Those attending the party (at least the two (or more) who are involved in the joketelling) share the same understanding of what constitutes a joke (for example, conventions such as punch-line, punning, pauses, acceptable subject-matter, etc.), and are thus likely to be from the same 'speech community'. Although the concept of speech community has been challenged, on the grounds that it is too imprecise, nevertheless as societies around

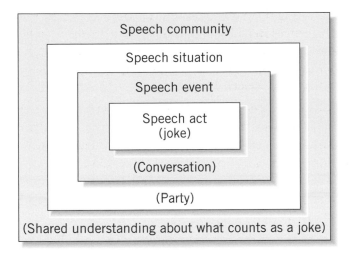

Figure 3.1 The context for the creation of meaning
Reproduced with permission from: E825 Study Guide, *Language and Literacy in Social Context*, David Graddol, Janet Maybin and Barry Stierer (Milton Keynes, Open University, 1994: 6)

the world become more diverse, it could be argued that imprecision, and the blurring of boundaries, is precisely what we should expect with regard to communicative behaviours. At this notional party, there could be members of several different speech communities, and individuals who arguably belong to more than one such community. Some of these notional communities might overlap. Figure 3.1 assumes that the people involved in the joke speech act do share the same norms of culture and language, and that the joke is successful. Hymes' model allows us to see that if the participants don't have this shared set of norms, the joke is likely to fail. Anyone who has unsuccessfully tried translating a joke into someone else's language will have first-hand experience of what this can mean.

Application of Hymes' model to everyday work situations

Social care workers can apply this model to everyday work situations, and a typical scenario is suggested in Figure 3.2.

In Figure 3.2 the social care worker elicits information from a service user by asking questions (speech act), which itself forms part of a longer conversation (speech event). You might be justified in wondering if the speech act and the speech event might be seen as the same thing. Hymes allows that in some instances this is the case. However, in our hypothetical interview there are likely to be other components of the speech event, such as a greeting, opening small talk and responses by the client, which can be classed as distinct speech acts (see a discussion of elements of conversation on page 69). The speech situation in Figure 3.2 is a formal interview, perhaps in an office in the Town Hall. The social worker may have a proforma to complete, by ticking or otherwise filling boxes. A precise outcome is thus required. When we come to define the content of the outermost square, the speech community, we can immediately see the potential for communication problems.

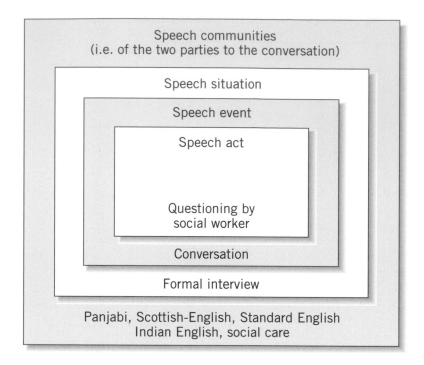

Figure 3.2 Interview with a service user (Hymes' model)

Different types of English

Even if both worker and service user are English speakers, they may be proficient in different types of English (for example Standard English and Indian English). Each of these varieties of English has specific assumptions built into it about what's appropriate in the context of a conversation, for example, in the degree of formality that needs to be built into the interview. On the other hand, perhaps both the social care worker and the interviewee are Glaswegians, and share the same form of local Scottish-English. However, the social care worker is also likely to be fluent in the discourse and language practices of social work. This speech community uses a more formal language structure and terminology. For example, instead of 'doing drugs', a person is said to 'practise substance abuse'; and when a worker makes sure that personal service user information is not disclosed to the wrong people he or she is 'implementing the written policy on confidentiality'. There are also issues of power attached to certain speech communities, and these are discussed more fully on page 75. The skilled social care worker who is fluent in the discourse practices of both the local community and social work may opt to switch to local speech norms in order to communicate more effectively with the interviewee, and to avoid the jargon and formality of the formal interview situation as far as possible. By so doing, he or she can demonstrate a genuine understanding of the person's circumstances. This kind of switching is not always possible, of course, but a professional can demonstrate empathy by picking up on expressions used by the interviewee where appropriate.

CASE STUDY – Sol: one person, many voices

Sol is a youth outreach worker in Central London. Born in South London of a family with roots in Jamaica, he has a broad linguistic repertoire, which enables him to switch his style of speaking to suit the context of situation.

He speaks Standard English with a South London accent when he is in the office, but when working with some of the local young service users he switches easily to the local version of Jamaican English. He writes his reports in good Standard English, and also makes use of the terminology found in local and national policy documents. However, when the team designed some leaflets to tell local young people about a new project to support Black music, he used his knowledge of Jamaican English, together with his familiarity of the expressions used by people in the music business, to give the wording of the leaflets more impact.

How many styles of speaking are you able to draw on when you work with service users? In other words, how broad is your linguistic repertoire?

Reflect on practice

Consider one conversation you've had at work recently — either with a service user, another colleague, your manager or someone whom you manage.

Put it into a diagram similar to Figure 3.2, setting out details of the speech act, speech event, speech situation and speech community or communities involved.

Hymes' model is a graphic reminder of the complexity of any speech act, irrespective of whether or not you agree that the concept of a 'speech community' is helpful. However, Hymes' work has also reinforced the ethnographic view that no language practice is essentially superior or inferior to another. What a structuralist would regard as 'variation and deviation' from a 'norm' actually has an organisation of its own, which is neither more nor less valid than standard ways of communicating. This idea will now be explored in the context of monolingual and multilingual speech communities.

Equality in variety: monolingual and multilingual communities

Every time we speak we reveal a considerable amount about ourselves. The words we choose and the way we put these words together can indicate to the listener aspects of our place of origin, our social background and the kind of education we have had, among other things. Perhaps you have moved from the area you grew up in and are now working elsewhere. However, you may still have retained your original accent and ways of speaking. This may, from time to time, cause you embarrassment if your new colleagues make fun of the way you speak. The experience of minority language speakers, or people with physical communication difficulties, can be much more problematic.

Consider your reaction to the examples in the box below.

TEXT 2: REGIONAL AND STANDARD UK ENGLISH

Speaker No. 1 We ain't got no money. We don't get nothin' from the Social, and we ain't got no savin's.

Speaker No. 2 We haven't got any money. We don't get anything from the DSS and we haven't any savings.

Would your reaction to and assumptions about the two speakers be different? Would you be surprised that speaker no. 2 doesn't have any savings? Perhaps you might assume that speaker no. 2 is more educated, and therefore might be expected to have a good job. Speaker no.1 actually does use several linguistic devices identified by linguists as typical of vernacular English (i.e., any form of English which varies from that considered as 'Standard' English), and vernacular forms have often been associated with speakers from 'lower' social groups or classes (and indeed, we should note that the use of the term 'lower' is itself a value-judgement). Vernacular forms include the double-negative ('we ain't got no'), the dropping of the letter 'h' ('aven't) and the dropping of the letter 'g' at the end of 'ing'. Reference to the DSS as 'the Social' is also typical usage among certain social groups. Some speech communities are still associated with assumptions about income, education and status in society. For example, if we hear someone speaking with a typical East End of London accent, we might make assumptions about his or her income, education or status in society. There are plenty of examples of people who confound this stereotypical way of looking at people, not least Fred Housego, the former Mastermind winner, who uses a London variety of English. Furthermore, there is evidence to suggest that speakers from all social groups use more vernacular forms in informal situations (Holmes, 1992). You may have been taught at school, or by your parents, to pronounce the letter 'h' at the start of a word, but do you really always do this? Do you never drop the 'g' at the end of 'ing'?

Linguistic repertoire

In fact, we all have a **linguistic repertoire** made up of different ways of speaking, and we adapt our speech to suit each situation. The relationship between language and social context is very complex (Halliday, 1993). It is not just our knowledge of grammar and vocabulary that is important, but also the social knowledge that tells us how to use the words appropriately. The combination of choice of words with the right sort of sentences, the formality or informality of the way we speak and the choice of the content are referred to as **register**. The ability to get the register right (and in the right language) is sometimes referred to as **communicative competence**.

TEXT 3: REGISTER: THE RIGHT WORDS FOR THE RIGHT CONTEXT

Example I May I get you something to drink?

Example 2 What are we all drinkin', then?

In Text 3, the first example is much more formal than the second. It is a polite question, appropriate between people who perhaps don't know each other too well, or who feel some degree of social distance exists between them. The second example is more typical of a person in the pub who is offering to buy the next round of drinks for a group of friends. Even within monolingual communities, it is vital to adapt speech to situation – you have to get the register right.

It's vital to adapt your speech to suit the situation. If you don't, the conversation may go wrong

Many people live in a bilingual or multilingual world. It has been estimated that half the world's population is bilingual, and many others speak more than two languages (Holmes, 1992 p.79). A significant number of people living in the UK are bilingual or multilingual, and constantly need to adapt their speech to suit the context of situation. Before the right register can be selected, the appropriate language must first be used. For example, members of a Panjabi family living in Southall (London) regularly select between Urdu, Panjabi, Hindi, and English in conducting their everyday affairs (Saxena, 1994). Once the right language has been chosen, the speaker must then use the appropriate register in order to communicate effectively. The linguistic repertoire of truly multilingual people is extremely sophisticated. However, the communicative competence of a multilingual person may have limitations. An elder from Bangladesh who is extremely comfortable with the subtleties of Bengali and Sylheti, for example, may not be so confident in using English, particularly when it comes to some semi-formal situations involving, say, the Housing Department or Social Services. As a social care worker you will need to be sensitive to the language problems of such a person when faced with the daunting prospect of an interview for assessment.

Reflect on practice

What speech communities do you consider yourself to belong to? How do these differ from the census categories that were listed in Chapter 1?

What speech communities do you think are represented in your workplace, either by staff or service users?

Do you speak differently at home from the way you do at work? Is the choice between different languages, or between different ways of using the same language?

Variety, prejudice and power: devaluing diversity

As a social care worker it is vital that you recognise the existence and significance of linguistic repertoires, and also the subtle system of value judgements, which can be inbuilt into the various discourses within any society. In the case of English, for example, linguists agree that there is nothing intrinsically 'superior' about the variety that has come to be known as Standard UK English. This is the version of English that is currently used through the United Kingdom to conduct business, codify laws and to write social work reports, amongst other things. Standard English is also the variety you will be asked to use to write your essays and your examination papers. However, if we trace the history of this variety of English back to the fifteenth century, we might argue that if William Caxton had not chosen to use the East Midlands variety when printing the first books in English, then the 'Standard' version we use today might have been very different. The East Midlands variety of English (which uses I instead of ich, and home instead of hame) was, as a result of Caxton's decision, codified and widely distributed throughout England in the form of printed books. This was one of the reasons why it eventually became accepted as the 'official' version of English. It subsequently developed into the Standard variety that we use today. We should also note that Standard English continues to change, and what is now considered 'correct' may be outdated and even out of use in a hundred years time (Graddol, Leith and Swann, 1996). However, there is still a great deal of snobbery about the way people speak, particularly towards speakers of regional varieties or people who just speak differently. The practitioner who values diversity will do well to remember that if Caxton had made a different choice, the UK Standard variety of English might have been closer to the speech of people who live in Birmingham or Glasgow. Varieties of English are linguistically no better and no worse than each other.

Reflect on practice ....

Have you ever made a judgement about someone mainly on the basis of his or her speech?

How important is it for someone to be able to use Standard English at work? Does it matter if a member of staff speaks with an accent that is different from what the majority of your service users expect to hear?

Caxton's decision to use the East Midlands variety of English for his books was not whimsical. His reason for selecting the East Midlands dialect was that this reflected usage amongst the literate and merchant classes of the south and east of England (in a triangle roughly bounded by London, Cambridge and Oxford). These were precisely the people to whom Caxton hoped to sell his books, which reminds us of how closely language use can be allied to power and influence within any society. Standard and national languages can be misused to exert power over people who do not have expertise in their use. An expert user of a Standard language may devalue the speaker of a regional variety of the same language. This may make a difference between the selection of interview candidates, or the way in which someone turning up at a social services helpdesk is greeted or dealt with.

Varieties of English

Furthermore, many forms of English have developed around the world, and these are recognised by some linguists as true varieties of English in their own right. Thus, Indian English is not an inferior form of the language, but is a variety that is unique to the Indian subcontinent and has its own particular practices. The rhythm of Indian English is different from that spoken elsewhere, which means that it can sound strange to someone used to hearing the stress-timed rhythm of UK English. Speakers of Indian English often use the tag 'isn't it?' in a way that a UK English speaker wouldn't, or leave out the definite article before a noun. Indian English might thus say 'Social Services office closes at six, isn't it?', rather than the standard English form 'The Social Services office closes at six, doesn't it?' . However, sometimes people who use Standard English (or another regional variety as used within the UK) regard world Englishes as somehow 'inferior'.

Such value judgements can also operate between speakers of completely different languages. In 1952, as a result of civil disturbance, the British Government in Kenya reorganised the education system, and English became the official language for schooling. The Kenyan writer Ngugi wa Thiong'o has described how, during this period, school pupils were physically punished and humiliated for speaking their own language, Gikuyu, in the school playground. Conversely, the use of English was rewarded, and expertise in the language became synonymous with intelligence and ability. The experience was so profound for Ngugi that after publishing four novels in English, from 1977 he was determined never to write in English again, but to use and promote the Gikuyu language in his published work (Maybin and Mercer, 1996).

Ngugi's experience of growing up in colonial Kenya is an extreme example of the effect of the use of language as a tool for social control. You might wish to object to the notion that acquiring English can be a bad thing, particularly since this is now spoken by millions of people worldwide, whether as a first language, one of a number of second languages or as an international language. Indeed, some people see the acquisition of English as a key to accessing the worlds of commerce, business and academic life, as well as the way to obtain jobs, wealth and influence.

Language as a tool to express identity

However, in many situations, there remain difficulties when speakers of different languages come into contact. We use language not only to communicate but also to express our identities. When people are forced to use a language that is not natural to them, or come up against a different variety of their own language, they may be disadvantaged. Even if they have chosen words which approximate to what they want to say, they may not get the register right in order to express their real meaning.

As a social care worker, you will need to develop a sensitive approach to interpreting what your service users say to you, particularly if you don't share the same first language. If the person sounds aggressive, for example, could this be because his or her own first language has a different rhythm or range of tones from your own? If the way you are spoken to evokes a negative emotional response in yourself, try to bear in mind that you may be misinterpreting the verbal signals your service user is giving off. Of course, it would be impossible for you to recognise and interpret exactly the vast range of such variations across all the speakers of different languages you encounter in the course of your work. As you acquire expertise with speakers of certain languages (e.g. speakers of Eastern European languages seeking asylum in the UK), you may begin to learn about such key differences. However, in general, it will be enough simply to bear these regional and cultural differences in mind when responding sensitively to your service users.

Reflect on practice ·

Consider a conversation you've had with someone during which you experienced a negative emotional reaction. Perhaps you became angry or irritated by the way things went.

Was this because of the content of the conversation, or was it because of the way things were said? Did you perceive the speaker as aggressive or hostile in some way, or did you feel that he or she was being rude to you?

On reflection, do you feel that your emotional response could be explained by the way the person spoke to you?

3.4 The everyday expression of diversity: conversations and scripts

In Chapter 2 we considered the contribution of our emotional response to the creation of meaningful psychological contact between human beings. For the social care worker, it is useful to recognise how discourse practices can help or hinder a positive emotional response. In this section we will review three aspects of discourse: firstly, how conversations are built up between people; secondly, how an imbalance in the power relationship between parties to a conversation can dramatically effect the course that that conversation takes; and finally, the implications of not having a spoken language as your first or preferred means of communication.

Working relationships: the subtleties of conversation

The way that a conversation is structured, from start to finish, plays a vital role in determining how successful that speech act will be. By way of introduction to this topic, consider the case study below.

CASE STUDY – A bad start?

Brenda, the manager of Abbey Hey Care Home, is standing in the lobby of the main building discussing an important matter with the deputy. Suddenly, a man rushes in and interrupts the conversation very abruptly.

'Mr Smith!' is all he says, in a very loud voice. He doesn't wait for a gap in the conversation, or say 'Excuse me!', or even 'Good Morning'. He hasn't noticed that there is a receptionist on duty who might be able to help him.

'Mr Smith, here!' he repeats, in a very insistent manner.

Brenda's initial response is irritation, as she feels that the man is being rude. However, she quickly recognises a number of factors that may be contributing to this. It sounds to her as if English is not the man's first language, and it may be that he doesn't know enough about how English is used in the UK to realise that his opening speech might be perceived as rude.

Within a few seconds, Brenda excuses herself from the conversation with the deputy and turns her attention to the newcomer. She doesn't let her initial irritation impair her ability to appraise the situation and respond appropriately.

What might your reaction have been if you were in Brenda's situation?

Many people in the UK who use Standard English as their first language do feel that it's rude if someone doesn't open a conversation with some kind of greeting. The exception to this would be in a case of emergency, when people feel justified in moving straight to the point. By and large, however, it is considered rude to move straight to the business in hand without some kind of initial opener. Take a look at Figure 3.3 below, which sets out some of the key recurring elements in conversation. These key elements are the greeting, 'small talk', the main business of the conversation and the close (see Maybin and Mercer, 1996, for a very thorough explanation and discussion of how conversations are structured).

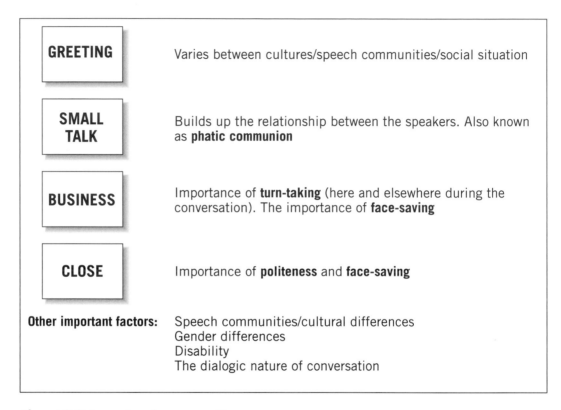

GREETING	Varies between cultures/speech communities/social situation
SMALL TALK	Builds up the relationship between the speakers. Also known as **phatic communion**
BUSINESS	Importance of **turn-taking** (here and elsewhere during the conversation). The importance of **face-saving**
CLOSE	Importance of **politeness** and **face-saving**

Other important factors: Speech communities/cultural differences
Gender differences
Disability
The dialogic nature of conversation

Figure 3.3 Aspects of conversation

Greetings

Greetings can be very simple, as in 'Hi! How are you?' They can also be complex. Contrast the more formal greeting 'Good morning, Your Worship, and welcome to the Cedars. We are delighted to receive you here today for the official opening of our new soft play facility.' Greetings will vary according to the formality of the occasion, the relationship between the speakers, and the speech communities to which they belong. In France, speakers must choose between the pronouns *tu* and *vous* when addressing an individual (*tu* is less formal and *vous* is more polite; *vous* is also the plural form for all situations). In Japan, the choices are far more complex (Holmes, 1992). The speaker first has to decide on the status of the other person in terms of family background, sex and age. The relative formality of the situation is also a factor. The choice is then between 'plain, polite and deferential' styles of speaking, which involves the way words are pronounced, the form of the words and the way they are put together. The speaker must sustain this choice of style beyond the greeting, but clearly it is important to get everything right from the start of the conversation.

For the social care worker it is helpful to bear in mind the importance of the greeting element in any conversation, not least because it is a vital aspect to establishing (or maintaining) relationships between yourself and your clients. Conversely, if your service user gets it wrong and the lack of a greeting (or an inappropriate one) produces a negative emotional reaction in you, then you may be able to deal with this more professionally by reflecting on why you have reacted in this way. The cause may lie in the way that language is used.

Small talk

The second key aspect of conversation is small talk, a kind of social grooming which Malinowski (see page 59) dubbed **phatic communion**. The purpose of small talk is either to build up the relationship established by the greeting, or to maintain already existing relationships. Consider Text 4 below.

TEXT 4: GREETING AND SMALL TALK BETWEEN COLLEAGUES

John: Hi Mary! Happy New Year! How are you doing?

Mary: Happy New Year! I'm not so bad. Yourself?

John: Yeah! Ate too much over the holiday. Usual thing.

Mary: Tell me about it! I can't resist those chocolate liqueurs.

John and Mary are two colleagues chatting together on their return to work after the mid-winter holiday. They need to re-establish their friendship after the break, and start the working day in a warm and friendly way. If they were so inclined, they could keep up the small talk about over-indulgence for some time, or they might wander onto other non-work related subjects. We should also note that they share the same (implied) concerns about food and weight, and they also celebrate the same New Year. Once the telephone rings and business resumes, talk in the office is likely to become more focused, although there may be times when colleagues resort to phatic communion during the day as a release from the tension of concentrating on work. Malinowski considered phatic communion to include gossip, comments on the weather, general enquiries about health, statements of the obvious and expressions of sympathy — in short, conversation which lacks a specific purpose other than to maintain the relationship between the speakers.

Small talk may not always be appropriate. If you were having a meeting with a member of staff to investigate a complaint against a colleague, you might feel that it would be better to move straight to the business in hand rather than to spend time on pleasantries about the weather. Your decision would be based heavily on the context of situation. However, it is worth remembering that small talk can sometimes be used in formal contexts to help along the more serious business aspects of the conversation. If you are required to interview someone in order to complete an assessment form of some kind, you might be able to build up an atmosphere of trust and friendliness by opening the interview with a warm greeting, followed by some chat on general matters before moving in to questioning and form-filling. Once again, the decision is yours. It might be the case that the person you are interviewing is too nervous or anxious to appreciate general chatter, and wants to get straight down to the task in hand (perhaps if the objective is to determine eligibility for a service). Clearly, it is up to you to respond appropriately, as you have the power to control the conversation in such a situation. We will return to the issue of power later in this section.

Closing a conversation

The close of a conversation is just as important as the opening. Closings often involve repetition of things that have been said earlier and reference back to previous topics. Polite withdrawal from the speech event is critical, whether or not this was a formal business meeting, or an informal conversation between friends. Text 5 sets out an example of closure at the end of a brief meeting between colleagues to discuss a service user.

TEXT 5: INFORMAL CONVERSATION CLOSURE

Jan: I have to go now, Helen. I've got another meeting. Thanks very much for that report on Mrs Wilson.

Helen: No problem. I've got another meeting too. I'm glad the report was what you needed.

Jan: Yeah, it's great. Just what I needed. Too many meetings...

Helen: I know what you mean, and it seems to be getting worse – hardly any time to get on top of things.

Jan: Yes, well, I've really got to be going. I'll email you about Mrs Wilson. Thanks once again.

Helen: I look forward to hearing from you. Take care, now.

Jan has to leave, but feels she can't withdraw without justifying this ('I've got another meeting'), and also by repeatedly thanking Helen for the file she needed. Helen supports this by saying that she also has a meeting, thus signalling that she, too, is happy for the meeting to close. Both speakers feel the need to reinforce the positive nature of their time together, and end their meeting without either of them losing face. If Jan were to get up and leave with a curt 'Bye!', then Helen would feel this was rude. When a person has no option but to cut short a conversation, he or she will often apologise for doing so. In such a situation, the one who has to leave may say something like 'I'm so sorry. I didn't realise it was that time. I really have to dash off and leave you!'

> **Reflect on practice**
>
> With respect to each of the following speech events, how important do you think the greeting, small talk, business and closure elements might be? Who is likely to take the lead in each scenario?
>
> - You have an appraisal interview with your manager.
> - You serve afternoon tea to residents in a care home.
> - You discuss future care provision for a person with learning disabilities and her relatives.
> - You meet a friend in a pub.

Losing face

The issue of **losing face** is an important element in any conversation, and there are two aspects to this. On the one hand, a person usually feels the need to be liked and admired (positive face); on the other hand, people don't want to feel threatened or to have their perceived status compromised (negative face). When language is used inappropriately, perhaps because the rules of two or more speech communities are in conflict during the speech event, then a person may perceive that he or she has lost face, and may become defensive (or even aggressive). Such misunderstandings can occur across two or more languages, and even between different speech communities within the same language. There is also evidence that men and women sometimes use language differently. A study of American, British, Polish and New Zealand speakers, for example, has shown that women use compliments more frequently than men, and that women are complimented more often than men (Holmes in Maybin and Mercer, 1996: 32). In some languages, such as Bengali, men and women may use different linguistic forms. One example from this language is that women may use an initial (*l*) where men use an initial (*n*) for some words (Holmes, 1992: 65).

Turn-taking

This is another important aspect of conversation. Turn-taking is the ability to recognise when it is acceptable to begin to speak, taking your turn after the previous speaker has finished. In many English speech communities, the basic rules are that only one person speaks at a time, and any damage caused by overlapping or interrupting has to be repaired fairly quickly (Maybin and Mercer, 1996). If the damage is not repaired, one or other of the speakers may lose face. However, there are some speech communities where overlapping is more the norm, and there may be some situations in which interruptions are considered acceptable (see section 3.5).

Language use amongst people with disabilities or mental health problems

There will be some people who may not be expected to use all the elements of conversation in the same way. People with visual impairments, for example, may not always be able to read the non-verbal cues given by speakers, although they may be especially sensitive to subtleties of oral expression such as tone of voice. In a group, it is possible they may not be able to pick up the non-verbal signals that an individual wants to take the conversational floor, and it may not always be obvious exactly who is speaking. Deaf people, although they are not necessarily able to hear a conversation, do recognise such devices as small talk and the importance of greeting, and do distinguish between different registers when signing (for example, between formal and informal communication). However, people with hearing problems can be disadvantaged, especially in groups, when it can be very hard to determine who is speaking, and understanding can be hindered by the failure of the speaker to position him or herself so that the deaf person can lip-read.

A person with a visual impairment may not pick up on non-verbal cues but may be sensitive to tone of voice

People with learning disabilities encompass a very wide range of abilities when it comes to using language. Some people, especially those with autism, tend not to conform to the basic speech patterns described in Figure 3.3. However, others are very good at using these conversational devices, and indeed this may sometimes lead the social care worker to underestimate the extent of their learning disabilities. Furthermore, recent research on young adults with learning disabilities who also display delinquent behaviours indicates that even fairly neutral forms of expression can be misinterpreted as hostile or threatening. These young people are unable to read the language cues, which would not present a problem for a person without such a disability (Smith and Griffin, 2002). This inability to read social cues in language may also extend to some people with mental health problems.

The foregoing paragraphs do not do justice to the complexity of the issue of language use amongst people with disabilities or with mental health problems. You will need to do further study in order to become more sensitive to the ways in which language use varies amongst people with disabilities, particularly if you are planning to make a career working with disabled people, or those with mental health problems. What is important at this stage is that firstly, you become aware of the great diversity of expression that exists. Secondly, when you encounter language practices that differ from your own, or from what you are expecting, you need to be prepared for the possible negative response it may effect in you. In Chapter 2 we considered how thought and emotion interact to create meaning, or to make sense of what is happening. When you encounter a language practice that doesn't conform to what you are expecting, for example when a person with a learning disability doesn't

Being aware that the conventions of different speech communities may vary helps you to value diversity

respond to your prompts, this may trigger some kind of emotional response within you. Furthermore, if you can't read the language cues that someone is giving you, the chances are that he or she can't read your cues either. If you are feeling frustrated or even disturbed by the mismatch of conversational styles and expectations, your service user may also be experiencing a similar response. In such a situation, being language aware gives you the knowledge (you already have the authority) to work with the person to bring about a positive outcome.

This awareness of how speech events work or break down is invaluable to the social care worker. It will help you to encourage clients to express their feelings, and to establish and maintain productive dialogue as necessary. Awareness of and respect for the conventions of different speech communities will help you to demonstrate that you respect and value your service users as individuals. Conversely, by failing to take such considerations into account, you may run the risk of abusing the power that lies within your role as a social care worker. In the next section, we will look more closely at issues of power within discourse.

Reflect on practice ....

Consider a conversation you have had that went wrong at some point. Was this in any way the result of a mismatch between expectations as to how the conversation should go?

Could it be that you were both from different speech communities and were not able to fully interpret the clues that the other one was giving out, either verbally or non-verbally?

3.5 The expression of power through language

It may seem like stating the obvious to say that a conversation is dialogic – that is to say it takes more than one person to create one. People build up episodes of conversation between them, and the ebb and flow of a particular speech event depends upon the relationship of the participants, the formality or informality of the context of situation, and also the speech communities to which the speakers belong.

Power in relationships: scripted conversations

When all parties are relatively equal in status, then the flow of speech might be fairly unpredictable, as speakers introduce new topics where appropriate. However, when there is a relative imbalance of power between speakers, and set within a particular context of situation, the speech event is likely to proceed to a predetermined outcome, and one of the participants is more likely to control the progress of the dialogue. Consider Text 6 below. In your opinion, who is in control of the dialogue?

TEXT 6: CONSULTATION WITH A GP

Doctor: Hello there, come in and sit down. How are you?

Patient: Erm... Hello doctor... not too bad. I'm still missing the wife though...

Doctor: Yes, of course. So what can I do for you today?

Patient: Well, doctor, I've been having these headaches and trouble sleeping...

Doctor: Headaches. OK, can you tell me exactly where you get the pain?

Patient: Well, it's sort of all over, well it moves about... it sort of starts at the back and...

Doctor: And how often does this happen?

Patient: Well I've been taking aspirin and it goes away, and then it comes back, erm...

Doctor: So would you say you get this headache – once a week, a few times a week or every day?

In this hypothetical consultation, the doctor takes the initiative by greeting the patient and inviting him to sit down. She follows up with the ambiguous 'How are you?' It is ambiguous because this is the place in a less formal conversation where speakers might make general enquiries about each other's health, without necessarily expecting to go into any great detail (phatic communion). The patient in Text 6 is disconcerted by this, as he is unsure whether it is an invitation to an episode of small talk, as it might be between friends. Remembering to greet the doctor in response (he is aware of the importance of the greeting part of any conversation), the patient decides to go for the non-committal, 'Not too bad', but then starts to volunteer some very personal (and potentially significant) information. He is still grieving for his wife. Clearly, the doctor is aware of the patient's recent bereavement ('Yes, of course'), but the appointment book is full and the doctor must move swiftly on to the task in hand – diagnosis of the patient's presenting symptoms ('So what can we do for you today?'). The patient begins to describe his symptoms, which are headaches and sleeplessness. Deciding to focus on the headaches, the doctor moves the conversation into a rapid and focused question and answer sequence, often interrupting the patient when his description starts to become imprecise, sharpening up the information she extracts by more detailed questions (this technique is known as 'funnelling'). It is almost as if doctor and patient are following a **script** in which the doctor is expected to take the lead, and her interruptions are accepted by the patient

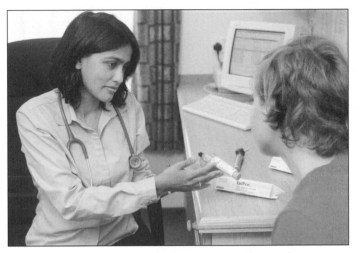

During a consultation, doctor and patient often follow a 'script' in which the doctor takes the lead

as a necessary part of the speech event. Arguably, he would not tolerate similar interruptions from friends during a chat in the pub. He might not be offended, but he would almost certainly not give up the conversational floor without a fight.

If the same man were in a session with a counsellor, would you expect the speech event to take a different course? Perhaps you might expect the counsellor to focus immediately on the person's grief rather than his headaches; you might also expect that he or she would not interrupt the client quite so much, if at all, and also that he or she would use the skills of reformulating and feeding back to the service user the story that he wants to present. In chapter 4 we will look more closely at the phenomenon of **re-storying**. It is sufficient here to note that the script for a counselling session is likely to be very different from that of a consultation with a GP, although the counsellor may still have more power than the service user and must be careful how he or she uses this authority if the story is not to be distorted.

There are many other situations in which scripts are enacted. In the classroom, for example, the teacher has the power to lead the discourse, and students are expected to respond appropriately. When a police officer is taking a statement from a witness, he or she has power to control the dialogue by virtue of his or her legal authority.

The discourse in courtrooms is even more rigidly controlled by protocol, the presiding judge having supreme control over what is said, and turn-taking is strictly prescribed. Witnesses respond to questions from barristers, and are directed to adhere to the matter in hand by the judge whenever they introduce irrelevant matter.

You may be able to identify the operation of scripts within your own place of work. When someone does the rounds with the medication trolley, for example, does the business of making sure that everyone is issued with the correct drugs override the more social activities of small talk? During an appraisal interview, would you expect the manager to take the lead in steering the conversation through the prescribed questions in order to achieve the desired outcome for the organisation? And when someone turns up at a social services reception area asking to be assessed for entitlement to services, would you expect it to be a social work professional who leads the conversation during the assessment interview?

How often do you have conversations at work where you have more power than the person you are talking to? How do you express this power in terms of language practices (e.g. taking the lead, responding to small talk, allowing turn-taking to take place)?

When is it important to take the lead? Are there times when this doesn't matter?

3.6 Deafness and discourse: disability or difference?

The title of this section is meant as a deliberate challenge to historical assumptions about deafness. This alternative approach goes right to the heart of what it means to value diversity, and challenges you to consider what attitudes you might need to adopt in order to practise in the field of social care and social work. As a starting point, we've chosen an extract from a poem by the deaf poet, Willard Madsen. This is printed as Text 7 on page 79. Madsen's poem asserts that 'only one small difference' sets deaf people apart from the hearing world (this line not reproduced). Yet hearing people often insist that deaf people must learn to speak and become like them, or be relegated to a 'deaf ghetto'. Madsen suggests that instead, the rest of the world should learn to sign in order to create 'one world at heart'. How did you react to this suggestion?

The notion that the attitude of the hearing world disables

The poet suggests that it is the attitude of the hearing world that disables people who cannot hear, and indeed there have been recorded instances of communities where deaf and hearing people have lived and worked side by side very successfully. On Martha's Vineyard, Massachusetts (USA) between the 1690s and the early twentieth century, there was a very high incidence of hereditary deafness. This was at a rate of about 25 per cent by the mid-nineteenth century. Consequently, everyone (hearing and deaf alike) learned to sign, and community members used both speech and sign in the same way as a bilingual person in a UK city might use, say, a variety of UK English and Gujerati, switching from one to the other as appropriate (Groce, 1991; Sacks, 1989). Furthermore, there were many advantages to having two communication systems. Many of the vineyarders lived by fishing, and sign was often used between workers in boats up to 150 yards apart to facilitate the task in hand. People in houses some distance away from each other used to communicate by using their spyglasses in order to read their neighbours' sign language. There are also anecdotes about people signing to each other to tell funny stories in church. Hearing people might also use sign when no deaf person was present. All residents on the vineyard were genuinely bilingual, and this served to reinforce the identity of all the islanders — deaf or hearing. Socially, there were no distinctions made between deaf and hearing people — deafness was simply not an issue with respect to the formation of friendships, or setting up of social activities.

TEXT 7: **NO!**

Extract from a poem by Willard Madsen

I'm tired of hearing
That old refrain:
'Teach the deaf to speak – to talk
And they'll be whole again!'

How well I know
That's just not so!
I live; I grow
And everyday
Quite simply tells me
'NO!'
…
You pat me on the back and say
'It's a hearing world you must live in
Or be quite simply,
Relegated to
A stigmatised
Deaf ghetto ghetto ghetto ghetto
A world of silence:
A world of signs:
A limited world
Apart from the rest!'

NO!
That's not the world at all:
Not the world I know:
My world is
Beautiful
Unlimited.
Not perfect, but
Neither void:
How can it be
When all around me
Are
Hands
Faces,
Whole beings,
Communicating?
And I understand all that's said;
No guessing,
Doubting,
Struggling,
To fill in the gaps –
Words unrecognised or missed!
…
Yes! Teach the deaf
To speak – to talk,
But teach them first
How to walk

With confidence,
With heads held high,
And full knowledge
To converse by
With 'words' flowing from the hand!
…
Let them carry
Throughout this land
A simple banner
Called 'Self-esteem',
And teach the world at large to sign –
To make us all
One world at heart
And not a world
That's set apart!
NO!

Source: *Language for the Eye: an Anthology of Deaf Writing and Publication*, ed. George Montgomery, Scottish Workshops Publications, 1995.

Models of deafness

This picture of life on Martha's Vineyard is in stark contrast to the ways in which deaf people are largely excluded from the hearing world today, which brings us back to Madsen's poem and the challenge it poses. Currently there are three models of deafness (Knight, 1998).

The first is the **medical model**, which is concerned to measure levels of hearing loss and to establish how this might be rectified in order to make the patient's hearing as 'normal' as possible.

The second is the **social model**. This is a challenge to the medical model in that it claims that people are not disabled by their physical or mental condition, but rather by society which does not allow them to achieve their maximum potential (for example, by discriminating against them in their efforts to obtain the kind of education they want, or in getting work). However, this model resembles the medical one in that it assumes that there is something called 'normal', and also that everyone in society will automatically aspire to the same norms.

However, some deaf people are currently challenging even the social model of deafness, and are promoting instead a linguistic and cultural model. This asserts that sign is a minority language, and that people who use it are a linguistic minority group, rather than disabled. Members of this group are proud to be **culturally Deaf** rather than simply audiologically deaf. The latter, by definition, renders Deaf people defective as human beings. People who see themselves as culturally Deaf thus reject the 'deficit model' as the impairment narrative (see Chapter 2). To be culturally Deaf is to be proud of the 'Beautiful Unlimited' world of which Willard Madsen writes in his poem, and there is indeed sound linguistic research to support the arguments for the existence of a Deaf speech community.

Sign language systems

You may be aware that there are a number of sign language systems currently in use worldwide. There are national sign languages such as those of Sweden, Britain and America, and then there are simpler systems such as Sign Supported English (SSE). Comments in this section are based on research into British Sign Language (BSL). Some years ago, all sign language was regarded simply as a kind of 'picture writing', having no subtlety or precision, and capable of expressing only the simplest of concepts. In fact, fully developed sign languages, such as BSL, are now regarded by some linguists as full languages rather than gestural codes. In BSL, for example, the elements of hand shape, position and movement recur in the same way as the phonemes (sounds) of spoken English, and tiny differences can indicate changes in meaning. BSL has its own complex grammatical system, and its expressiveness is enhanced by many non-manual features. Because BSL (like other signed languages) is visuo-spatial, the signer can make several gestures simultaneously. Signing is thus often referred to as 'multi-channelling', and it is a medium by which complex concepts can be conveyed. BSL has many non-manual markers (or gestures) which can be used to signal turn-taking, sentence boundaries, conditional clauses, topic-comment structures, questions and negatives, all of which can be signalled at the same time as the hands are being used to indicate words or concepts (Brennan, 1991). Sign has been described as 'language in four dimensions', that is, the time dimension is added to the three spatial dimensions accessible to the signer's body (Sacks, 1991).

British Sign Language is regarded as a language in its own right by some linguists

Concept of register in BSL

In section 3.2 we considered how important it is for a speaker to get the register right. A person must dip into his or her linguistic repertoire to produce language that will match the occasion and the perceived relationship between parties to the conversation.

This concept of register also exists in BSL, and the signer must choose between Frozen, Formal, Informal and Intimate modes of communication. The multi-channel system is very sophisticated, and the person who signs can put a great deal of information into the speech act. Furthermore, certainly within the UK, deaf people recognise and use conventions similar to those of the hearing community with respect to conversational practices such as greeting and small talk. BSL also enables a signer to indicate turn-taking (see above), and deaf people expect these conventions and adhere to them. Problems arise only during the interface between sign and speech, when it is very easy for hearing people to exclude deaf people through failure to observe the obvious stratagems of positioning oneself so that the deaf person can read the face, or by exercising self-restraint in turn-taking (perhaps by using a physical signal to indicate a wish to speak). Deaf people may often interrupt a conversation simply through lack of awareness that someone else is already speaking. The problem is obviously more acute in groups. If several people suddenly start laughing, for example, a deaf person may feel excluded and even wonder whether he or she is the butt of a joke. This apparent 'failure' on the part of the deaf person to observe group norms in conversation may even be wrongly associated with limited intelligence or capability.

CASE STUDY – Excluded from the group

Chris is an adult deaf student studying for a social care qualification at a College of Higher Education. He has been allocated to a group for a piece of project work, but has been excluded from the decision-making by his colleagues. The others have allocated Chris one of the simpler tasks, which they have decided should present him with fewer problems.

Chris is very angry, and after making representations both to his colleagues and to his tutor, has asserted his right to take part on an equal basis to the others, and has renegotiated his role in the project. However, this was a battle he could have done without, and it has left him feeling both annoyed and a little suspicious of the others.

Have you ever made a decision for someone else because you thought you were doing them a favour?

This case study illustrates how a deaf person can be marginalised by hearing people. Conversely, during a trip to Paris by a group of both hearing and deaf students, one of the non-deaf people discovered he had forgotten to bring shampoo. Unable to speak French, he was reluctant to go into a store to ask for what he wanted. With great confidence, one of the deaf students went into the shop and bought some shampoo without experiencing any problems at all. By deft use of a modified signed communication she bridged the Anglo-French language gap and came to the aid of her hearing colleague. Who was 'disabled' here?

Diversity in perception of deaf identity

We noted above that some people regard themselves as culturally Deaf rather than simply audiologically deaf. However, it is important to recognise that not all deaf people see themselves as culturally Deaf, and also that others may consider themselves to have membership of several speech communities (including the Deaf community). Someone who has been deafened later in life may have a very different approach to this than someone who was born deaf (and is thus **prelingually deaf**), and for whom Sign is very much a first language. On the other hand, the existence of this very well-defined Deaf culture constitutes a challenge to all hearing cultures, because it asserts that Sign has an equal value to spoken languages. Furthermore, by accessing the Deaf community, deaf people acquire their own normality (Brien, 1991). Strictly speaking, you don't have to be audiologically deaf to be a member of the Deaf community (for example, you may be able to sign and also be welcome at Deaf social events because of your personal links to a Deaf person, or because you are active on behalf of the community). However, ultimately membership of this community carries with it a well-developed alternative to the deficit model of deafness operating in the hearing world. Culturally Deaf people are replacing old models and discourses of disability and exclusion with new narratives that value the different status that being deaf brings. The Deaf community has developed its own cultural norms (for example, speech may be discouraged and a refusal to sign frowned upon), and its own linguistic repertoire. Indeed, some audiologically deaf people are actually reluctant to have surgical interventions such as cochlear implants (which can restore some degree of hearing), as they would lose the unique identity that goes with being culturally Deaf. By asserting their difference (and indeed rejoicing in it), Deaf people are proudly defining their identity in the same way as gay and lesbian or black people have done.

CASE STUDY – Disabled or different?

Rob, who was born deaf, has been offered a cochlear implant to enable him to hear for the first time. His mother Rachel, who was also born deaf, is objecting to the operation. She argues that Rob can communicate perfectly well with his friends by using BSL. He is also a proficient lip-reader and can make himself understood to non-deaf people. Rob, who is now 11 years old, attends a special unit in a mainstream school (where there is a deaf teacher), and he is currently thriving there.

Rachel feels that if Rob were able to hear, he would lose his identity as a member of the Deaf community. Furthermore, he might not be fully accepted by hearing people, as he might still have some kind of hearing impairment even after the operation.

What do you think of Rachael's point of view? What would you advise her to do if you were involved with this family in a professional capacity?

There are a number of challenges here for the social care worker. At the very least, the assertion of Deaf identity is a warning to hearing people not to make assumptions about the relative 'superiority' of speech and its desirability. However, if you find the arguments of the Deaf community persuasive, why not push this reasoning a little further and extend it to other groups that have fallen victim to the deficit model?

Other people can and should assert the right to celebrate their difference in the face of what the majority regard as 'normal', whatever that may be. Working positively with diversity is an attitude of mind as much as it is about adherence to policies, codes or laws. To celebrate diversity involves embracing a different narrative from the 'grand narrative' of the importance of being 'normal' that is pervasive in our society.

Reflect on practice

How do you react to the following statement?

'Everyone has the right to live as normal a life as possible.'

Summary

○ All discourse has a cultural context.

○ Meaning is created from the social knowledge of the speaker and listener, not just by the spoken word.

○ Everyone has a linguistic repertoire of different ways of speaking, whether he or she is monolingual or multilingual.

○ The combination of word choice, formality or informality of speech and the content of what we say is known as register.

○ Getting the register right is referred to as communicative competence.

○ Standard English is not necessarily linguistically superior to regional varieties. This is true of other languages.

○ Sometimes the choice of a language (or between varieties of the same language) is determined by issues of power and control.

○ Some conversations follow 'scripts' in which one person determines the outcome.

○ People often make value judgements about other people based on the way they speak.

○ If someone doesn't follow the conversational rules you are expecting, then you may experience some kind of emotional reaction.

○ Sign languages such as BSL are complex, four-dimensional communication systems, and can be regarded as languages in their own right.

○ There is a difference between being audiologically deaf (not being able to hear) and being culturally Deaf.

○ Culturally Deaf people see themselves as a linguistic minority rather than as disabled.

○ Valuing diversity is attitudinal, rather than a matter of simply following laws, policies and guidelines.

CHAPTER 4

Many voices: expressing diversity through narrative

Introduction

In Chapter 3 we considered aspects of discourse with particular reference to the elements of conversation, and how these may be affected by imbalances in the power relationship between parties to the speech event. We studied the experience of the Deaf community, and suggested that the concept of 'speech' should be widened to embrace signed communication. In this chapter we move on to consider another aspect of discourse – that of the narrative or story – which permeates the whole business of communication between individuals or within groups. The focus is on the oral or signed narrative, although our discussion will extend to include written aspects of storytelling.

Because the creation of narratives is such an important part of everyday life, it is vital for the social care worker to be able to recognise its significance, particularly with respect to service users. Narratives are used to express aspects of self, as well as to entertain or to explain, and will contain essential clues about the teller's identity (or identities). Not only will you need to listen sensitively to such disclosures, but you must also recognise how narrative is produced jointly, and that as a listener you will influence the way the story is told. Finally, as a practitioner you will have responsibility for retelling or re-storying the narratives you are privileged to hear. Re-storying offers you an opportunity to demonstrate respect for diversity.

Aims This chapter aims to enable you to explore:

4.1   Describing narrative: function and type

4.2   Respecting diversity: collaboration in the creation of a narrative

4.3   Telling tales: re-storying the narrative

4.1 Describing narrative: function and type

Some disciplines distinguish between the concepts of 'story' and 'narrative', ascribing specialist meaning to each. For the purpose of this section (and throughout Chapter 3), the terms 'story', 'narrative' and 'autobiography' will generally be used interchangeably to indicate the same concept – that of the telling or retelling of events in a specially constructed way. Where terms are used in a specialist manner, this will be clearly explained.

What is a narrative?

Broadly speaking, the telling of a personal narrative involves the reconstruction of an event or episode. In Western societies, such a telling usually proceeds in chronological order, moving in sequence through the progress of the event in question. In creating such a narrative, the teller will inevitably select from a range of facts about that episode in order to present a particular viewpoint about it. This viewpoint will be made clear to the listener by a number of devices such as tone of voice and the ways in which what happened is described. This aspect of narrative is known as an evaluation. The teller is often concerned to present him or herself in a positive light, and this will have an effect on the selection of events, and the way in which the various protagonists are described. In telling a story, a person is creating or presenting an aspect of him or herself. Storytelling is thus a vital part of the creation of personal identity. However, it takes more than one person to create an oral narrative, and the response of listeners has an important effect on the way the story is eventually told.

In this and section 4.2 we will explore the different forms that narrative can take, and how this varies between cultures and speech communities. We will also look at the role you play as a social care worker, firstly as a listener and co-creator of personal narratives, and secondly as a reteller of the stories you hear.

Reflect on practice

Do you find that there are some stories about yourself that you frequently tell to others? What do you think these stories reveal about you?

If you were to write a novel based on your own life history, who would be the main characters? What would be the main plot, and what sub-plots would you include? Which bits of your life would you choose to leave out?

The function of narrative: creating and expressing identities

Oral or signed narratives exist in many different forms, ranging along a continuum from the loose fragments of autobiography which occur within conversations, through the more structured storytelling of the skilled raconteur, to the grand set pieces of professional or cultural storytellers. A specific example will serve to illustrate, and to open the discussion. Text 1 is a transcription of a spoken narrative told by Clara Vaughan at the age of 82. Clara was born in Manchester in 1893, and often used to reminisce about events that happened when she was a young woman. This telling was tape-recorded in 1975 by John Forristal, and forms part of a longer sequence of conversation and oral storytelling. In this extract, Clara is describing an incident that happened during her time working in a munitions factory during World War I. She tells how a dispute between herself and the charge hand brought production to a temporary halt until it was resolved by the supervisor.

TEXT 1: DISPUTE ON THE FACTORY FLOOR

Clara: And another time – erm – the crane driver – I waved to her – to – a shell – pick it up – well, so I put it into my lathe

And as she was coming down with the crane the charge-hand come across and he's taken it away

I said, you can't take that it's mine

Oo, he said, er. I've got a lathe empty over here – I said, well, *my* lathe's empty, I said, I've called her down for it

Anyhow he took it
And – er – I said, well, I said, I'm not doing any more work for you I said... I don't want any more shells

So he said, oo, well, you'll *have* to do – and I'll put you one in your lathe, like, and – er – he put it in

And I said, well I'm not going to do it
So he said, well, I'll start it for you

Well, he started it, well when he come to the end I had to stop it
Otherwise it would have smashed all the works
So – I stopped it – and I said – I wasn't going to do any more
I said, well in fact, I said, if it'd been daytime I'd have walked out on you
Being on nights, y'know, 10 o'clock till 6 I couldn't walk out

John: Yes

Clara: And I can remember me standing in the middle of the floor – and all the – all the bosses round me

John: Yes

Clara: And I was telling them what, y'know, what I wouldn't do – this and that, and they were trying to persuade me

And then – er – Miss Harrison – she was, like, one of our Supervisors

She came up, like, and was talking

So I said, oh well, alright Miss Harrison, I said, I'm doing it – I said, not for any of these *men* here   (*very loud*)

I said

I'm doing it because you've asked me

So, I said, I'm going back and doing my work... little rows we used to have (*laughing*)

Types of oral story

Text 1 is typical of the stories that Clara regularly recounted to her family members. She was a skilled and entertaining raconteur, whose stories were set pieces, which she would retell on request. On each occasion the telling would be very similar to the time before. Linguistic researchers have defined four **genres** (types) of oral story:

● those which include the setting out and then resolution of a crisis for the purposes of entertaining the listeners (narrative and anecdote)
● those making a moral point (exemplum)
● those involving the factual retelling of an incident or situation, including some kind of appraisal (recount).

This is not a linguistics textbook, but it is interesting to observe that Text 1 arguably appears to fall into the first of these categories. Clara clearly sets up in stages the crisis resulting from the disagreement between herself and the charge hand, then goes on to show how it was resolved. The gradual build up and the theatrical way in which Miss Harrison is described as defusing the situation put the story into the category of entertainment. Clara varies her tone of voice to indicate how the conflict escalates. This obviously cannot be picked up from the transcript, and the anger and contempt she puts into the phrase 'not for any of these *men* here' needs to be heard to be appreciated.

This expression of contempt alerts us to another, very significant, function of narrative. In Chapter 2 we argued that the telling of stories is closely bound up with the expression of self and of personal identity. In Text 1, Clara casts herself as a strong-minded woman, capable of defending her rights against authority in general, and male authority in particular. This is a theme that recurs in her stories (many of which tell of events which took place either before or during the conflict of 1914–1918), and it is arguably indicative of a high level of self-esteem and personal sense of self, particularly her sense of identity as a woman. Narrative psychology recognises the importance of storytelling as 'a way of organising episodes, actions and accounts of action', and indeed some scholars see narrative as 'an organising principle for human life' (Crossley, 2000: 46). Another way of describing this is that each person is a narrator of selves, and the stories that each individual tells about him or herself are unique to that person (Harre, 1998). Such stories represent that person's experiences, cultural background, thoughts, memories and even expectations for the future. In this sense, each person is living and telling his or her own story at the same time as events are retold, cast in a form in which the teller presents to the external world a particular self or selves. Of course, the person listening to the story may choose to interpret it in a different way from that presented or intended by the storyteller. This will be explored in more detail below in section 4.2. For now, we will continue to focus on the creation of identity through narrative.

Reflect on practice

When you tell stories about yourself, what kind of 'self' do you consistently present?

Are there people you work with (colleagues or service users) who are always telling stories about themselves? Are there consistent patterns or themes in the events they describe, or in the ways they talk about themselves and other people? Do these stories provide clues to how they like to be treated or what they really want?

In a residential establishment for men with learning disabilities, Esplanade, a study of storytelling by the residents revealed that 'localised tellings' were performed (Croft, 1999). These tellings are different in structure from those told by people who do not have a learning disability, but nevertheless they can be identified as narratives, particularly as the tellers demonstrated a strong impulse to share their stories with listeners. The stories of the Esplanade residents Kyle, Lee and Don are of interest for several reasons. Firstly, the tellings made no reference to Esplanade or to events taking place there but instead focus on aspects of the storytellers' own lives. In this respect, the tellers were creating personal space in which they could escape the behavioural routine that dominated life in the house. A second point is that each of these men had his own distinct way of telling his stories, expressing his individual identity very strongly. Finally, the researcher had to adapt her own listening style to accommodate the preferred narrative technique of each teller. Here, we should note that with respect to people with learning disabilities we should expect as much diversity in storytelling as from people who are not so disabled. Each person with a learning disability is unique, and creates selves through narrative in the same way as everyone else. The listening may demand a great deal of skill and flexibility, as the approach used by the researcher at Esplanade demonstrates. We will consider the role you play as listener in section 4.2. For now, we continue to explore how identities are created through narrative.

Text 1 and the example of the men at Esplanade provide good examples of how individual selves are created and presented, but, of course, individuals may also take aspects of their identity from membership of groups. This kind of expression of self is very common in, for example, Japanese society, where people tend to define and present themselves in relation to others, according to differences and likenesses (Harre, 1998: 159–60). Within large organisations, too, individuals may choose to define themselves in terms of the prevailing organisational culture, using specialised terminology and casting themselves in roles that they perceive as potentially desirable to their managers.

TEXT 2: INTERVIEW FOR INTERNAL PROMOTION

Interviewer: Tell us why we should consider you for the post of Training Manager in social services?

Candidate: Well, I'm totally committed to the concept of modernising the social care workforce, and I'm absolutely convinced that this is the best way forward – matching skills to job competencies – mapping everything against the TOPSS strategic objectives – implementing the LDAF framework and so on. My track record is good, too. In my current post we now have 20 per cent of staff that have completed NVQ, and a further 20 per cent are registered. We're using TSP funding to support this...

In the short piece of narrative in Text 2, the storyteller casts him or herself in a proactive role – that of taking the initiative in improving training for staff who work with people with learning disabilities. Shared jargon is used to increase a sense of identity with the interviewing panel (for example, TOPSS for Training Organisation for the Personal Social Services), and the candidate is keen to demonstrate that he or she has embraced the national training agenda for social services. The narrative here is about someone who is knowledgeable, keen, and who is demonstrably able to produce results. This person may tell a different story with a different audience, however. In a different context, this manager may want to appear more caring than results driven.

Reflect on practice ••

What kind of self do you present when you are applying for jobs?

CASE STUDY – Gary: different place, different story

Gary is a 25-year-old man with a mild learning disability who lives at home with his parents. He enjoys going to a day centre, and also works in supported employment for 3 days a week. Tim, his Key Worker, finds Gary to be a very happy and lively person at the day centre, where he is very active in the drama group and also enjoys team sports.

It is felt that the time is right for Gary to move to a supported living facility, and Tim is making the necessary preliminary enquiries to start the process going.

At the centre, Gary is very chatty, and constantly talks about his move to his own place. When Tim makes a home visit, however, there is a significant change in Gary's behaviour. His mother does all the talking, and Gary seems a little distressed by the questions that are being asked.

His mother insists that Gary doesn't want to leave home. Tim suspects that Gary isn't able to express himself freely in his parents' company.

The context of situation can make a big difference to the way that people express themselves. What would you do if you were Tim?

A study of the discourse of Mexican workers entering the United States has shown how such people often use ethnic markers to identify characters in the stories they tell (de Fina, 2000). In Indian English, people often use Indian kinship terms to indicate the importance of their own cultural conventions, even though they are using the English language. For example, the term *didi* or *di* (elder sister) may be used as a term of respect, even if the person referred to is not a blood relative (Maybin and Mercer, 1996). Ascribing ethnicity to oneself and to other protagonists in conversation and in storytelling is an affirmation of both personal and national identity, and is especially important to people who are displaced from their original homelands by necessity rather than choice. However, it is important not to jump to conclusions about a person's identity based upon his or her apparent ethnicity. The issue of national or ethnic identity can be made more complex when a person makes a move to another country, spending many years there and bringing up a family in the new location.

CASE STUDY – No place like home

Sue is now 40 years old, and moved from Hong Kong to live in Scotland 20 years ago, when she also got married.

In Hong Kong she spoke Cantonese; her new husband's family speak Hakka, a different variety of the Chinese language. Although she has made an effort to learn Hakka, over the years Sue has found it easier to communicate with her Scottish-English speaking friends than with her Hakka-speaking Chinese family.

Sue thinks of herself as both Scottish and Chinese, but whenever she goes home to Hong Kong (which is not very often) she experiences a strange feeling of not belonging. When anyone asks her 'Where are you from?' her answer can vary. Sometimes she says she is from Hong Kong, sometimes from Scotland. In terms of the census (see Chapter 1) Sue would be described as 'Chinese'. Her personal reality is far more complex.

Is your situation similar to that of Sue? Do you know anyone else (either a friend or a service user) who might experience a similar sense of having several national or cultural identities?

(This case study is based on data presented in Ang-Lygate, 2000.)

It is really important not to prejudge a person's chosen identity on the basis of ethnic appearance. A recent report based on the annual Labour Force Survey reveals that many people whose ethnicity, according to the census definition, may be, for example, Pakistani, Bangladeshi or 'mixed race' are absolutely adamant that their national identity is British (Frith, 2004). A recent article in *The Independent* newspaper featured an Indian doctor who moved to Britain ten years ago and now lives and works in York. This person feels very strongly that his national identity is British. One of his reasons for this is that he feels more comfortable with many cultural forms of expression of the speech community within which he now works. An example he gives, in telling his story, is that in Britain people are more reticent about expressing emotion, which is not the case in India. This man's wife is Irish; both Hindi and English are spoken at home; and in the prayer-room are images of both Hindi gods and Jesus (Venkatesan, 2004). As the world becomes more of a global village, because of the increased mobility of individuals and the widespread use of the Internet (which enhances communication, business and the spread of common forms of expression), it is reasonable to suggest that we will see the development not only of diversity within societies, but also diversity within individuals as people assimilate aspects of other speech communities into their personal repertoire of values, beliefs and behaviours. The narratives that people tell about themselves will increasingly reflect this diversity.

Finally (and disturbingly), it has to be acknowledged that sometimes people will create narratives purely in order to justify certain attitudes or prejudices. Text 3 forms part of a telling by Debbie, who works at a day care facility for people with physical disabilities. She has recently had a negative experience with three of her colleagues who are Asian, and who like to speak Bengali amongst themselves.

TEXT 3: THE ROOTS OF PREJUDICE

Debbie: And then there was this time when – I had just gone into the staff room and they were the only ones there – I know I never used to feel like this before – and they never made me feel like this before, I never used to think anything of it, I mean, we're all the same aren't we... and then they...

Manager: Debbie, can you say exactly whom you mean by 'they'?

Debbie: Those three from the agency, those Asian girls.

Manager: OK, so tell me about what happened when you went into the staff room.

Debbie's narrative is expressed by degrees, and has to be helped along by questioning from her manager. This is a very common process in the creation of everyday narratives. She emphasises the difference between herself and her Bengali-speaking colleagues by referring to them continuously as 'they'. As the story proceeds, she explains how they were talking in their own language and laughing together. She believes that they were talking about her, and in fact she subsequently uses this incident to justify a suspicion of all Asian people. Unfortunately, this phenomenon of creating narratives that justify prejudice is not uncommon, and is a negative aspect of the storytelling process.

Aspects of narrative: set pieces and gradual disclosures

Personal narratives can take many forms. At one end of the scale is the published autobiography, in which an individual retells life events, casting him or herself in a certain role (that of intrepid adventurer, perhaps, or the brave survivor of a traumatic event). In such a work, some life events are highlighted, others are played down or omitted, and everything is sequenced in such a way as to entertain the reader. Not all life storytelling is so formal, however, and some is so 'mundane' in character that we might not even have considered it to be an autobiographical narrative (MacLure, 1993). CVs and job application letters, for example, fall into this category, as a job applicant will select from events in his or her working life to present the most favourable persona to a prospective employer. This will involve leaving out experience that is not relevant to the application, presenting instead those aspects of employment history that appear to best satisfy the requirements of the personal specification. The CV thus creates or reinforces one aspect of personal identity, that of the working self.

With respect to oral storytelling, it is possible to identify a similar broad range of styles. At one end of this spectrum is the skilled tale-teller who, in some cultures, preserves cultural traditions and knowledge along with narratives about individuals. In Niger, for example, the verses recited by Hausa oral poets tell that language is so powerful it should be used very carefully, and sometimes a spokesperson or intermediary is necessary in order to tell the tale safely (Hunter and Oumaru, 1998). In Western societies there are also people who are able to construct narratives in an entertaining and structured way, some of whom make a living from this skill (the performances of the comedian Billy Connolly come into this category), and others who restrict their performances to entertaining their friends in the pub or at parties. The structured aspect of oral narrative will be explored more fully below. However, such performances do not happen all the time, and people are just as liable to reveal aspects of their identity in autobiographical fragments within wider conversations. There are also times when people are expected to disclose autobiographical details of their lives, such as in consultation with the doctor, the therapist or the social care worker. In such circumstances, the storyteller will go through the same process of editing and selecting material, in order to present life events or personal details that are relevant to the situation. The telling may not be so flamboyant as a narrative told to entertain, as the teller may be constrained by the circumstances of the speech event – giving personal details in an interview room with a social worker taking notes, for example, can be inhibiting. In this section, a number of personal narratives will be examined in a little more detail to illustrate the range of forms that oral storytelling can take.

In Text 1, Clara Vaughan retells a piece of narrative that is a self-contained set piece. It has a clear beginning, middle and end, and characters who play distinct roles in an unfolding drama. It presents the listener with a crisis situation, building up the tension systematically and setting out the place and situation very clearly. The tension builds as a sequence of events unfolds, and drama is added by Clara's tone of voice. The listener is left in no doubt about Clara's attitude and the significance of what happened (in her view); the crisis is finally resolved, rather dramatically, by the intervention of Miss Harrison. In concluding the narrative, Clara returns us, as listeners, to the present, by adding a comment, the 'little rows we used to have'. Her laughter at this point indicates that however angry she may have been at the time, she can now safely consign the event to the past, retelling it purely for the enjoyment of her audience.

Clara's narrative broadly follows a classic pattern identified by the linguist Labov in a study of oral storytelling in the USA (Reissman, 1993; Maybin and Mercer, 1996). The classic components of an oral story, according to Labov, are shown in Table 4.1.

Table 4.1 Labov's study of oral storytelling

CLASSIC COMPONENTS OF AN ORAL STORY	
The abstract	A summary of the story to come
The orientation	Details of place, characters, etc.
The complicating action	The events as they unfold
An evaluation	The significance of the events, including the narrator's viewpoint
The resolution	What happened in the end
A coda	Indicates to the listener that the story has ended

Clara's account of the factory dispute contains all of Labov's classic components of an oral story except, perhaps, the abstract – but since it comes in a sequence of stories about her time at the factory, her opener, 'and another time', is actually a link between similar episodes. Her linking expression signals to the listener to expect another story about an argument.

However, not all personal narratives are as well organised as Text 1. It is important to remember that Clara felt very comfortable surrounded by family members, who encouraged her in the process of storytelling. People in other situations may not be so happy to disclose aspects of themselves in such a revealing way (as in the case of Gary in the case study on page 90), and they may not have the confidence or experience in using this classic narrative format, even if they belong to a speech community that traditionally uses this style. Furthermore, narratives can also unfold within a more conversational structure, and, as already discussed, can be quite mundane in their telling.

Simon and Ed are care workers in a home for older people. They are chatting in the staff room during a break. Simon has a negative opinion of his current managers, and starts to tell Ed about a situation when lack of forward planning led to the unit being dangerously understaffed for a number of hours. Text 4 constitutes part of Simon's telling.

TEXT 4: OVERNIGHT CRISIS (GRADUAL DISCLOSURE)
Simon: It's like I've already said – we can't have all this – all this messing about with the rotas – did I tell you about when the rota got changed just like that and we had trouble covering – nobody cares about us on the floor – and they're doing it again...

Ed:	When was this?
Simon:	Ah – about 6 months ago – before you came over – big fuss – no one to cover on a Friday night and somebody just had a heart attack – and they tried to cover it up – Tess was sick – I had Margaret's sixtieth to go to – booked up ages before – Could happen again if they don't get their act together…
Ed:	Hang on – who changed the rota? I never knew someone had a heart attack…

Simon signals that a story is about to be told when he says 'It's like I've already said…' His telling has to be helped along by Ed, who feels obliged to interrupt in order to clarify some of the details. Simon's justification for giving this account in the first place (his evaluation) is that the current management are incompetent, and a potentially dangerous situation might happen again. He distances himself from management by referring to them as 'they' all the time, which also means he can avoid specifically accusing any individual of bad planning. His account is rather emotional, and he tends to digress from his main point so that Ed's specific questioning is necessary in order to elicit more details from the narration. Storytelling by gradual disclosure is very common, and has been referred to by researchers as 'mundane autobiography' as it often comes about during the course of everyday conversations (Maclure, 1993).

Reflect on practice

Are you aware of having helped someone to tell a personal story in the course of your work? Is this something you do frequently?

Is storytelling formally encouraged in your place of work (for example, by reminiscence sessions)?

We have already described how Kyle, Don and Lee, residents at Esplanade (a home for men with learning disabilities) expressed aspects of their personal identity through creative tellings or narratives (see page 89). Although these narratives do not display the same structure as those of people who are not learning disabled, the researcher was able to identify them as narratives for several reasons (Croft, 1999). Storytellers identified events, linking them together using the complicating action device identified by Labov. Secondly, tellers demonstrated a very strong impulse to share their tellings with listeners, another key aspect of the use of narrative. Kyle, for example, who told a story of himself as a bee charmer (amongst other things), enjoyed the act of storytelling so much that he would carry on for as long as there was someone willing to listen to him. The collaborative nature of the storytelling process is illustrated by the experience of the researcher at Esplanade, who had to change the way she listened to each man quite significantly in order to encourage the stories to emerge.

Narratives across cultures

So far, our examples of narratives have been drawn from English-speaking communities in the USA and Britain. However, narratives differ significantly across cultures, and just as conversations display cultural features of the speech communities in which they take place, so storytellings also bear the same cultural hallmarks. Furthermore, narrative forms are conveyed to children at a very early age by their parents (Yusun Kang, 2003). As a speaker of English in the USA or the UK, on hearing a narrative you would probably be expecting to hear a lot of evaluation expressed by the storyteller. That is, you would be expecting the teller to give you a lot of clues about the significance of the events, especially his or her own viewpoint. The story might be, for example, about a visit to hospital where the staff were not very sympathetic, and might also include an expression of the teller's own anger about the way he or she was treated. However, Chinese, Korean, Japanese and Turkish stories contain much less evaluation of this kind than American and British stories. Similarly, the structure of a narrative may vary across cultures. Stories from Central America, for example, will often not follow the same linear timeline as their counterparts in the USA and Britain. Instead, one single narrative might include a sequence of non-related stories, a format that might be quite baffling to a listener from outside that speech community.

At any time, you may come across someone who tells stories in a very different way from that which you are used to

So why does the social care worker need to know all this? There is certainly no suggestion here that you should become an expert in the subtle nuances of language use in all speech communities from Caracas to Chesterfield. It is simply important for you to be aware firstly that there can be great differences in the way that people from different speech communities produce narratives. You need to recognise that at any time in your working life you may come across someone who has a totally different approach to storytelling from the one you are used to. Furthermore, in the same way as failure to observe expected conversational norms may produce an emotional response in either or all of the participants, so can the use of an unfamiliar narrative style have the same negative effect. You will need to be patient and flexible when you encounter an unfamiliar narrative style, not least because your response will influence what happens, and how the narrative unfolds.

In section 4.2 we move on to consider ways of listening, and how a narrative is the result of collaboration between teller and listener.

4.2 Respecting diversity: collaboration in the creation of narrative

Whilst it is clear that we do tell stories about ourselves to ourselves (self-talk), human beings have a tremendous need to tell their stories to others, an act which links our inner understanding with the outer world, and also helps us to be clearer about our beliefs, thoughts and feelings (Gersie, 1997). Inevitably, the telling of personal narratives is collaborative, and listeners can help or hinder the process of narration.

How narratives emerge: collaboration in telling stories

The way a story emerges depends heavily on the purpose of the storyteller at that moment in time, the identity of the listener or listeners, and the context of the telling (Halliday, 1993; Harre, 1998). If the context of the situation changes, it is highly likely that the way personal stories are told will also change. However, the process remains collaborative, whether the context is formal or informal. Text 5 is a further extract from Clara Vaughan's narrative.

TEXT 5: PROMPTING A NEW TOPIC

John: What was that about the Clayton Anilyne Company?

Clara: That was on Fraser's side – he had this place built, Mr Fraser

John: That was your husband's Father?

Clara: Yes – just before the 1914 War – when the War came on, the Government took it over…

In this part of the conversation, John directly prompts Clara with a question, to which she responds. He then further interrupts with a request for clarification. Clara briefly answers in the affirmative, and then begins a new section of narrative about the factory owned by her father-in-law. Although Clara always acknowledges such interruptions, she feels free to take issue when she doesn't agree, and often won't allow such interruptions to deflect her from the process of storytelling.

TEXT 6: INTERRUPTING A NARRATIVE

Clara: …when the Committee got in touch with the Father – course the men on the Committee were business men as well – and – erm – they said to Dad, like, with his War experience – he joined up the day War started – or the day after – and – erm –

John: **The day War broke out!**   (*very loud*)

Clara: August 4th – I think it was – 1914 – I didn't know him then – and when he went before this Committee…

In Text 6, John feels compelled to interject in a rhetorical way. However, not only does Clara respond by supplying the date that the First World War began, she very quickly resumes the thread of this particular story. This is clearly a context of a situation in which Clara feels confident.

Groups of people will also work together to shape the storytelling process. In a study of English-speaking, London-based Greek Cypriots, Lambrou (2003) found that what began as a group interview eventually became a collective conversational and storytelling activity. The researcher's role as a questioner and interviewer was gradually pushed into the background as the group took control of the speech event. By collaborative speech acts such as prompts and requests for clarification, group members elicited stories from each other and contributed to the telling, yet at the same time respecting the storyteller's right to dominate the conversational floor. However, sometimes an interruption by a group member might impair the flow of a story, making it necessary for the narrator to respond (like Clara did with John), and sometimes bringing the telling to an early conclusion. Sometimes, a personal narrative would trigger a similar story in another group member, who would then take over from the preceding narrator.

In this example, it is arguable that the conversational skills of the researcher, and her willingness to take a consciously passive role, actually facilitated the creation of stories by the group, and allowed an informal atmosphere to develop. In a more formal context, narratives may be inhibited. In Chapter 3 (see page 76) we saw how a hypothetical GP controls the dialogue with a patient, in order to elicit only the information that she considers important. The patient's account of his illness is thus circumscribed by the relative power of the GP within the discourse. We suggested that there are some situations in which people follow scripts, that is to say, the conversation will take a predictable course dictated by the context of situation and the relationship between the participants. As a social care worker it is highly likely that you will find yourself in situations where, by virtue of your role and/or the immediate task, the conversation will follow such a script. Examples already suggested include the assessment interview (with respect to a person's physical or financial needs), or the initial interview at the front desk in a social services reception area. The way in which you handle the conversation will affect the nature of the information your client presents. Some of this information may emerge in the form of a personal narrative, and you will need to use your judgement on:

- how far you allow the storytelling to proceed unchecked (so as not to restrict the possibility of the disclosure of other relevant information)
- how far you shape it along certain lines (perhaps by encouraging the speaker to develop a particular storyline)
- how far to inhibit or close off storytelling because it just isn't possible to benefit from it at that time.

Reflect on practice

When you are telling stories about yourself, or what has been happening to you, does it make any difference when the tellings are made to different people? Do you give a different emphasis to the same story when it's being told to another person or a different group of people?

Do you tell different stories to different people?

When you are listening to a new service user telling you about personal needs, how far would you let him or her go in telling a story about something if you felt it wasn't relevant to what you wanted to know?

The next section describes some key conversational tactics that can be used to enhance (or otherwise) the creation of a personal narrative.

Shaping the narrative: empowering the storyteller

When someone starts to deliver a piece of personal narrative, every sound that you utter (or not) can enhance or inhibit the storytelling process.

There is an activity that is sometimes used during training courses where participants work in pairs to experiment with different ways of listening. One member of each pair is instructed to speak for 2 minutes about something that is of interest or importance to him or her. The others, who are the listeners, are asked variously either to keep absolutely silent, or to keep interrupting the speaker. Both these ploys drive the speakers to distraction (as well as causing some distress to the people who are supposed to be listening), and there is a great feeling of relief all round when the 2 minutes have ended.

Listening in complete silence (**passive listening**) is something that many people find very unnatural. Listeners often want to make some kind of response to a speaker, even if it is just to give small **acknowledgement responses** (such as 'mmm', 'yes', 'I see', etc.) every few seconds. When a trainer is working with small groups, individuals will spontaneously nod or make small sounds of encouragement as he or she talks to them. Completely passive listening is usually only tolerable in formal situations such as a lecture, or in the theatre (although some establishments such as Shakespeare's Globe on Bankside, London, are now actively encouraging spontaneous audience participation and reaction to events on stage). Some people, however, use silence as a tool to intimidate whoever is speaking, and the lack of an encouraging response can be extremely discouraging to a speaker (although some communities, such as that of Aboriginal people in Australia, don't find long silences intimidating). Head nods and other facial expressions can also be used as effective acknowledgement responses. If a person starts to disclose something by way of a personal narrative, one of the worst things you could do might be to listen in silence and with a blank or bored expression. Storytellers need support and encouragement.

Too much **interference** might impede the telling of a narrative. A speaker can tolerate a certain amount of interruption (see above, Texts 5 and 6) such as when a listener asks for clarification, or demonstrates support for what is being said by a sympathetic utterance such as 'I know what you mean!' **Reflective statements** will also encourage a speaker, where the listener feeds back to the speaker crucial parts of what has just been said, such as 'That must have been very hard for you!' However, critical interference as, for example, where the listener expresses strong disagreement or is disparaging about an aspect of the speaker's narrative, can eventually impede the telling. Tone of voice can also affect the way in which an interruption is perceived. Different way of listening are shown in Table 4.2.

Tone of voice can affect the way an interruption is perceived

Table 4.2 Collaborating in building the narrative: different ways of listening

Passive listening	Can be inhibiting in many speech communities
Acknowledgement responses	Tiny signals (verbal and non-verbal) to encourage the speaker
Interference	Prompts and request for clarification can be helpful, but critical interference is not conducive to building a narrative
Reflective statements	Can encourage and help build a narrative

Reflect on practice ••

Ask a colleague to work with you to check out your listening skills.

Get him or her to talk to you for about 5 minutes on any topic. Practise listening in an active way, remembering especially to use acknowledgement responses and reflective statements to help the speaker in his or her task. However, make sure you don't interrupt too much and disrupt the speaker's flow.

Ask the listener to use the checklist on page 104 to rate your performance. If you get a low score, it may be you need to work on these aspects of listening. If you got a high score, congratulations – you're a good listener.

Skilful questioning

If skilful listening is on one side of the coin when it comes to building narratives, then skilful questioning is on the other. There is a technique used by skilled interviewers known as 'funnelling'. This method is often used by interviewers to elicit stories or information, and starts from the asking of **open questions**. These are questions that cannot be answered 'yes' or 'no', and often begin with 'how', 'what' or 'why'. In contrast, **closed questions** may be answered with a 'yes' or a 'no' (see the examples in Figure 4.1).

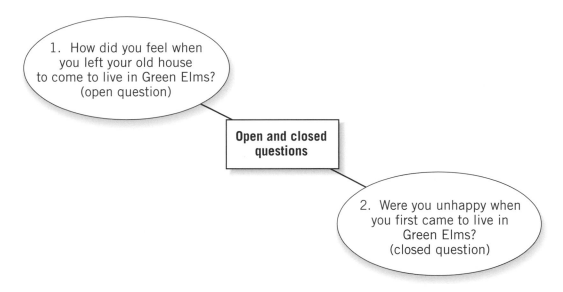

Figure 4.1 Examples of open and closed questions

Of course, someone who doesn't feel like answering may refuse to give a detailed response to a question like number 1 in Figure 4.1. He or she might avoid answering by replying 'I can't remember', or 'I don't know', but it is not possible just to say 'yes' – another strategy has to be found if the person doesn't want to talk. Conversely, a very talkative person is not likely to stop at a simple 'yes' or 'no' in reply to question 2. He or she may go on to elaborate on his or her response without any further prompting. However, the open question is more likely to encourage a person to talk freely, and can prove a very fruitful starting point, as the person answering the question is free to select the topic or angle, and to proceed to develop a narrative around it.

Closed questions can, of course, be useful when the listener wants to check out a point of detail in a narrative. In Text 5, John interrupts Clara to ask, 'That was your husband's Father?' This is both closed and specific, and requires a simple 'yes' or 'no' by way of response. Clara deals with it quickly and resumes the story. If you are required to control a conversation (because of time or other constraints) you can also use closed questions to summarise or to bring things to a close. These are not necessarily the kind of questions that will enhance the collaborative production of a narrative (see Figure 4.2).

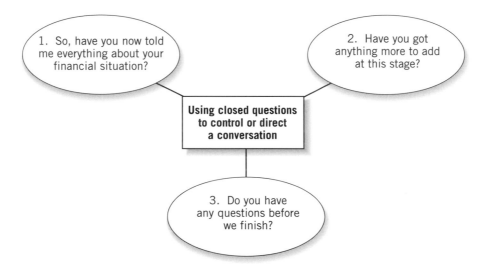

Figure 4.2 Examples of closed questions

A listener can also use **specific questions** when clarification is being sought. Examples of specific questions are shown in Figure 4.3. If carefully and sensitively

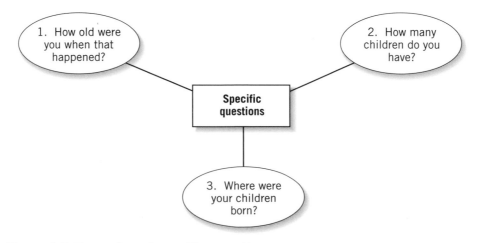

Figure 4.3 Examples of specific questions

put, such questions need not necessarily impede the flow of a narrative, although a forceful question may sometimes result in the redirection of a narrative's flow. However, when posed in the right way, they also indicate that the listener is taking a sympathetic interest, and is concentrating on the details of the story.

Leading questions can also affect the flow of a narrative, especially if the storyteller has to spend too much time dealing with such an interruption. Leading questions indicate that the questioner is expecting a particular answer. If that answer is not what the storyteller wants to give, more time will need to be spent in dealing with the question before he or she can return to the main storyline (see Figure 4.4).

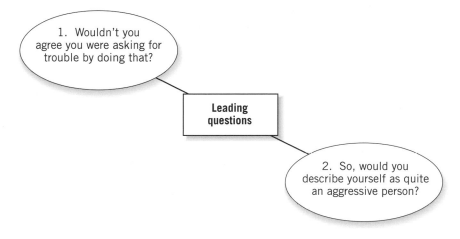

Figure 4.4 Examples of leading questions

Finally, **reflective questions** fulfil the same function as **reflective statements**, in that they reflect back to the speaker something he or she has just said. You can do this to show the speaker that you are following and understanding the emerging narrative, and that you are sympathetic to the angle that the teller is seeking to present (see Figure 4.5).

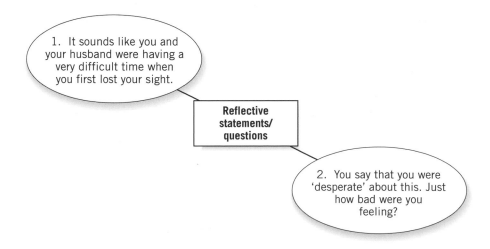

Figure 4.5 Examples of reflective statements/questions

Reflective questions differ from leading questions in that the questioner will often re-use or paraphrase the storyteller's own words, rather than trying to impose a new concept into the narrative.

Table 4.3 is a checklist to help you determine whether or not you are using these different listening and questioning techniques. If you feel you need to develop these further, you can redo the questionnaire in a couple of weeks to see if you have made progress.

Table 4.3 Skills checklist

HELPING ALONG THE NARRATIVE: HOW DO YOU RATE YOUR SKILLS?		
Give yourself a score out of five for each of the following aspects of collaborating with a storyteller to help the narrative along. Check things out again in a couple of weeks to see if you are doing anything differently. (Alternatively, listen to a colleague talking for a few minutes, and then ask him or her to give you a rating on your performance as a listener.)		
	Today's score	
I use acknowledgement responses to signal that I am listening.		
I try not to interrupt in a way that stops the flow of the narrative.		
I use reflective statements to signal that I am listening.		
I use appropriate questions to clarify aspects of the narrative.		
I am sensitive to the other person's body language.		
I am sensitive to tone of voice and facial expression.		
I recognise that cultural differences can affect what is said, tone of voice and body language.		
I recognise that physical or sensory difficulties and differences can have an impact on communication.		
I am able to adapt my conversational style to suit the situation.		
I do not respond negatively when I encounter a conversational style I am not used to.		
TOTAL		

Of course, there will be variations in the way people need or like to be listened to. Some of this will depend on the practices of the various speech or cultural communities to which people belong.

One group of people who may display a distinctive narrative style and who may require greater flexibility in being listened to are people with learning disabilities. We have already seen how Kyle, Lee and Don, residents at Esplanade (a home for men with learning disabilities) used personal narratives to express identity. We also considered how their telling differed from the format often used by non-learning disabled people. The researcher who collected these stories has described how she had to adapt her way of listening to accommodate the telling style of each man (Croft, 1999). With Don, for example, she found that it was best to listen quietly without interrupting. Kyle, however, took the lead in his telling, and the researcher used acknowledgement responses and reflective statements or questions to show that she was listening. Kyle would even get up and move outside the house into the yard, followed by the researcher, as he continued his telling. For Lee, more specific questioning produced the best results, and the researcher found that he was more comfortable when she took on the more proactive role of interviewer.

As a social care worker, you have the power to choose to work sensitively with your clients by being language aware. You will need to recognise that the nature of a speech act is affected by the relationship between the participants, the context of situation and the purpose of the interaction. You will need to keep in mind that people belong to different speech communities and, as such, they may have different expectations of what language does and how it should be used. Your response to a client can help or hinder the expression of self through language in general, and through narrative in particular. The decision to keep silent or to use acknowledgement responses, carefully chosen empathetic reflective statements or questions, a willingness not to interrupt and to adapt your listening style to suit the narrator will all make a difference to the story that emerges.

Reflect on practice

If you haven't already done so, make a copy of the checklist on page 104. Use it to analyse your listening technique in a number of different situations.

Are you satisfied that you are able to empower a person to tell his or her stories freely and fully?

Do you find that you listen differently to service users than to staff?

4.3 Telling tales: re-storying the narrative

When celebrities are asked about things they read about themselves in the press, they often say that they don't recognise themselves. Reporters take certain aspects of a person's life and elaborate on it so much that the person's character has been changed beyond recognition.

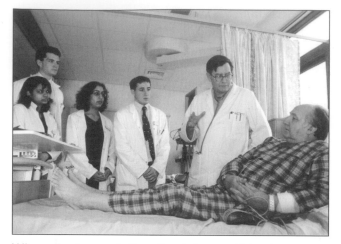

When doctors retell patients' narratives to colleagues, the re-storying often becomes a stylised presentation

Such tabloid articles are extreme examples, but in fact re-storying occurs continuously, and is an inescapable fact of life in many cultures. People retell the narratives of others in speech, sign and in writing and the re-storying (in whatever mode) can be formal or informal, to a greater or lesser degree. In terms of speech or sign, the most informal kind of re-storying takes place in the context of everyday conversation. 'Did you hear about Navdip?' someone might say. 'She had an accident on her way to work on Tuesday…', and the story would proceed, possibly using new words in the retelling. There are also, however, more formal modes of spoken (or signed) re-storying. Research into the oral reports of doctors, as presented to their colleagues on ward rounds, shows that such accounts retell patients' own narratives about their illnesses, turning them into stylised presentations which include certain key phrases, and also involve the use of a particular tone of voice and facial expressions (Misselbrook, 1997; Ratzan, 1992). Similarly, a study of the final arguments of lawyers during their summing up presentations found that these formal oral performances re-story the subject of the trial in very specific ways. This research found that defence lawyers tend to focus on witness testimonies to present a revised narrative of the case, whilst prosecution lawyers focus on the alleged events (Carranza, 2003). In both instances, lawyers are using the narratives of witnesses selectively (and in conjunction with other evidence) to re-story events.

Reflect on practice

When you retell a story that someone has told you about a personal experience, do you find that you sometimes add your own point of view about what happened?

Do you make your personal view clear when you are retelling a story? In retelling the stories of service users, how important is it to distinguish between what that person actually said, and how you are interpreting that particular telling?

Written re-storyings also range from the formal to the informal. At one end of the scale might be an account of something described by a mutual acquaintance set down in a letter between close friends or family members. At the other extreme might be the case study such as you might be required to make in the course of your work with service users. Such documents are extremely important, and need to satisfy the requirements of your organisation in terms of its recording policy. Sometimes they can even become key documents in legal proceedings. Such case studies and reports are subject to the requirements of the Data Protection Act, and there will be strict procedures relating to their storage and who is allowed access to them.

However, whether the re-storying is formal or informal, oral or written, there will always be an element of input by the person responsible for the retelling. This may take the form of the simple addition of a personal opinion after recounting the events themselves (perhaps an expression of sympathy or of disapproval). On the other hand, the retelling may involve the emphasis of some elements of a narrative, and the downplaying or even omission of others. More extreme versions of re-storying can involve recasting the subject of the narrative in a specific, perhaps one-dimensional role. Consider the following case study.

CASE STUDY – Recreating service users

At a mental health day centre, a new system of working with service users has been introduced. This system is known as 'Strengths', and it emphasises goal-setting and achievement on the part of the centre users. Care workers have to use the terminology of the Strengths programme when writing up their case notes and reports. Written records at the centre thus focus solely on individuals' goals and their attainment (or otherwise). The form of re-storying portrays service users as goal-directed individuals, whose main concerns are with practical tasks such as the regular cleaning of their accommodation, or the attainment of good budgeting skills.

However, when care workers talk about the service users, they employ a different kind of language. They speak constantly about needs, levels of dependency and the nature of individuals' illnesses. They don't use this language in their written reports, but between themselves (for example at team meetings) they often speak about doing things 'for' service users, and often use concepts such as 'low functioning'. This kind of language creates a different kind of service user – someone who is very limited by illness and heavily dependent on the intervention of care workers in order to remain within the community.

What kind of narratives are created in your workplace about your service users?

This case study is based on research from a day centre in the United States (Floersch, 2000). It is arguable that the voices of the service users themselves are only faintly heard in the midst of all this re-storying activity, although the researcher did not conclude this explicitly. Despite being consulted about what they wanted their goals to be, it doesn't appear that they were given any choice about whether or not to have goals in the first place. The Strengths programme required that they have goals, the authority had adopted the Strengths programme and, therefore, all service users had to have such goals.

You might want to argue that both these modes of re-storying are valid, as they serve a particular purpose, in this case, that of supporting people in the community. You might consider that a detailed exploration of clients' personal narratives is the province of the therapist or psychologist. However, you might wish to take an alternative approach, and query whether the application of a broad policy of keeping people in the community sometimes does not fit individual needs. By editing out the potentially rich scope of personal narratives to focus only on goal attainment or dependency, or by concentrating on people's disabilities or illnesses, workers might be missing vital clues to service users' real wants or needs. Diversity can be masked by the imposition of a particular policy or way of working, which often takes the form of a specific discourse about clients and about the business of working with them.

Whatever your view of this particular debate, it is essential that you keep in mind the role you play in constructing and re-storying narrative. We have already looked at ways in which narratives are collaboratively constructed during the speech event. It is important to remember that there are also cognitive and emotional processes involved in this. When you listen to a narrative unfolding, you are inevitably processing the information you are given, both in terms of your emotional response (you might feel sympathy, or anger, for example), and in your cognitive processing of the data (perhaps disbelief, approval or disapproval). In so doing, you are creating a new, 'virtual' version of the original narrative.

Reflect on practice

Does your organisation have guidelines about writing case notes or records?

Do the guidelines require you to focus on particular aspects of a service user's life (for example, his or her ability to do certain tasks, needs for specified services, etc.)?

How far do the guidelines allow you to express a service user's individuality?

It is interesting that the notion of re-storying is paralleled in some aspects of current literary theory, and before you start to think that this book is here flying off at a tangent, please remember that right now you are engaged in the act of reading. Just as the role of the listener in constructing a narrative is now considered to be very important, so the role of the reader in 'creating' a written text is now emphasised by some literary critics (Tompkins, 1981; Selden, 1989). In particular, it has been suggested that there is a distinction between the actual text (the book or document that preserves the written word) and the virtual 'work' which exists in the reader's head (Iser, 1980). As a reader of this book, you are engaged in the task of absorbing and making sense of the information and arguments we have presented. Perhaps you may not agree with some of the things we have suggested. We hope that you won't allow us to 'position' you as a reader just because this is a printed text, and printed matter (especially in book form) is often seen as being 'authoritative'. We hope that rather you will engage in a kind of dialogue with this book. Although you can't check things out or question us directly, as you go along you can make notes of things you disagree with, points to discuss with your fellow students or your tutor, and issues you want to follow up. At the end of your reading, you will have a version of this book in your head. By going through the cognitive processes of questioning, analysing and editing (and also perhaps by responding emotionally to some sections or examples in the text), you will have re-created *Diversity and Rights in Care* to a form that you understand, and that you can re-use in your own written and oral activities, both as a student and as a practitioner. We hope that you will see the task of reading as an active process in which you contribute to the development of your own understanding, knowledge and cognitive skills.

Of course, there are limits to the extent to which you can re-story someone's narrative, whether in oral or written form. If you were to tell someone that *Diversity and Rights in Care* promotes discriminatory practices this would be at best a misrepresentation, and at worst a total fabrication, depending on how far down this line you go. If a service user told you that he or she had a physical impairment that caused serious mobility problems, and then you went on to report that this person was experiencing no significant difficulty in this respect, you would have exceeded the permitted limits of re-storying.

However, provided that the original narrative is not changed beyond what is reasonably supported by its content, the act of re-storying (whether by speech, sign or the written word) is of itself neither inherently good nor bad. A good example is that of the case notes or reports you will be required to produce as a social care worker. The Social Services Inspectorate (SSI) has published *Recording with Care*, which is a report on the writing, storing and use of such written records (Goldsmith and Beaver, 1999). It is quite likely that you will be, or are already required to adhere to these recommendations when producing written reports on individual service users for your organisation. This report recommends that a good case record should include:

- details of individual contacts made with the service user
- the work to be done together with objectives
- the procedure that is to be followed
- the assessment of need
- the care plan, and
- the timing, process and outcomes of reviews.

Inevitably, such a care record is a re-storying, which focuses on the service user as a person with personal needs, who is also the subject of a care plan, and of specified goals and targets.

We are not suggesting that you are doing something wrong in writing a care plan and focusing on particular aspects of a service user's personal narrative. Indeed, it is inevitable that the provision of a specific service will require its own recording formats in order to make delivery of those services more efficient and effective. It is, however, important for you to recognise that in writing case records you are, in reality, re-storying a personal narrative, and also that it is essential that you do this responsibly and with respect for the individuality of each of your service users.

How much opportunity do your service users have to tell their own stories?

If they do have the opportunity to tell their own stories, how are these tellings used?

We have suggested that re-storying is an inevitable fact of life. It is vital that you recognise this inevitability and use this knowledge responsibly. Re-storying a narrative demands integrity, and a commitment to valuing the personal narratives of your service users. Although we need to recognise that such narratives may themselves change in response to the key factors of context of situation, the participants in the creation of the narrative and the purpose for which a telling is created, it has to be recognised that telling and re-storying one's own narratives is a perfectly natural and valid phenomenon. In reality, stories are told and retold in a far more dynamic and fluid way that may be very different from that described in a case report, which seeks to capture the 'truth' of a situation by means of the written word. Oral re-storying by professionals can also seek to present captured 'truths', where an individual's circumstances are re-storied in terms of absolutes such as 'limited ability' (as in the discourse of case managers at the Midwestern mental health centre we described above).

Ultimately, everyone has the right to tell his or her own personal stories. Frameworks such as *Recording with Care* are clearly necessary to provide structure and organisation, but ultimately such structures do not fully address the deepest human need to express identity. As a listener, you cannot avoid having an impact on a telling, and as a social care worker in particular, you cannot avoid re-storying that narrative. This is a tremendous responsibility. However, having an awareness of how diversity is expressed through language in general, and narrative in particular, will help you in rising to the challenge of the Care Standards. Sensitivity and flexibility in your response to how people use language (your colleagues as well as service users) will empower you to establish and sustain working relationships in a way that truly respects and values diversity.

Summary

○ A narrative can be defined as the retelling of an event(s) or episode by a storyteller, who in so doing presents a particular point of view about that episode.

○ The creation of narratives is an important aspect of discourse in many societies.

○ Narrative has many social functions including:

  – entertaining

  – explaining or describing

  – expressing national, group or personal identity.

○ People with learning disabilities use narrative to express personal identity in the same way as people who do not have a learning disability.

○ Identity may be more complex than membership of a single ethnic or social group.

○ Narrative types range from snatches of personal autobiography along a continuum to set pieces of formal storytelling.

○ The structure of narratives varies between cultures and speech communities.

○ A narrative is ultimately the product of collaboration between the teller and the listener(s).

○ A mismatch of narrative styles may be disconcerting for both teller and listener.

○ The way you listen will affect the way a narrative is told.

○ The telling of a narrative may differ from what you expect to hear: you will need to adapt and respond flexibly in the way that you listen.

○ When you re-story a service user's narrative, for whatever reason, you need to do this responsibly and sensitively.

CHAPTER 5

Moral rights

Introduction

This chapter explores some of the traditional ethical theories that have been used to establish the moral rights of service users. The argument put forward is that no single 'perspective' provides an adequate basis for defining moral rights when used on its own.

The chapter adopts a view, advanced by Clark (1999), and argues that moral rights can be established by prescription. The rights of service users can be derived from an analysis of codes of practice and other national standards. Ethical theories are still important in so far as they inform the analysis, justification and development of a human rights culture.

Equality, the celebration of diversity, and freedom from discrimination are seen as key human rights. This chapter adopts the view that care organisations should seek to create a human rights culture in which service users' rights are balanced with responsibilities.

This chapter explores rights of respect for diversity, freedom from discrimination, independence and choice, dignity and privacy, confidentiality, effective communication, security and safety and the right to take risks.

The chapter concludes with comments on establishing good quality care.

Aims *This chapter aims to enable you to explore:*

5.1   Rights, values and ethics: theories

5.2   Putting theory into practice

5.3   Promoting human rights

5.4   Establishing good quality care

5.1 Rights, values and ethics: theories

Moral and legal rights are important in care work because servi
services because of issues that create vulnerability.

Vulnerability

Some older service users may be physically frail; they may need assistance in order to
be able to eat, assistance with bathing and personal care, assistance with getting
dressed, going to bed and mobility. Such individuals may experience a loss of control
over their daily living. They may perceive themselves as vulnerable in so far as they
cannot control the extent to which their needs are likely to be met. Some service
users may experience learning difficulty. Some people with a learning difficulty may
perceive themselves as dependent on their carers to organise appropriate daily
activities to ensure their needs are met. Some older service users may be
disorientated. People with dementia may feel that they are unable to interpret and
control their surroundings without appropriate support. Children are often unable
to make wise decisions or choices due to limited understanding of the world.
Children may often have to rely on adult guidance in order to be safe.

In all the instances above, service users have to rely on carers to meet their needs.
Having to rely on others might expose a person to the risk of not being able to
control how his or her needs are met, or if needs are met at all. As well as
vulnerability with respect to needs, service users can also be at risk of exploitation,
abuse and physical or emotional damage resulting from unmet need, exploitation, or
abuse.

A widely accepted model for interpreting human need was developed by Abraham
Maslow (1908–1970). Developed within the Humanistic perspective, Maslow's
original five-stage hierarchy of human need is an enduring icon from twentieth
century psychology. The extensive use of this model in a wide range of management,
counselling and social care contexts testifies to its plausibility. Although Maslow's
hierarchy may be perceived as a simplification, it provides a useful tool for
summarising the range of human needs. There was a time when welfare was
understood as the provision of food, shelter and warmth. Maslow's levels of need
encompass social, emotional and cognitive human functions as well as the need to
maintain the physical body of a person.

Within Maslow's theory people might be perceived as being vulnerable on different
levels, as shown in Figure 5.1. Maslow argued that the first four levels of need, (that
is, physical need, safety, belonging, and self-esteem) were deficit needs. Self-
actualisation was a different kind of need – a 'becoming need'. Deficit needs have to
be met before an individual can move on to fulfilling his or her potential and
actualising – or making real – a self that he or she could become. The goal of living is
to fulfil human potential, but according to Maslow the majority of people in Western

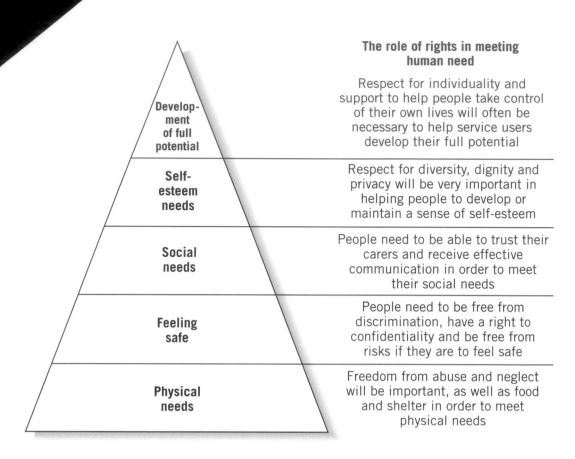

Figure 5.1 Maslow's hierarchy of human need

society spend their lives wrestling with needs to achieve safety, belonging and establishing self-esteem. Only a minority of people successfully establish a safe, socially secure, and worthwhile interpretation of themselves.

Levels of vulnerability are worth thinking about because within this theory, care workers' deficit needs may often be construed as unmet. Service users may be vulnerable to the performance of care staff, which has the power to influence the quality of their lives. Carers may well have emotional safety needs and unmet identity and self-esteem needs. Some carers may have difficulty in perceiving themselves as powerful and may feel vulnerable with respect to the responses of colleagues or service users.

Moral rights

The concept of moral rights has often been explained in terms of arguments about how to create a fair and just society. Historically, the problem of defining moral rights has centred on the issue that there has never been general agreement on theories of society and on the conduct that is necessary to achieve an ideal model. One way of trying to escape the problem of a lack of moral consensus is to admit that different individuals and communities value issues differently. By describing moral rights in terms of values we can escape the problem of a lack of social consensus about the ideal society. Values can, therefore, represent beliefs that we hold to be central to the understanding of how people should behave. We can construe ourselves as 'choosing values', and we can accept that other people in different knowledge communities could choose different values.

Values

On the surface, it seems to make sense that individuals or communities can choose to value certain principles. Once these principles have been defined it is possible to deduce moral rights that might follow from these principles. Chris Clark (2000) argues that the concept of values is problematic, in that 'the ideas of value and values resist satisfactory definition' (26). Clark argues that philosophers, economists, sociologists and psychologists often use the term values in different ways. Moreover, Clark points out that the idea of values is often circular. When a person believes in something such as 'the importance of individual independence' we might call it a value, but calling our belief a 'value' is circular. We believe in something because it is a value and it is a value because we believe it. The concept of 'value' adds nothing to the original statement about importance!

Chris Clark (2000) provides an extensive philosophical critique of the usefulness of values and concludes: 'the conclusion to be drawn from all this multiplicity and complexity of usage is this: there can be no final definition of the concept of value; the meaning of "value" cannot be definitively translated into other concepts that are safely beyond the reach of misunderstanding or controversy.'

The assumption that values guide behaviour is open to doubt

Some people assume that behaviour is motivated by internal mental mechanisms that are controlled by values. Such a theory might fit a narrative that was popular in Europe during the first part of the last century. This story explained that the highest human achievement was rationality. Humans were evolving away from emotional responses and the truly enlightened 'man' would live 'his' life purely on the basis of logically deduced reasoning. Providing one's conduct is purely logical, it is safe to assume that values and logic together will determine behaviour. This assumption achieved realisation in the mythical race of Vulcans central to the Star Trek series. However, there is little current support within psychological literature for value systems coupled with logic as an explanation of human behaviour.

Clark's critique of values acknowledges that there is something important behind social workers' attempts to clarify important guiding principles. Different social groups and different knowledge communities may, indeed, value things differently. His argument is simply that the term 'values' has the potential to mislead us into thinking that we have discovered a mechanism for regulating behaviour. It may be misleading to suppose that attempting to justify moral rights in terms of values could achieve anything useful. Rights are justified because we value them, and we value them because they are rights!

Ethics

It is tempting to say that we value rights such as independence because personal independence will create a happier world. Naturally, philosophers can put forward far more complicated versions of such an argument. The problem with this kind of argument is that it focuses on practical, and, in theory, measurable issues to do with the nature of physical reality – i.e., what constitutes a happier world? In order to accept such an argument a vast amount of scientific analysis and reasoning would be required – and scientific analysis is always open to interpretation! In practice, arguments about the possible nature of the universe are likely to be unhelpful in providing a justification for moral rights. The philosopher G.E. Moore (1873–1958) was famous for his statement 'you can't get an "ought" from an "is"'. Ethical judgements and moral rights cannot be justified with reference to scientific arguments about how things are. Rights are socially negotiated, and this negotiation cannot be reduced to a matter of scientific inquiry or empirical questions.

Historically, there have been two grand theories of ethics within European philosophy. Neither of these systems has ever been fully adopted or accepted by the diverse groups and communities that exist in Europe. The two theories are worth noting because they identify issues that are still used to justify ethical decisions.

KANT

Immanuel Kant (1724–1804) produced a theory of ethics based on the principle of logical consistency. A superficial explanation of Kant's ideas is that society needs social conventions such as 'telling the truth'. Government, commerce and social relationships depend on negotiation – trust is an important issue. If everyone tells the truth then society works. If nobody tells the truth then social cohesion becomes impossible. Kant's argument is that if telling the truth is a good thing then everyone should do it! Every member of society has a moral duty to conform to key social conventions. It would be logically inconsistent to allow some people – perhaps people with power and privilege – to break this code of conduct. In some ways, Kant's theory was a forerunner of the principle of equal opportunities and anti-discrimination. He would have held that it was not consistent, logical or, therefore, reasonable for members of one section of society to treat others less favourably than they would expect to be treated – at least with respect to social conventions such as telling the truth. Treat others as you would like to be treated is a moral proposal that embodies the principle of consistency that was stressed in Kant's ethical philosophy.

For all its initial appeal, Kant's philosophy has not proved to be generally plausible or widely accepted. In practice, moral decisions can often be very complicated. Kant's theory was challenged with a question about what he would do if he knew that he could save a person's life by diverting a potential murderer with a simple lie. Kant maintained that the principle of logical consistency, or duty to the truth, should override consideration of possible consequences. Few people in the United Kingdom today would be likely to accept such a theory.

Consistency is not enough to justify actions

MILL

The philosopher John Stuart Mill (1806–1873) advanced a second grand theory of ethical reasoning. Mill argued that social conventions should be justified in terms of their potential to bring about greatest happiness for the greatest number of people. There is a range of fundamental principles, such as 'justice', that can be justified as a basis for the law using the principle of greatest happiness for the greatest number of people. Mill's philosophy is all about the consequences of laws, policies and procedures. A law cannot be morally justified if it creates more unhappiness for people than happiness. A policy must be morally wrong if it does not result in an increase in human happiness. And the happiness of an elite social group cannot be used to justify the unhappiness of a larger social group who are perhaps exploited. Mill's theory is a democratic theory focused on the good of all. The theory of social consequences was designed for application at a strategic level, i.e., to law, policy and procedure.

Mill was aware of the problems that individual people would face if they attempted to use the theory in their own private life. On an individual level people would almost certainly make biased judgements. If you feel hungry, would you consider stealing a colleague's sandwich? If you apply the principle of greatest happiness you can easily resolve that your colleague is not really hungry – otherwise he or she would have already eaten the sandwich. The happiness that eating will bring you must surely outweigh any unhappiness your colleague will feel about the loss of his or her lunch. But the principle of assessing consequences in terms of greatest happiness of the greatest number is best left to democratic debate. Within a democracy, the institution of property (ownership of the sandwich) might be argued to bring more happiness to more people than allowing a 'free for all'. If this is the case, then eating your colleague's sandwich is morally wrong and classified as theft. The principle of 'property' is justified in terms of consequences, not the principle of 'Who gets to eat the sandwich?'

The greatest happiness of the greatest number might not always work out the way you hoped

Once again, this theory (known as utilitarianism) has failed to establish itself as the definitive system of moral reasoning. There are insurmountable problems in predicting how legislation and policy will actually turn out in practice. Quite apart from problems of predicting the future, there are also obvious problems with the concept of 'happiness'. What constitutes happiness, how to assess relative happiness, and how to quantify happiness in society, are questions which we cannot expect answers to any time soon! On the other hand, many people within the United Kingdom today would accept that the consequences of actions are very important when considering moral issues.

Neither Kant's nor Mill's ethical theories have been extensively adopted as they stand. But what if they were synthesised together?

SEEDHOUSE

David Seedhouse (1988) combines the theories of utilitarianism and Kant's principle of consistency into one theory. Seedhouse argues that when an ethical decision needs to be taken workers should consider the following (see Figure 5.2).

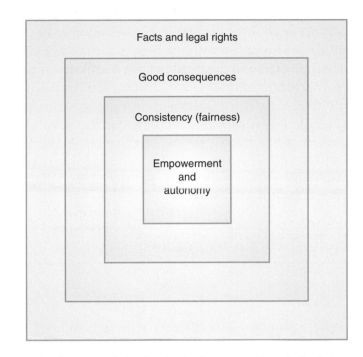

Figure 5.2 The principles which should influence ethical decisions, based on Seedhouse's theory

- The facts of the situation. Decisions depend on workers collecting all relevant details about service user need, legal rights and so on.
- The extent to which a decision may create a good outcome for everyone. This principle is similar to Mill's utilitarianism.
- Fairness and consistency in any decision that is taken. People have a right to an equal quality of service or treatment. People must not be discriminated against. This principle can be construed as associated with Kant's focus on consistency.
- The degree to which the decision empowers vulnerable service users and increases their control over their own life (autonomy). Decisions should not result in 'control' of others unless this is definitely in the greater interests of the majority of people.

Health and care work in a democratic society take place in the context of beliefs about individual rights, choice and freedom. David Seedhouse (1988) argues that health and care work should not simply be about meeting physical needs or curing disease and illness. Seedhouse quotes the World Health Organisation's definition, 'Health is a state of complete physical, social and mental well-being, not merely the absence of disease, illness and infirmity'. Seedhouse goes on to argue that 'Curing disease and illness and increasing the length of life remain important, but not as important as creating and increasing the autonomy of people who request, or need health care [and] respecting people's choices even if they conflict with given advice' (1988: 9). The central purpose of health and care work is to improve quality of life and this means enabling people to take control of their own life or to 'be autonomous'.

Seedhouse argues that the need to develop human potential defines humanity. The question 'What is a human being for?' can be answered by producing a list of potentials. So the freedom and autonomy to develop potential are argued to be the central principle of ethical decision-making. Seedhouse states, 'It is possible to develop the argument of this book that the fullest degree of morality, or of ethical intervention, is that which enables persons equally, without discrimination, to achieve the fullest enhancing potentials of which they are capable' (1988: 81). Seedhouse's model for ethical decision-making combines the principle of consistency, the importance of considering consequences and the central humanistic principle of self-actualisation into one framework for guiding the decisions of health and social care workers.

5.2 Putting theory into practice

Radical social work

Understanding people's needs in terms of theories of human potential has been perceived to have one major weakness. Humanistic theory focuses on the individual. In many care situations this makes intuitive sense. A care worker seeking to build a relationship with a new resident may well perceive himself or herself as working on an individual basis with another individual person.

When working with a distressed family a social worker might miss something of critical importance if he or she ignores broader social issues. A breakdown in family relationships might be associated with the stress of attempting to live on a low income. Why does the family have a low income? Perhaps the reason is that there is little chance of the adults gaining employment. These family members cannot gain employment because of low educational attainment. Why have these family members gained so little at school? This answer needs to be explained in terms of structural disadvantage. People are not born into exactly the same opportunities and advantages. People born into low-income families may experience a wide range of difficulties that could result in a stressful life with limited opportunities. An individual's ethnic group membership might expose him or her to racial discrimination. Women may find their career opportunities to be restricted because of gender discrimination.

Issues such as low income, racism and sexism cannot be understood or explained purely with reference to individuals. Understanding why a family cannot manage financially will necessitate a study of how society is structured. Radical social work theory emphasises the importance of challenging existing political and economic systems with the aim of creating a fairer, or more just society. There may be a risk of 'blaming the victim' if we perceive individuals to be solely responsible for their difficulties, or if we perceive people to be in some way defective because they are service users.

Within the radical perspective, rights are justified with reference to the need to change society in order to limit disadvantage. Justification of individual rights would not be sought in terms of individualistic theories of potential, happiness or even consistency.

As Sarah Banks (2001) states, 'However, the recognition and challenging of structural oppression – the recognition that the very rules and structures within which society operates reflect basic inequalities in power and that therefore fundamental and revolutionary change is required – is at odds with the emphasis on individual freedom of both Kantianism and utilitarianism; it calls for a more radical analysis and approach' (2001:59).

Most people employed in care or social work would accept the importance of exploring structural explanations. But there is a tension between individualistic traditions and the radical analysis of the need to change society. Banks (2001) writes: 'the rhetoric of anti-oppressive practice is generally couched in terms of challenging structural oppression. Yet as this rhetoric is incorporated into mainstream practice, it is questionable sometimes whether "empowerment" and "anti-oppressive practice" consist of anything more than enabling individual users to gain confidence and offering "individually sensitive practice" that takes account of, for example, a user's dietary and religious needs and their personal experience of oppression.'

A focus on structural issues is important – but can it be the only issue?

Deriving practice principles from just one ethical 'perspective' may result in consequences that are unacceptable to a range of people. Yet the principles of maintaining consistency, concern for consequences, promoting human potential, and achieving structural change are all vital issues in any service that provides care for people.

Ethics as prescription

There are many different standpoints and shades of view when it comes to defining and justifying moral systems. Ultimately, no simple, single moral explanation for defining rights is likely to establish itself across all the diverse 'communities of knowledge' that exist within the United Kingdom. So what is left?

Chris Clark (2000) in his book on social work ethics offers what might be perceived as a pragmatic solution. This is that professional ethics can simply be prescribed. A professional group can define its identity by devising a code of ethics or a code of practice. The rights and duties of members of a professional community can, therefore, be prescribed. Clark writes: 'in any field of professional ethics there are two main aims, the prescriptive and critical. Ethics as prescription aims to instruct how professionals ought to deal with morally problematic situations, while the critical aspect examines the premises and arguments on which prescriptions are based' (2000: 46).

If people choose to undertake a career in social care they can be perceived as taking up membership of a social group and taking on an identity as a professional carer. This field of work has a prescribed code of practice that defines a range of service user rights. Just because the code refers to, or infers, rights does not mean that the code is perfect or correct in any ultimate way. The code can and should be critiqued using ethical perspectives.

For example, from a humanistic perspective, are the provisions of this code likely to promote the fulfilment of human potential? From a radical perspective, does this code challenge structural disadvantage? From a utilitarian perspective, is this code likely to promote a balance of greatest good? If aspects of the code could be demonstrated to be either inconsistent, productive of negative consequences, condoning of structural inequality or limiting of human potential then there would be a major argument for review and revision of the provisions of the code. Whilst none of these ethical perspectives enjoys universal adherence, perspectives do at least provide a foundation for evaluation of prescribed codes. But codes exist because people design them. Naturally, people design them in order to meet perceived needs. But the rights identified within the GSCC Code of Practice are ultimately simply prescribed. Whether they are ultimately morally appropriate and sufficient is an issue for debate. Ethical debate will need to identify the assumptions and starting points involved.

The General Social Care Council (GSCC) Code of Practice for Social Care Workers

The General Social Care Council has designed a list of statements that describe the standards of practice required of social care workers. This code is designed to apply to all social care workers in the United Kingdom. Figure 5.3 illustrates the principles in this code.

There are a range of moral rights that managers of care services and authors in the field of social care have assumed 'ought' to apply to service users. The list of rights in Table 5.1 on page 124 can be regarded as being prescribed by the GSCC Code of Practice for Social Care Workers. This table lists eight moral rights. Some issues, such as freedom from discrimination and confidentiality, are also the focus of legal rights, but the GSCC code may be regarded as providing broader rights for service users.

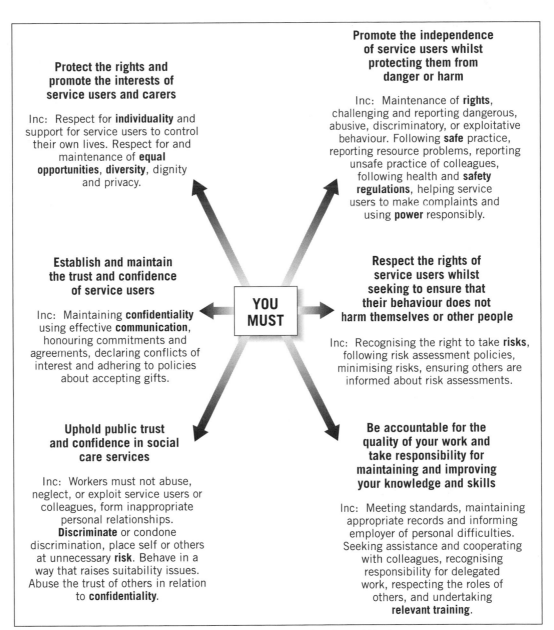

Protect the rights and promote the interests of service users and carers

Inc: Respect for **individuality** and support for service users to control their own lives. Respect for and maintenance of **equal opportunities**, **diversity**, dignity and privacy.

Promote the independence of service users whilst protecting them from danger or harm

Inc: Maintenance of **rights**, challenging and reporting dangerous, abusive, discriminatory, or exploitative behaviour. Following **safe** practice, reporting resource problems, reporting unsafe practice of colleagues, following health and **safety regulations**, helping service users to make complaints and using **power** responsibly.

Establish and maintain the trust and confidence of service users

Inc: Maintaining **confidentiality** using effective **communication**, honouring commitments and agreements, declaring conflicts of interest and adhering to policies about accepting gifts.

Respect the rights of service users whilst seeking to ensure that their behaviour does not harm themselves or other people

Inc: Recognising the right to take **risks**, following risk assessment policies, minimising risks, ensuring others are informed about risk assessments.

YOU MUST

Uphold public trust and confidence in social care services

Inc: Workers must not abuse, neglect, or exploit service users or colleagues, form inappropriate personal relationships. **Discriminate** or condone discrimination, place self or others at unnecessary **risk**. Behave in a way that raises suitability issues. Abuse the trust of others in relation to **confidentiality**.

Be accountable for the quality of your work and take responsibility for maintaining and improving your knowledge and skills

Inc: Meeting standards, maintaining appropriate records and informing employer of personal difficulties. Seeking assistance and cooperating with colleagues, recognising responsibility for delegated work, respecting the roles of others, and undertaking **relevant training**.

Figure 5.3 The GSCC Code of Practice for Social Care Workers: an outline summary

Table 5.1 Moral rights

MORAL RIGHTS OF SERVICE USERS	SOURCE OF PRESCRIPTION WITHIN GSCC STANDARDS
Diversity and the right to be different	**1.1** treat each person as an individual **1.2** respecting and promoting individual views **1.6** respecting diversity and different cultures and values
Equality and freedom from discrimination	**1.5** promoting equal opportunities **5.5** care workers must not discriminate **5.6** care workers must not condone discrimination
Control over own life, choice and independence	**1.3** supporting service users' rights to control their lives and make informed choices **3.1** promoting the independence of service users **3.7** helping service users and carers to make complaints **3.8** recognising and using power responsibly
Dignity and privacy	**1.4** respecting and maintaining the dignity and privacy of service users
Confidentiality	**2.3** respecting confidential information
Effective communication	**2.2** communicating in an appropriate, open, accurate and straightforward way
Safety and security	**Principle 3** promote independence while protecting service users including health and safety policies; appropriate practice and procedures. **4.2/4.3** follow risk assessment policies, take steps to minimise risk **5.2** must not exploit service users **5.7** must not put self or others at risk
The right to take risks	**4.1** service users have the right to take risks – help them to identify and manage risks

Reflect on practice

How far does the service you work in – or a service that you know about – promote the rights that are set out above?

Do you ever need to justify the policies and procedures used in this work setting? If so do you use any or all of the principles below?

- Maintaining consistency
- Concern for consequences
- Maximising human potential
- Challenging structural disadvantage and discrimination.

Moral rights may also be regarded as prescribed with reference to NVQ Standards and National Minimum Standards. The National Care Standards Commission has produced National Minimum Standards for a range of care settings. This commission was established by the Care Standards Act 2000 and these Standards define the quality of care that service users may expect. Local employers' policy documents may also refer to the principles prescribed by the National Care Standards Commission and the General Social Care Council.

5.3 Promoting human rights

Equality, rights and responsibilities

It is possible that a Human Rights Commission may be established and this commission would take over the work of the Race, Gender and Disability Equality Commissions. 'Liberty' (which was formerly known as the National Council for Civil Liberties) published a consultation paper issued by the Joint Committee on Human Rights in March 2003. This consultation paper sets out an argument that equality is essentially an area of human rights and that equality issues can be subsumed within the field of human rights.

The Joint Committee states:

'We support the establishment of an Equality and Human Rights Commission which would have both equalities and human rights issues within its remit. The Human Rights Act treats equality as a fundamental human right, as do many international human rights treaties. But human rights have something else to offer: a holistic approach to equality.'

'Human rights should be mainstreamed throughout the commission and its work. In practice this would mean that every issue considered by the Equality and Human Rights Commission would be looked at from a human rights perspective as well as an equality perspective.'

'There also exist human rights issues that do not necessarily involve discrimination but should fall within the remit of the new commission, for example: the treatment of older people and disabled people in residential care homes.'

'Mainstreaming human rights would have an additional benefit: it could help to provide the 'glue' that will enable a range of different equality areas to work closely together and resolve their differences. It is inevitable that, from time to time, there will be clashes of opinion between different equality strands.'

A culture of human rights

The consultation paper goes beyond arguing for human rights as a guiding and unifying principle for interpreting equality and anti-discriminatory issues. The paper argues that a focus on human rights should result in 'cultural change': 'There is a pressing need for an approach to human rights which emphasises the need for cultural change: this is something that NGOs [non-government organisations] alone can never deliver. An Equalities and Human Rights Commission, through education, issuing good practice guidance and undertaking other capacity building, has a vital role to play in filling this gap.'

As the Human Rights Commission consultation paper identifies, an individual's rights have to be balanced with responsibilities towards others. A culture of human rights would involve clarifying the boundaries of individual liberty and perhaps clarifying responsibilities that can be attributed to diverse members of society. The consultation paper states: 'It will be important for the Equality and Human Rights Commission to think carefully about how it approaches human rights issues. We believe it should avoid a legalistic approach, working instead on showing how human rights are something which we all can and should uphold in our lives by promoting the values and principles that underpin human rights standards.'

Tensions

The summary of the O2 NVQ Unit analysis states that the worker is expected to be 'proactive in promoting people's rights and responsibilities; equality and diversity; people's right to confidentiality.' The Standards recognise, however, that these areas often have a number of competing tensions 'within people themselves, between different people and between people and organisations'. Some tensions may not be easily resolvable. In Chapter 2 we argue that there are different 'knowledge communities' with different constructions of what is true or plausible. The radical social work perspective would interpret rights from the standpoint of achieving structural change in society; more traditional ethical approaches would focus on an individual perspective. Focusing on prescription within codes of practice, or national standards, may not provide a tension-free answer, but it may provide the only practical way forward in a post-modernist world (see Chapter 2).

Table 5.2 represents a potential starting point for discussing the boundaries of individual service user rights and potential service user responsibilities with respect to 'a culture of human rights'. The issues identified are perceived as being consistent with the GSCC Code of Practice and the model of ethical reasoning put forward by David Seedhouse (1988), that is, the principles are logically consistent, aimed at promoting socially positive outcomes, and aimed at promoting, as opposed to limiting, human potential.

Within a human rights culture, rights will be perceived as carrying responsibilities with them. An individual can expect respect but he or she has the responsibility not to interfere with or damage other people's rights. You have a right to be free from discrimination but a responsibility not to discriminate against others.

Table 5.2 Individual service user rights and responsibilities within a culture of human rights

MORAL RIGHTS OF SERVICE USERS	RESPONSIBILITIES WITHIN A HUMAN RIGHTS CULTURE
Diversity and the right to be different Including an individual's right to express his or her own identity/self-narrative and interpretation of life from the standpoint of different social group memberships	**To respect diversity in others** Including an acceptance that other people have a moral right to interpret life differently. A moral responsibility not to discriminate against others on the basis that own identity/social group membership is morally superior to that of others
Equality and freedom from discrimination Including freedom from discrimination on the basis of race, sex, ability, sexuality, religion	**Respect for the equality of others** Including respect for, and not discriminating against members of other social groups
Control over own life, choice and independence Including the freedom to choose their own lifestyle, self-presentation, diet and routine	**Respect for the independence, choice and lifestyle of others** Including arriving at a balance between the impact of own choices and the needs of other people who may be affected by the service user's choices – including care staff
Dignity and privacy Including the right to be responded to in terms of own interpretation of dignity and respect, that is, in terms of own identity/self-narrative	**To share or disclose own assumptions about dignity and negotiate boundaries with others** Including boundaries associated with health and safety or the identity needs of other users or carers
Confidentiality Including rights as established in law and local codes of practice	**Respect for the confidentiality of others** Including others' legal rights, and rights established in local codes of practice
Effective communication Including appropriately clear and supportive communication that minimises vulnerability	**Communication with others which does not seek to increase their vulnerability** Including communication that respects diversity and which is not discriminatory, prejudiced, or intended to create a sense of threat in others
Safety and security Including physical safety, living in an environment that promotes health and emotional safety. Security of property, and freedom from physical, social, emotional, or economic threat	**Contributing to the safety and security of others** Including behaving in a way that does not compromise or threaten the physical or emotional safety and security of others
The right to take risks Including taking risks as a matter of choice, in order to maintain own identity or perceived well-being	**Not to expose self or others to unacceptable risks** Including a willingness to negotiate with respect to the impact of risk on others

Respect for diversity (the right 'to be different')

If care work is about supporting vulnerable people, then it is vitally important that care workers can support and promote the identity needs of service users. Without respect for diversity, service users' self-esteem needs may not be met. In addition, service users may perceive their identity to be threatened. A loss of emotional safety might undermine needs at a more basic level of Maslow's pyramid. Care work ought to involve supporting people to develop and maintain a clear sense of who they are, together with a feeling of self-worth. A person's sense of identity is often founded on his or her social group membership. People also have different personalities – they enjoy different things and develop different ways of understanding life experience.

Care work involves celebrating the fact that people are different or 'diverse'. This chapter argues that we live within different 'communities of meaning'. If this viewpoint is accepted then it is vital that service users should never be expected to fit the assumptions of care workers. Service users have a right not to be judged in terms of assumptions about what is normal, or what is the right way to live.

Within a rights culture, service users must expect at least to respect the diverse nature of other people's identity and social group membership. But inevitably tensions are likely to occur.

CASE STUDY – Belief systems

Suppose you are talking to a 90-year-old woman in a care home. This service user is not diagnosed to have any kind of dementia. She says to you: 'I like it here, because my mother comes to visit me.' You might ask: 'But how old is your mother then?' The resident quickly states: 'Oh, my mother died 20 years ago – that's what I mean, she comes back from the other side to comfort me – when the time comes she will guide me across to the next world.'

How does this statement make you feel?

If you hold beliefs similar to this person, then this might be a natural and completely unchallenging conversation. But for many people such a conversation will create a feeling of tension and uneasiness. Some religions teach that the dead may be resurrected, but they do not come back in this way. Some atheists may believe that ghosts do not exist. The behaviour of this resident is a threat to the assumptions and belief systems of many people. On an emotional level, people may become angry when they feel threatened. Anger might result in hostility towards the resident and a reaction of labelling her as having a mental health problem.

But from the resident's point of view, her experience is positive and supportive. A human rights perspective would stress each person's right to his or her own religion and spiritual beliefs. Carers also have a right to their own beliefs. A conversation might need to acknowledge the woman's experience without judging it from the carer's perspective.

Freedom from discrimination

Receiving a worse service than others because of your age, gender, race, sexuality, or ability, could strike at the heart of a service user's sense of self, self-esteem and feeling of self-worth. When services or workers make assumptions about people, discrimination can easily follow. Architects in the 1960s designed buildings with steps and stairs – no lifts or ramps. As well as issues to do with economy, it is possible that people simply did not think about the needs of diverse groups. So disabled people were discriminated against. Making assumptions that everyone eats the same food, everyone shares the same life history, and everyone celebrates the same religious festivals results in excluding people and discriminating against them. Discrimination can damage a person's ability to construct and maintain a viable identity (see Chapter 2).

Thompson's PCS model for understanding discrimination

Neil Thompson (1997) identifies three levels where discrimination and anti-discrimination practice can take place. These three levels are analysed as being P, C and S levels (see Figure 5.4):

   P stands for personal and psychological
   C stands for cultural and conformity to norms
   S stands for structural and social forces.

Discrimination can work on any of the three levels. Historical beliefs about gender role and about the superiority of ethnic groups influence the social and political structures in which we live. Some organisations may still value male employees more highly than women. Men may find it easier to gain promotion because organisations

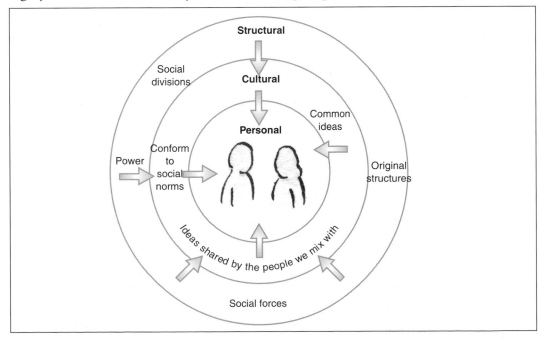

Figure 5.4 Thompson argues that discrimination can be understood on three levels

have built-in or structural systems that make it easier for men to succeed. Structural economic systems may result in some black communities living in more deprived housing conditions. Stressful housing conditions may represent one factor that can reduce life chances and opportunities.

On the cultural level we mix with groups of people who share values and ways of behaving. A great deal of discrimination happens because people conform to the expectations of others. People might, for instance, join in with jokes about a particular minority, not because they hold personal prejudices, but because they want to fit in with others. On a personal level, our own beliefs are often translated into our verbal and non-verbal behaviour. Our personal practice has a direct and immediate effect on others.

On an individual level, Thompson (1997) makes the point that workers can make a major difference to the quality of a service user's life by checking their own assumptions and their own behaviour. On a personal level, discrimination may result from emotional reactions as well as resulting from belief systems. Building an understanding of each service user's identity and working within a culture of human rights might enable an individual to identify and challenge emotional responses. A belief system that incorporates a human rights perspective might enable an individual to contribute towards an anti-discriminatory culture. Every individual has the power to develop his or her own skills and to employ appropriate skills when he or she interacts with others. Resource constraints may be argued to limit personal effectiveness, but there is nearly always something that could be achieved within person-to-person dialogue.

On a wider cultural level, individuals can 'make a difference'. Individuals can analyse what is happening and can challenge others to try to change group norms and values. Organisations must introduce management and quality systems, which aim to ensure that workplace norms and expectations conform to national standards and codes of practice for care.

Reflect on practice ·

The impairment narrative might create a focus for discriminatory assumptions in a service for people with physical disabilities. On a personal level, how could you ensure that you do not promote this narrative? On a broader cultural level, how could you challenge assumptions associated with 'handicap'? How far can ideas like self-advocacy assist service users to see themselves as different rather than defective? At a structural level, National Standards may identify the importance of 'the social model of disability'. How else could discrimination be tackled at this level?

Where quality systems incorporate a focus on rights, the culture of an organisation may become non-oppressive. On the very widest structural level, individuals may feel that they have little influence. Setting up quality standards and systems is a government function and the standards and the resources, which services have to operate within, are strongly influenced by political views and values. Individuals may need to join pressure groups, or become involved in political debate in order to influence the structural level of discrimination.

Some obvious types of discriminatory practice are shown in Figure 5.5. It should be possible to monitor your own and others' behaviour in order to minimise such risks.

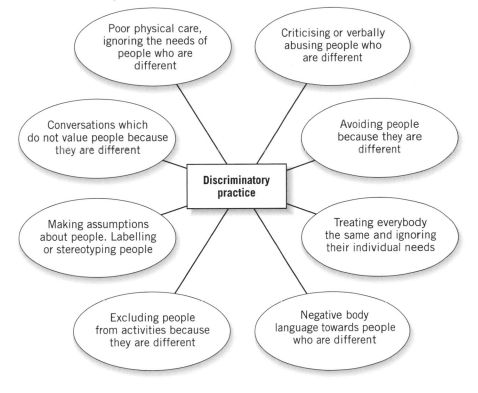

Figure 5.5 Types of discriminatory practice

Discrimination may result in the outcomes shown in Figure 5.6.

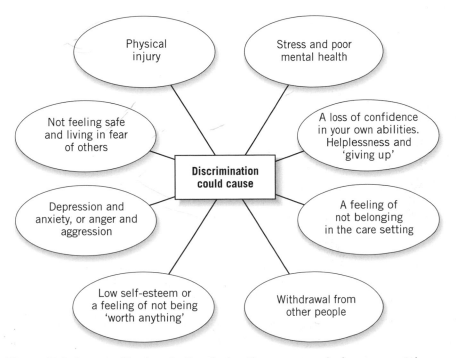

Figure 5.6 Some effects of discrimination on people in care settings

The right to control your own life, independence and choice

A sense of self, a sense of belonging and self-esteem, are often developed or maintained by involving people in their own care as much as is possible. Wherever possible, service users should be helped to take control of their own care. When people cannot do things for themselves they can still be asked to say how they would like care to be given. Wherever possible, service users should be given the power (empowered) to do things for themselves. Feeling independent may increase a person's self-esteem. Feeling out of control may threaten a service user, increase his or her vulnerability and reduce self-esteem.

If people are to be independent, then they must be free to make choices. Part of being an adult is to make day-to-day choices about personal appearance, diet, and so on. Where people have serious disabilities or illnesses, or when they are very young, care workers sometimes limit what they are allowed to do – usually for health and safety reasons. Where service users are deliberately restricted there should be clear reasons for doing this, and normally those reasons should be recorded in writing so that they can be checked. Where service users have difficulty in expressing their wishes, care workers should try to find ways of helping them to choose what they want or need.

If a person feels that his or her wishes and needs are not being respected this is likely to damage that person's sense of belonging and self-esteem. We may feel that we don't matter – almost don't exist if we cannot make important choices.

CASE STUDY – Smoking

Nasil argues that he has a right to smoke – it's his life and he has a right to choose how he lives and dies. Nasil attends a day centre that has a no smoking policy inside the building. Nasil will often go outside to have a cigarette, but he complains that the cold damp air is unpleasant and bad for his health. 'Us smokers are discriminated against', he says. 'Why should we have to put up with being cold just because other people have got different habits?'

What are Nasil's rights and what are his responsibilities in relationship to smoking?

Adults have a right to choose to smoke even though smoking usually damages health and might shorten a person's life. Smokers have a responsibility not to put other people's health at risk because people have a human right to health. Other people, including care staff, should not have to breathe in tobacco smoke. This means that in most places today, smoking is only allowed in specially set-aside areas.

In the past, service users' responsibilities may not have been a major focus because service users generally have less power than staff and managers of services. Service users are generally vulnerable, whilst care workers generally have a degree of control over their own lives. But just because a person is vulnerable, it doesn't mean that he or she has a right to interfere with other people or, for instance, threaten people with racist or sexist behaviour.

CASE STUDY – Eating

Graham is a 38-year-old man with learning disability. He gets great pleasure from eating and particularly enjoys sweet things such as honey and jam. Graham is overweight and the staff think that he should go on a diet for health reasons. Graham cannot understand their ideas and becomes angry if he can't have his usual eating pattern.

What are Graham's rights and responsibilities? In general, Graham has a right to choose to eat lots of sweet things. He also has a right to be overweight! People may choose their own diet and lifestyle. Graham has a responsibility not to behave in a way that might definitely injure him or shorten his life. Graham doesn't understand the issues of diet and health, so it is difficult for the staff, or for Graham, to finally decide what should be done.

In situations like those described in the case studies, an **advocate** should be appointed to help to decide on the balance of rights and responsibilities. An advocate will try to understand the needs and wishes of a service user and then argue for them. In Graham's situation the advocate argues that Graham should continue to enjoy his favourite food, but that care staff should keep an eye on his weight in case the level of risk increases.

The balance between rights and responsibility will often involve difficult ethical decisions. It may be important to involve an advocate and there may be a need for negotiation and problem-solving work between advocates and care staff/managers. Such work may need to identify the ethical principles and assumptions used to assist in arriving at a decision.

Dignity and privacy

For people to feel that they belong and that they are worth something, they need to receive respect. People may need assistance with very personal tasks in a care setting. People may need help with food, help to dress and wash, and help to use the toilet. With all these activities, it isn't just a matter of performing a behavioural task. If an individual is simply treated as being nothing but a body, it is likely to undermine his or her identity. In Chapter 2 we explained the theory of self-narrative. If individuals are treated very differently from the way they have always expected to be treated then we might expect individuals to have to change their understanding of self. In short, being treated with the lack of dignity and respect is likely to result in a loss of self-esteem and an experience of emotional threat.

Showing respect for other people usually involves understanding their feelings and wishes. Respect involves making sure that people have privacy when undressing, washing or going to the toilet. Respect involves not expressing negative attitudes towards difficulties that people may have with daily living activities, such as washing, dressing and personal care.

There is great diversity in the beliefs that people hold with respect to the meaning of touch, the significance of keeping areas of the body covered and the appropriateness of being cared for by a member of the opposite sex. Some people perceive touch as comforting. Holding hands, or an arm round the shoulder, implies care. For other people, a stranger putting his or her arm around you implies that the stranger has power and dominance. For some people, all physical contact is associated with sexual behaviour. Some people feel safer if staff that provide physical care wear a uniform. The act of wearing a uniform makes physical contact acceptable within the storyline that these people live by.

Showing respect for dignity must involve becoming aware of the service user's interpretation of physical care. Care staff will need to negotiate a way to work with service users that is perceived as dignified and private by the service user. This may not always be straightforward.

CASE STUDY – Providing support

Palvinder is a 30-year-old man with a learning difficulty, who uses a wheelchair. He attends a local college and has a good relationship with a male support worker. Palvinder will only accept physical support to transfer from his wheelchair from this one particular support worker. He becomes upset and withdrawn if other workers seek to help him. Palvinder cannot explain his reactions, but he has clearly formed a set of interpretations and expectations around physical support. These expectations will include belief systems associated with socialisation.

How should other care workers respond to this situation, given that they will need to provide support in the future? How can they come to understand Palvinder's interpretation of the situation?

The right to confidentiality

Care services have to keep detailed information on people in order to meet their needs. Care workers also have to find out a great deal of personal information about service users in order to ensure they can work effectively and maintain service user rights. It is vital that this information is only shared with people who have a genuine need to know it.

If care workers were to pass information on to friends, neighbours or other members of the public, it could have the following effects.

- The service users could feel that they didn't matter; their sense of self and self-esteem could be damaged if they even thought personal details could become public.
- People could lose trust in a care worker if they thought their personal details were being discussed and talked about by others.
- Service users could lose control over their lives if relatives or neighbours know details of their medical conditions and make assumptions. For instance, if neighbours find out that a person has cancer, they may assume that they will go into hospital and maybe die. It could be difficult for the service user to deal with this.
- Service users' property and personal safety could be at risk if information on their savings and where they are kept were to be made available. If it becomes public that a person keeps a door key under the flowerpot in his or her front garden, he or she could be burgled. If a service user is known to be forgetful, criminals who see the potential for exploitation could target him or her.

The right to effective communication

Respecting diversity, avoiding discrimination, showing respect for dignity and offering choices, all depend on understanding the people that you work with. Before we can understand people, it is necessary to communicate with them.

Communication is not just a matter of giving and receiving information. Communication requires active listening as well as appropriate verbal and non-verbal skills. If people do not feel that they are understood and listened to, they may have difficulty maintaining a viable self-narrative. Poor communication may result in a lack of self-esteem and a negatively re-storied self. Poor communication may result in more serious problems than simply being misinformed.

Communication requires active listening and appropriate verbal and non-verbal skills

CASE STUDY – Re-storying

An older service user, whose aches and pains are simply dismissed as 'it's your age, love', is not simply being patronised or being treated with a lack of respect. This short and simple comment represents an example of 're-storying'. The care worker's story is that the service user is impaired and that nothing can be done because of age. This may not be the service user's interpretation but with enough exposure to this way of thinking it might become his or her interpretation.

How can care workers prevent themselves from re-storying service users?

The right to security and safety

Many people come to understand themselves in terms of the possessions that they own and relationships with other people. Some people associate a sense of being with personal space. When strangers invade a person's personal space and if personal possessions are removed, such actions may undermine the personal narrative of that individual. For example, a wedding ring might represent a small 'scrap gold reward' for a thief, but that same scrap of gold might be a vital symbol of a lifelong relationship for an older service user. The loss of such a ring might create a sense of powerlessness and even a feeling of 'self' being violated. Perhaps you are no longer the person you used to be, if you have no control over the symbols of your identity.

A right to security and safety is vital in order to enable service users to maintain a successful self-narrative. Security and safety are about emotional needs as well as protection from physical harm or abuse.

Emotional safety

Most people understand themselves to be more than simply a physical body. Most people develop a sense of self, sometimes described as a sense of identity, and this sense of self, or identity, includes social relationships and a sense of social worth. Physical threat activates a physiological stress response within the body. A threat to self or identity activates the same physical stress response.

What if...

What if you had to go to hospital for an assessment? Many people feel threatened because they fear the possible consequences of surgery. But you might also feel threatened in terms of identity or sense of self. You may become an 'appendicitis' or a 'back problem'. You may feel that 'you' have been reduced to a malfunctioning 'bag of bones'. An exclusive focus on physical issues involves re-telling the story of who you are, in terms of language and thoughts that you are not used to. It may be that you will perceive this as a lack of dignity or respect.

The right to take risks

Humanistic theory places the development of human potential at the heart of ethical reasoning (Seedhouse, 1988). It can be argued that unless individuals are free to make choices and to take risks it is difficult to learn and develop. If care services take complete control of service users' daily living routines then it may be possible to maximise safety from external threat. For example, if children are not allowed to play outside when there is snow, we can be confident that they will be safe from falls. However, such a restriction may also limit children's learning and experience and limit their enjoyment of life. An over-protective environment may restrict the development of human potential. We may maximise security against external threat only to create the internal stress of limited potential.

The issue of risk is, therefore, a matter of balancing competing issues when undertaking a risk assessment. It can never be right to simply seek to maximise safety from physical hazards.

CASE STUDY – Risk assessment

Mrs Barber lives alone and receives home care support in order to cope with shopping, cooking and cleaning. Mrs Barber does not appear to be sensitive to the temperature in her home. She has a fully functioning central heating system, and has been assessed to have adequate financial resources to pay heating bills. Mrs Barber frequently turns the heating system off in order to save money. She will talk about the importance of avoiding waste and her desire to leave some money behind for her son.

Mrs Barber's carer frequently points out the risks of living in a cold home – including hypothermia. Mrs Barber says that it's her right to choose how to live and that she is not prepared to take orders from other people. However, she will put the heating on for the home care worker 'because she wouldn't like her to feel cold'. A risk assessment for Mrs Barber would need to take into account the competing tensions between the risk to health of under-heated premises and the risk of infringing Mrs Barber's moral right to make her own choices and live 'within her own story'.

How far does Mrs Barber have a right to live in a cold home?

Evaluating systems

NVQ Unit O3 requires senior staff to evaluate systems to 'promote the rights, responsibilities and diversity of people'. The unit summary states: 'The worker is also expected to evaluate the systems and structures of others and seek to improve these if they do not promote the rights of people.' In part, this requirement will be actioned by analysing an agency's policies, procedures and provisions in relation to the appropriate set of National Minimum Standards relevant to the service sector.

The National Care Standards Commission or NCSC started work in 2002. This organisation aims to make sure that care services, including private and voluntary hospitals and nurses' agencies in England, meet quality standards. Wales has its own Care Standards Inspectorate. The NCSC produces a set of regulations and National Minimum Standards that care services must achieve. There are different sets of Standards for different care services. The Standards provide very detailed guidance on how services must be delivered. Care services have to be registered with the NCSC and the NCSC inspects services to make sure that they are providing quality care. The NCSC also investigates complaints about care services. The Commission for Social Care Inspection (CSCI) took over the inspection role of the NCSC in England in April 2004.

National Minimum Standards involve extensive analysis of the quality of care that must be provided by specific services. Standards identify equality and human rights issues, as discussed below. These Standards provide a system of definition that will enable measurement of quality, and a way of identifying shortfalls in provision. Although Standards provide a basis for monitoring services, they do not provide a system for guiding relationship work or for explaining how individual needs, lifestyles, or respect for dignity may become a positive focus for quality care work.

We would argue that assisting individuals to develop or maintain a self-narrative should be central to many of the issues identified in Table 5.3. Narrative work can be explained (see Chapters 1–4), but listening and conversational work is hard to measure – it does not easily lend itself to a culture of inspection. Just because it is not easy to measure and monitor does not mean that it should not be a focus for concern. People are not simple and any attempt to reduce services to focus only on 'that which is easy to measure' may not accord well within a human rights culture.

Consider the time-honoured story of the 'drunk and the lamp-post', which has been around for at least 50 years. The story goes that a drunken person is crawling around a lamp-post. A passer-by asks, ' What are you doing?' 'I lost my keys,' replies the drunken person. The passer-by asks, 'Where did you lose them?' 'Oh – down the road,' replies the drunk. 'Then why are you looking for them here?' asks the passer-by. 'Ah it's easier to see here,' explains the drunk.

Things that are easy to measure may not always be the important things that need to be considered when interpreting quality. A service that goes beyond minimum standards might do so through a focus on human rights, diversity and the quality of interpersonal work on offer.

An example of the principles set out in National Minimum Standards for Care Homes for younger adults (adults between 18 and 65 years of age) is set out in Table 5.3. Some terms that imply service user rights are noted in bold.

Table 5.3 The National Minimum Standards for Care Homes for Younger Adults: a summary of principles

NO.	STANDARD
	Choice of Home Standards 1–5
1	The registered person produces an up-to-date statement of purpose, setting out the aims, objectives and philosophy of the home, its services and facilities, and terms and conditions; and provides each prospective service user with a service users' guide to the home.
2	New service users are admitted only on the basis of a full assessment undertaken by people competent to do so, involving the prospective service user, using an **appropriate communication** method and with an independent **advocate** as appropriate.
3	The registered person can demonstrate the home's capacity to meet the **assessed needs** (including specialist needs) of individuals admitted to the home.
4	The registered manager invites prospective service users to visit the home on an introductory basis before making a decision to move there, and unplanned admissions are avoided where possible.
5	The registered manager develops and agrees with each prospective service user a written and costed contract/statement of terms and conditions between the home and the service user.
	Individual Needs and Choices Standards 6–10
6	The registered manager develops and agrees with each service user an individual plan, which may include treatment and rehabilitation, describing the services and facilities to be provided by the home, and how the services will meet current and changing needs and aspirations and achieve goals.
7	Staff respect service users' right to make decisions, and that right is limited only through the assessment process, involving the service user, and as recorded in the individual service user plan.
8	The registered manager ensures that service users are offered opportunities to participate in the day-to-day running of the home and to contribute to the development and review of policies, procedures and services.
9	Staff enable service users to take responsible **risks**, ensuring they have good information on which to base decisions within the context of the service user's individual plan and of the home's risk assessment and risk management strategies.
10	Staff respect information given by service users in **confidence**, and handle information about service users in accordance with the home's written policies and procedures and the **Data Protection Act 1998**, and in the best interests of the service user.
	Lifestyle Standards 11–17
11	Staff enable service users to have opportunities to maintain and develop **social, emotional, communication and independent living skills**.
12	Staff help service users to find and keep appropriate jobs, continue their education or training, and/or take part in valued and fulfilling activities.

NO.	STANDARD
13	Staff support service users to become part of, and participate in, the local community in accordance with assessed needs and the individual plans.
14	Staff ensure that service users have access to, and choose from a range of, appropriate leisure activities.
15	Staff support service users to maintain family links and friendships inside and outside the home, subject to restrictions agreed in the individual plan and contract.
16	The daily routines and house rules promote **independence**, **individual choice** and freedom of movement, subject to restrictions agreed in the individual plan and contract.
17	The registered person promotes service users' health and well-being by ensuring the supply of nutritious, varied, balanced and attractively presented meals in a congenial setting and at flexible times.
	Personal and Healthcare Support Standards 18–21
18	Staff provide sensitive and flexible personal support and nursing care to maximise service users' **privacy, dignity, independence and control over their lives**.
19	The registered person ensures that the health care needs of service users are assessed and recognised and that procedures are in place to address them.
20	The registered manager and staff encourage and support service users to retain, administer and **control** their own medication, within a **risk management** framework, and complying with their home's policy and procedures for the receipt, recording, storage, handling, administration and disposal of medicines.
21	The registered manager and staff deal with the ageing, illness and death of a service user with sensitivity and **respect**.
	Concerns, Complaints and Protection Standards 22–23
22	The registered person ensures that there is a clear and effective **complaints procedure**, which includes the stages of, and time scales for, the process and that service users know how, and to whom, to complain.
23	The registered person ensures that service users are **safeguarded** from physical, financial or material, psychological or sexual abuse, neglect, **discriminatory abuse** or self-harm or inhuman or degrading treatment, through deliberate intent, negligence or ignorance, in accordance with written policy.
	Environment Standards 24–30
24	The home's premises are suitable for its stated purpose; accessible, **safe** and well maintained; meet service users' individual and collective needs in a comfortable and homely way; and have been designed with reference to relevant guidance.
25	The registered person provides each service user with a bedroom which has usable floor space sufficient to meet **individual needs and lifestyles**.
26	The registered person provides each service user with a bedroom that has furniture and fittings sufficient and suitable to meet **individual needs and lifestyles**.

NO.	STANDARD
27	The registered person provides service users with toilet and bathroom facilities, which meet their assessed needs and offer sufficient personal **privacy**.
28	A range of comfortable, **safe** and fully accessible shared spaces is provided both for shared activities and for private use.
29	The registered person ensures the provision of the environmental adaptations and disability equipment necessary to meet the home's stated purpose and the individually assessed needs of all service users.
30	The premises that are kept are claimed, hygienic and free from offensive odours throughout and systems are in place to control the spread of infection, in accordance with relevant legislation, published professional guidance and the purpose of the home.
	Staffing Standards 31–36
31	The registered manager ensures that staff have clearly defined job descriptions and understand their own and others' roles and responsibilities.
32	Staff have the competences and qualities required to meet service users' needs and achieve Sector Skills Council work for strategy targets within the required time scales.
33	The home has an effective staff team, with sufficient numbers and complementary skills to support service users' assessed needs at all times.
34	The registered person operates a thorough recruitment procedure based on **equal opportunities** and ensuring the **protection of service users**.
35	The registered person ensures that there is a **staff training** and development programme which meets Sector Skills Council workforce training targets and ensures staff fulfil the aims of the home and meet the changing needs of service users.
36	Staff receive the support and supervision they need to carry out their jobs.
	Conduct and Management of the Home Standards 37–43
37	The registered manager is qualified, competent and experienced to run a home and meet its stated purpose, aims and objectives.
38	The management approach of the home creates an open, positive and inclusive atmosphere.
39	Effective quality assurance and quality monitoring systems, based on seeking the views of service users, are in place to measure success in achieving the aims, objectives and statement of purpose of the home.
40	The home's written policies and procedures comply with current legislation and recognised professional standards, covering topics set out in appendix 3. (Appendix 3 lists 33 areas that must be covered in a home's policies and procedures.)
41	Records required by regulation for the protection of service users and for the effective and efficient running of the business are maintained, up to date and accurate.
42	The registered manager ensures so far as is reasonably practicable the **health, safety and welfare** of service users and staff.
43	The overall management of the service (within or external to the home) ensures the effectiveness, financial viability and accountability of the home.

In addition to National Minimum Standards for each care setting, senior care staff will need to ensure that provisions, policies and procedures accord with the GSCC Code of Practice for employers of social care workers.

A summary of the Code of Practice for Employers of Social Care Workers is set out in Table 5.4.

Table 5.4 The Code of Practice for Employers of Social Care Workers: an outline

1	**Employers must make sure people are suitable to enter the social care workforce and understand their roles and responsibilities.**
2	**Employers must have written policies and procedures in place to enable social care workers to meet the GSCC's Code of Practice for Social Care Workers.** This includes written policies on: ● confidentiality ● equal opportunities ● risk assessment ● record keeping ● acceptance of gifts ● substance abuse. Effective systems of management and supervision. Systems to report inadequate resources. Support for workers to meet the GSCC Code of Practice.
3	**Employers must provide training and development opportunities to enable social care workers to strengthen and develop their skills and knowledge.** Including: ● induction ● workplace assessment and practice learning ● supporting staff to meet eligibility criteria ● responding to workers who seek assistance.
4	**Employers must put into place and implement written policies and procedures to deal with dangerous, discriminatory or exploitative behaviour and practice.** Including written policies and procedures on: ● bullying, harassment, discrimination ● reporting dangerous, discriminatory, abusive, or exploitative behaviour ● minimising the risk of violence and managing violent incidents ● support for workers who experience trauma or violence ● equal opportunities ● assistance to care workers in relation to health needs.
5	**Employers must promote the GSCC's Codes of Practice to social care workers, service users and carers and cooperate with the GSCC's proceedings.** Including: ● informing workers of the code, informing social care users and using the code to assist decision-making ● informing the GSCC of any misconduct, cooperating with the GSCC in investigations.

5.4 Establishing good quality care

By itself, the law cannot make sure that discrimination doesn't happen or that people's rights are always respected. It can often be very difficult to prove that discrimination has happened and it can be costly in time, energy and money to fight legal battles.

Policies, procedures and rights in practice

The Standards of good practice set out by the NCSC and GSCC can provide an effective basis for ensuring that employers develop procedures to protect service users' rights. Care services are inspected to ensure that the quality of the service they offer reaches the required standards. Each service will have policies on equal opportunities and confidentiality to guide staff behaviour. These policies will be designed to meet legal requirements as well as NCSC Standards. Together with policies, each care organisation will have procedures for staff to follow in order to ensure that service users' rights are respected.

Reflect on practice

The care service you work for (or know about) will have a range of policies and procedures designed to meet NCSC Standards. But how effective are these policies at creating a culture of human rights within your organisation? What else is needed in order to influence organisational culture?

Laws provide the background to policy making and policy and standards guide managers when they design procedures.

Just because policy and procedure documents say that care workers must meet certain standards, this does not mean that they will! The CSCI will undertake inspections of care services and can respond to complaints; but even inspection and complaints procedures cannot guarantee that every service user's rights will be respected. The quality of service that an individual receives will be influenced by the following factors:

- the level of physical and staff resources (including the number of staff available to work)
- the amount and quality of staff training
- the amount and quality of staff supervision and support
- the degree to which staff work in a culture of rights
- staff morale including the sharing of a common narrative purpose and how tired or stressed staff perceive themselves to be
- the quality of leadership and teamwork within a care service – do staff share a narrative that gives them a sense of purpose in their work?
- the degree of cooperation between different services.

Over time, standards and inspections might assist in the development of quality care services. But a lack of resources, or the inability to establish a 'human rights culture', could still result in a poor quality of service to an individual, despite the existence of Minimum National Standards and inspection procedures. It is possible that the establishment of a Human Rights Commission in this country would drive the implementation and improvement of standards, but no definite plans are yet in place. It is possible that a culture of human rights might in itself be sufficient to create a quality, supportive environment even where resource problems exist.

What is good quality care?

What is required from managers and deputy managers? Firstly, social care mangers need to be constantly aware that the social care profession is working at the interface between private individuals and public responsibilities. Focus on both personal and professional domains is essential. Both must be the focus of skill and commitment.

Within this broad remit there are three key areas.

- **Knowledge** The attainment of the Degree in Social Work or a Foundation Degree or the NVQ 4 Registered Managers' Award indicates the ability to conceptualise the complex issues involved in working with service users.
- **Skills** Without the personal motivation and the qualities to put knowledge into action, knowledge alone will not improve the quality of life for others. Skills, including communication skills, are needed at an interpersonal and inter-professional level.
- **Vision** The influence and power of the manager cannot be understated within social care. The best managers are those people who can create a palpably strong image of the type of emotional and physical environment they are trying to achieve. Social care involves the interlinking of multiple worlds – the service users' and staff's own history, experience, knowledge and expectations, the professional world of care standards, medical care, the expectations and emotions of relatives represent a few of these worlds. Which should take priority? The best services have a clear vision – a shared narrative that is worked out in practice – a model of care accepted as the normal culture by staff, relatives and residents. Quality services are characterised by attention to the personal, attention to small details, attention to creating a sense of a positive and interesting way to live as a service user. The importance of leadership cannot be underestimated and it is essential to use available resources such as training, staff meetings, open communication and a style of management that encourages care staff to take responsibility and reflect on their own actions. In practice, the best results may come with a combination of high support and high challenge (see Figure 5.7).

Social care work can be experienced as one of the richest and most diverse in the field of employment. The daily complexity of moving between the minutiae of the individual to the essential standards of an organisation can be challenging but very rewarding. A combination of skills and knowledge is essential but above all the social care manager needs a heart and a vision for the emotional and environmental experience of the service users and their carers.

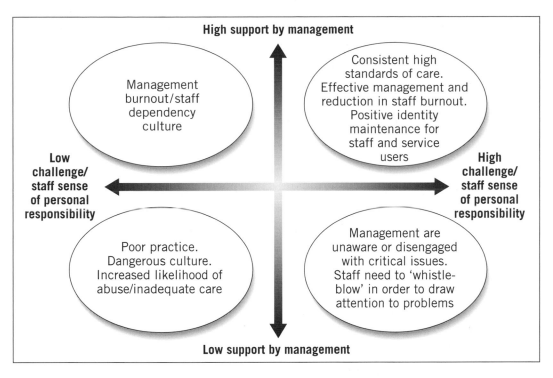

High support by management

Management burnout/staff dependency culture

Consistent high standards of care. Effective management and reduction in staff burnout. Positive identity maintenance for staff and service users

Low challenge/ staff sense of personal responsibility

High challenge/ staff sense of personal responsibility

Poor practice. Dangerous culture. Increased likelihood of abuse/inadequate care

Management are unaware or disengaged with critical issues. Staff need to 'whistle-blow' in order to draw attention to problems

Low support by management

Figure 5.7 Results of staff challenges and support within care homes

Summary

- ○ The concept of values does not provide a useful way for explaining moral rights.

- ○ Principles of maintaining consistency, concern for consequences, promoting human potential and challenging structural disadvantage and discrimination, provide principles to guide action.

- ○ In the final analysis, rights exist because of prescription.

- ○ Moral rights are implied by codes of practice and National Standards.

- ○ Service users are perceived to have moral rights of respect for diversity, freedom from discrimination, independence and choice, dignity and privacy, confidentiality, effective communication, security and safety, and the right to take risks.

- ○ Equality, respect for diversity and freedom from discrimination are central human rights. A human rights culture would aim to promote equality amongst other rights.

- ○ Human rights carry responsibilities towards others. A human rights culture will seek to balance individual rights with responsibilities.

- ○ Balancing rights and responsibilities involves skilled acts of judgement. The ethical principles outlined at the beginning of this chapter may be useful when attempting to balance rights and responsibilities.

- ○ Policies and procedures based on National Standards will not necessarily in themselves result in better quality services. A range of factors can influence the culture within a service; these factors might include a shared human rights narrative.

CHAPTER 6

Social care and law

Introduction

Social care workers operate at the interface between public and private worlds. In relation to the formal requirements of working in this field, social care workers need to be aware of the relevant law, policies and regulations affecting social care provision. However, too frequently the private world of the individual service user is overlooked, as the formal aspects of social care seem to take pre-eminence. It is essential to give equal weight to the private world of the service users in terms of their life stories, needs, emotions and expectations. Their life stories and pre-written narratives about themselves, as well as the nature of care settings, need to be understood and integrated into daily practice, if care is truly to meet people's needs. Over the last 20 years the formal requirements around social care provision have mushroomed, and it is, therefore, essential to have a solid grasp of them. However, the essentially individual and personal nature of relationships between service users and carers needs equal attention.

In order to understand and effectively assimilate the purpose and meaning of social care law and policy, four elements need to be identified and understood:

- the government's past and present approach to social policy
- the relationship between law, policy and rights in social care
- the role of the local authority in terms of assessment, care management, purchasing/commissioning, and adult/child protection
- the law and policy directly affecting social care provision and practice.

This chapter will address the first two elements. Chapter 7 will address the remaining two elements.

Aims *This chapter aims to enable you to explore:*

6.1   Social policy: the government's past and present approach

6.2   The relationship between law, policy and rights in social care

6.1 Social policy: the government's past and present approach

Social policy is perhaps an off-putting term, implying a depth of heavy political philosophy that is beyond everyday understanding. In essence, it means the relationship between the State and the individual in so far as the State identifies that it has responsibilities towards individuals social care needs. Understanding how the State defines its relationships to its citizens is essential in comprehending why we have our current laws. In social care, especially, law is not made in a vacuum but reflects deeply rooted beliefs about how and when the State should intervene in the life of its citizens. A summary of the historical relationship between the State and social care is contained in Tables 6.1 and 6.2.

Table 6.1 Relationship between State and social care until the end of the 19th century

17th century	State has minimal role in social care Church holds primary responsibility
18th century	Industrial Revolution Fear of revolution Urbanisation Parish system unable to cope Economic necessity for sustained labour supply
19th century	Concept of deserving versus undeserving poor Charity and morality heavily intertwined Government role in provision of health and education Social care provision punitive

Table 6.2 Relationship between State and social care in the 20th and early 21st centuries

Early 20th century	Increased State involvement Old age pension – Pension Act 1908 World War 1 (1914–1918) Expectations post-war of a 'land fit for heroes'
1930s	Depression Mass unemployment Rise of Fascism
1940s	Labour Beveridge Report 1942, blueprint for Welfare State Major policy change State as key universal provider and organiser of social care Fear of Communism

1950s and 1960s	Consensus politics Slight changes to welfare provision, but universal provision supported by all parties Institutions still have primary role in provision of social care
1970s	Oil crisis Recession 3 million unemployed Conservative philosophy: State has minimal role – individual alone is responsible for own welfare Business/market model introduced into social care Local authority role redefined
1980s	Social care legislation fuelled by spiralling costs of institutional social care Beginnings of integration of health and social care 'There is no such thing as society', Thatcher 1987
1990s	NHS and Community Care Act 1990 Role of local authorities = assessing and purchasing private, voluntary and independent care 85 per cent of local authority budget to be spent in independent sector
1997 to date	Labour Government Softening of terms 'Partnership not competition', 'Best value not competitive tendering' Core concepts of market/business culture intact Local authority role = a) purchasing/commissioning services; b) assessment; c) adult/child protection; d) limited/specialist service provision

Social policy from 1940 to 2004

From the 1940s there had been a general consensus amongst all parties that the State had a fundamental and universal responsibility to provide social care for individuals and families. This was summed up by the phrase 'from cradle to grave' (Beveridge Report, 1942). However, this State provision could only continue when there was a healthy and vibrant economy and full employment. By the 1970s the recession started to bite. Unemployment topped 3 million and people's expectations of health and welfare were increasing. This was combined with a rapid increase in the number of older people versus a reduction in the proportion of people working and contributing National Insurance and tax.

Developments in health care led to increasing demands for new treatments. The crisis in funding was also reflected in the spiralling cost of residential and nursing care. Until 1993 there was no assessment of need for individuals prior to their admission into private residential care; funding from the Department of Social Security was dependent only on fulfilling financial criteria. The DSS budget for private care spiralled from £10m in 1979 to £2,575m in 1993 (Laing and Buisson,

1996: 110–11). The fields of social care, health, and education were seen to be unaccountable and not focused in their aims and objectives.

The radical shift in political philosophy introduced by the Conservative Government in the 1980s had major implications for local authority performance and responsibility. The market and business culture was introduced for the first time into the social care field. The role of local authorities was re-defined as one of assessing and commissioning services and acting as purchasing brokers in the field of service provision. Their role as service providers was substantially reduced, retaining instead a limited role to provide specialist services that would not be economically viable in the private sector.

Cost, efficiency and planning were the key aims of social care from the 1980s, although the three stated aims were empowerment, autonomy and choice. Funding was taken away from health authorities and social security and given to local authorities in 1993. This was to reverse the perverse incentive towards residential and nursing care and restore the core aim of people remaining in their own homes. This was seen as a much more cost-effective option, where the demand for services would be regulated through assessment and strictly defined criteria about who was eligible for service provision. The targeting of resources to those most in need was also part of the business ethos that was introduced. Local authorities imposed ceiling limits to prevent spending on individual care packages from rising too high. In practice, they vary from one authority to another but an average indicator would be in the range of £200–300 per week per individual (in terms of the real cost of services in 2004) or, in service terms, around the equivalent of home carers calling three times per day. In the 1990s the government specified that 85 per cent of each local authority's budget in the adult sector must be spent within the private, independent and voluntary sector. This was based on the fundamental reasoning that the economic forces that could be exerted by local authorities in the marketplace would ensure maximum value for taxpayers' money. These policies were successful in their objective to end open, unlimited budget demands from organisations such as local authorities. Instead, central government has been able to establish tightly controlled fixed budgets at local level. The amount awarded is based on the complex Standard Spending Assessment formula; local authorities provide information each July and are advised of the amount awarded every November.

Redefinition of the State's responsibilities

Over the last 20 years there have been major changes in the way the government has defined the responsibilities of the State towards individuals. These changes directly affect the roles, tasks and responsibilities of the social care workforce. The main change has been the move away from the State undertaking to provide care and support on a universal basis.

The relationship between local and central government has, therefore, been radically redefined. Power and control have continued to be centralised. Government has now taken a much more directive approach in defining the processes, structures, aims and objectives of local government and the social care independent and voluntary sectors (see Figure 6.1). This has been achieved in part through the use of law and guidance, implemented through the Department of Health. Professional bodies such as the General Social Care Council, TOPSS (Training Organisation for Personal Social Services), and SCIE (Social Care Institute for Excellence) have also been created (see Figure 6.2). This resulted in responsibility being devolved to local authority level, whilst power and control have spiralled upwards to a centralised level. Although this is a political decision, it has significant consequences for individual social care workers at the local level. In psychological terms, a sense of responsibility without power can be a potent combination in producing personal reactions of stress. There is little argument

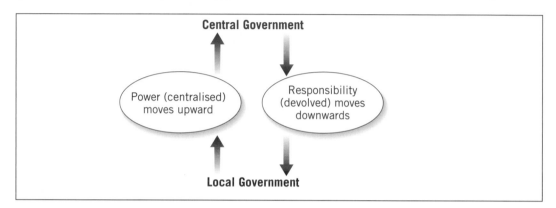

Figure 6.1 Trends in power and responsibility since the late 1970s

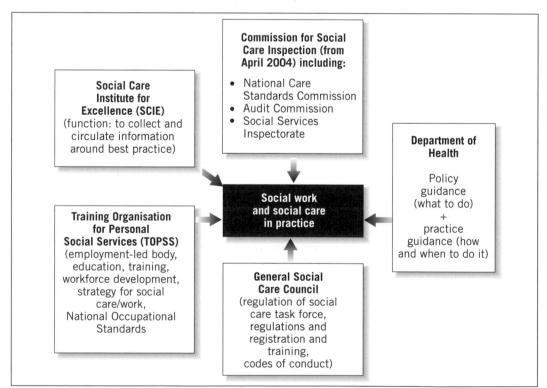

Figure 6.2 Government and professional bodies inputting to current social care practice

about whether social care work is a highly stressful occupation, but clarity is needed about the structural causes of this common experience.

Process, procedures and time limits

The plethora of guidance, legislation, regulations and local policies that has evolved since the 1980s has primarily focused on process, procedures and time limits. The effect has been to place a sense of unrealistic demands and responsibilities on social care workers. The focus on 'computerised' practice has led to a major reduction in the time that social care workers can spend in direct contact with service users due to pressures of completing the paperwork. The focus on outputs and measurable achievements as demanded by the business culture has therefore had a significant impact on practice and reduced the amount of time spent in direct work with the service user. Indeed, in the case of Victoria Climbie, one of the concerns referred to in the Laming Report (2003) was the lack of time spent in direct work with children. This is symptomatic of a much more widespread situation in social care, where feedback from social care workers reveals a general consensus that over the last 10 years there has been at least a 50 per cent reduction in direct work with service users and carers. Introduction of complicated computer software packages often involves duplication of work from paper-based assessment frameworks and very significant amounts of time are taken to record key events. In practice, the generalised nature of some of the care plans means that a second, more detailed, document is required to convey the individuality of the service user and this also takes significant time to record. However, computer software is still not in place to allow dialogue between medical and social care agencies on a countrywide basis. The current Children's Bill is looking at files on all children, but the technology needs to keep pace with the age-old problems of effective communication between agencies.

Current political belief under the Labour Government is a blending of the two previously polarised approaches to social policy. At one end, the State is seen as the universal provider of services, whilst the counter-view, as held by the Conservatives in the 1980s, is that individuals and families are solely responsible for their own welfare. Labour's approach is often referred to in policy as 'the third way'. In other words, the State should not be overly intrusive and the main responsibility lies with individuals, but the State will work in partnership in a focused way to provide support, targeted on those in most need, in a way that does not encourage dependence. Under New Labour the aggressive vocabulary of business culture has been toned down. Current terminology refers to partnership rather than competition – 'best value' has replaced 'competitive tendering'. Nevertheless, the core concepts of the marketplace and the business culture in social care remain largely intact.

Shift towards a technical-rational approach in social care

There has been a major shift in the culture of social care over the last 20 years towards a technical-rational approach. This is indicated by the emphasis on measurable outputs that can be monitored through statistics. Planning is seen as

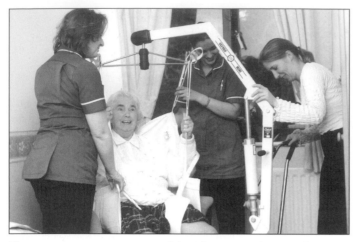

How can you measure subjective experiences in terms of the quality of care?

essential, with increased accountability for agencies and individuals involved in social care work. The technical-rational model is based on workers achieving measurable standards by following pre-set processes that are quantifiable and within tightly defined time scales.

The ethos of the previous culture in social care was to focus and emphasise the importance of the personal qualities of social care workers. Key issues were centred around workers' commitment to values as the essential attributes of a good care worker. This adherence to values now is not as strongly apparent as 20 years ago. This is perhaps due to the inability to define and agree common values to the satisfaction of all, combined with the imprecise nature of measuring subjective experiences in terms of quantifiable outputs.

Reflect on practice

Reflect on your understanding of the wider social policy picture and where this has had an impact on your daily experience. Think about whether you have blamed the social worker or the local authority in the past, and reflect on your updated understanding of the position.

6.2 The relationship between law, policy and rights in social care

Perception of automatic rights to services

Within popular perception, there is a belief that automatic rights to services exist in the field of social care legislation. This is strongly tied to the compensatory notion of disadvantage, where people experiencing ill health or disability should be able to access services quickly and easily, at little or minimal cost to enable them to cope as independently as possible. Notions of social justice strongly underpin this approach and it can be seen as a positivist approach (Cull and Roche, 2001). During the 1970s there was a distinct move towards the notion of clearly defined rights for people who were disabled, as championed by Alf Morris, MP; there was the beginning of a consensus around the moral imperative of the State to compensate for disadvantage. The Chronically Sick and Disabled Persons Act 1970 and the Disabled Persons Act 1986 adopted this approach. However, the sharp reversal of political thinking in the

1980s by radical Conservative philosophy led to a major retreat from a rights-based approach. Thus, although the Disabled Persons Act 1986 was passed, many key sections were never enacted.

Many people contact social services with the perception that there is an underlying entitlement to something, even if they are not sure what it is. In practice, their experience is very different from their expectations. Many service users and carers experience real difficulties in accessing social care services. Often the reality of contact can encompass long delays and experiences of conflict and/or confusion are also not uncommon. There is clearly a large gap between the public perception around rights and the actual reality.

Confusion exists around the entitlement of individuals and families to services

Whilst it is clear that legislation requires local authorities to provide services, there is much confusion surrounding the entitlement of individuals and families to those services. Some of the legislation covering service provision includes the Health Services and Public Health Act 1968, s 45 (power to promote the welfare of older people), the National Health Services Act 1977, Schedule 8 and s 21 (provision of home help), the National Assistance Act 1948, Part III, s 21 (duties and powers to provide accommodation for vulnerable adults and older people) and the Mental Health Act 1983, s 117 (after-care services for people discharged from specific compulsory admission sections). However, accessing these services is a very different process. Whilst it is intended that the threshold to an assessment should be low and, in the case of a person who is disabled, access should be automatic, under NHSCCA 90, s 47(2) that is not always consistent with practice. Ongoing shortages of qualified social work staff often result in long delays before an assessment is carried out. The reality that much social work is related to crisis work adds to the problems of a timely response to people waiting for an assessment.

Accessing services is built on the cornerstone of good quality assessments of need and risk (3rd Key Objective, Policy Guidance 1990, Community Care in the Next Decade and Beyond, see Table 7.1 on page 167). However, the assessment of need is made against local authority eligibility criteria, which are in turn affected by the pressures of limited resources. Local authority eligibility criteria are not static and react to changes in the budget.

The significant geographical variations by the government in outcomes for service users led to the introduction in April 2003 of Fair Access to Care. It is intended to avoid the post code lottery of service provision by setting four categories for eligibility for services: critical, substantial, moderate and low. An individual's needs and risks to independence are the key areas to be assessed.

Funding issues

The right to know how much proposed care is going to cost is another area that has become increasingly complex. Funding and charges for residential and nursing services are complex and confusing enough. However, the field of charging for domiciliary services is also now less than straightforward. The local authority has the discretionary power to charge for domiciliary services under the Health Services and Social Security Adjudication Act 1993, s 17. In 2001, the average amount recouped by local authorities for domiciliary care services averaged 12 per cent of the direct cost. Ten authorities chose not to charge at all for services, whilst other local authorities made much higher charges, with the highest rate of recoupment being in excess of 25 per cent (Select Committee on Health Memoranda 2001). The introduction of Fairer Charging in 2003 strongly discouraged flat-rate charge banding and implemented individual financial assessment, based on detailed information related to disability as well as income and savings. In practice, it is a matter of importance that service users have some indication of the likely ongoing costs. Prior to Fairer Charging, flat-rate charge bands were often used, based on benefits and savings set against the real cost of care. As such, it was possible to give service users and carers a fairly clear idea of potential charges at the time of the assessment of need. Following the introduction of Fairer Charging in 2003, this is no longer possible with any great degree of accuracy. Maximum and minimum costs might be indicated and some authorities such as Kent have devised ready reckoners to allow assessors to give some indication of potential costs. However, these are, by their very nature, complex, given the number of factors that the financial assessment has to cover.

In practice, the service user may have to wait many weeks for a detailed financial assessment. Although in many cases local authorities do not charge for services until this has been completed and agreed by the service user, many people find this process intrusive and unsettling. There may also be concerns about the accuracy of these assessments in cases where service users may have memory impairment and also in situations where people do not routinely keep bills and receipts. The assessment forms can be lengthy (in excess of ten pages) and there may be a need to check back on the previous utility bills. Receipts for disability related expenditure are also likely to be needed. Calculating costs of this type of expenditure is far from straightforward. Many people find the level of financial detail needed unacceptable or anxiety provoking. There are considerable variations between authorities with regard to maximum charging. Some authorities use a limit such as £30,000, above which a maximum cost of £200 per week will be charged. Many authorities state that the real cost will be charged in full for people with savings over £20,000. If a person declines to complete the financial assessment then the full charge is levied automatically. The continuing discretion for local authorities to make their own decisions on charging continues (DoH Guidance, September 2003). This is an example of where the quest for individual fairness has led to highly complex assessment systems that make it difficult to give clear individual information to service users and carers at the time when it is needed.

The reality of social care practice plays out the tension between need and resources on a daily basis. The ever-increasing regulation of practice through DoH guidance is seen by central government as the appropriate way of addressing these issues. However, these stresses and tensions are often experienced by individual social workers and it is one of the contributory factors to burnout within social care work. Whilst DoH guidance, regulations and professional bodies do give clear instruction in terms of standards, objectives, time scales and procedures, the sheer volume of these requirements is staggering. At the BASW Conference 2002 one social services director advised that he had calculated that there were 315 current separate pieces of guidance, regulations or directions relating to child care services alone, all of which had to be implemented and complied with. This is within a national picture of shortages of qualified social care staff. Currently, there is a significant vacuum and absence of meaningful dialogue around the vexed issue of resources versus need. The circular arguments of central government blaming local authorities and vice versa have ensured this area has been sidelined to an unproductive political stalemate situation.

Approaching service users

In the absence of a positive rights-based approach, encompassing absolute rights to services, how can a social care worker on an individual basis aim to work towards a 'rights-based' approach? The answer, in practice, lies with the *way* social care workers communicate and engage with service users. This has been described by Smales (1991), who identifies different ways social care workers can approach service users. These are:

- questioning approach
- procedural approach
- exchange approach.

The questioning and procedural approaches focus on the worker as the 'expert' and primary attention is paid either to extracting information (the questioning model) or to relate information to eligibility criteria, policies and procedures (procedural model). See Figure 6.3.

In practice, a rights-based approach is best served by the exchange model (Smale, 1991). Energy is invested into engaging and establishing a relationship that promotes communication. Needs and problems are jointly explored and defined between the service user, carer, other agencies such as health or housing and the care manager. Service users' sense of satisfaction with both process and outcome seems most strongly correlated to this model. The experience for the care worker is more

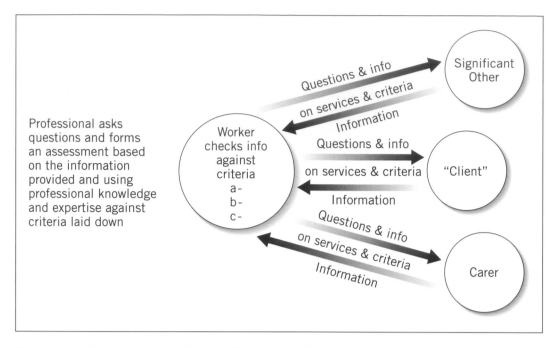

Figure 6.3 The procedural Model (Smale, 1991)

enriching and this model sits most closely to the core social care values of partnership and equality. In terms of the equality of power sharing, this model does acknowledge the vulnerability and lack of power experienced by many service users. Sharing of power and reciprocity in terms of information, options and choices forms the core of this approach. In practice, there is strong pressure for care managers and assessors to use the questioning model, as this is how the current multi-page assessment forms are structured. See Figure 6.4.

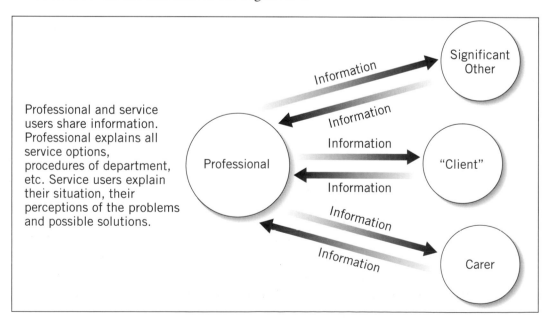

Figure 6.4 The Exchange Model (Smale,1991)

Process and method

Current initiatives such as the Single Assessment Procedure for Older People (all local authorities to be compliant by 2004) can be criticised for the absence of dialogue around the process and method of using tools and scales to assess the needs of older people. Social care workers may identify the task as the completion of the forms rather than the assessment of the person. The real task is to empower service users and carers to convey the reality of their experience and difficulties. Likewise, the procedural model focuses on eligibility criteria and the boundaries and process of accessing services rather than the service users' needs. The danger of conscious or unconscious adherence to the questioning or the procedural model is that power and control are vested in the assessor. To obtain resources, the assessor has to justify the application in terms of eligibility criteria and level of risk. However, the danger of the latter two models is that information will be captured but not the service user's own narrative. A rights-based approach will be facilitated by focusing on the person's narrative in order to effectively and mutually address his or her needs. The danger of the questioning and procedural model is to extract information in a sterile way that reduces social care work to a mechanistic process. To work as near to a rights-based approach as possible means establishing dialogue and a meaningful relationship within which to negotiate the complexities of need versus resources. In order to achieve this, there needs to be much tighter attention to the process of assessment. Current multi-page standardised assessments need to be used with sensitivity. In many cases, completion of the forms is seen as the primary objective where forms are the 'master' and the assessor is the slave to their completion. Many assessors lack the professional confidence to identify that forms should be the slave to the assessor and seen as a guide and a tool rather than an end in themselves. Burnout with this type of sterile 'conveyor-belt' social work is common and is often just as unsatisfactory and unhelpful to the service user. The recovery of process, as well as outcomes, needs to be effected if social care workers are to work towards a rights-based model of practice.

157

Personal value base of the individual care worker

This argument raises immediate issues about the personal value base held by the individual social care worker. The current emphasis on measurable outcomes and production of standards and regulations has led to a significant move away from the role of professional and personal values within social care practice. The counter-argument was that these were so ill defined and ill applied to practice as to reduce their usefulness. There seems to be little focus on process; rather the outcome-based approach gives scant consideration to this area.

The notion of rights is also a dynamic concept affected by the perception of the appropriate role of the State in the intervention into the lives of its citizens. The universalist model from 'cradle to grave' no longer attracts the consensus of political agreement. The concept of the business objectives and market forces within social care remains strongly established. In addition, the notion of rights and social care work has to address the tensions between the right to individual liberty versus the right of vulnerable adults and children to protection. The focus on the rights of the individual to live free from State interference was perhaps more evident in the 1960s, following recognition of the oppressive role of many large institutions (Goffman, 1961). In terms of what is seen as appropriate social care intervention, competing values strongly influence outcomes. For example, in the case of an older person living alone in squalor and refusing social work intervention, the social work response deemed appropriate in the current social care climate would perhaps be different from that of 20 years ago. The pre-eminence of individual liberty as a core value, thus allowing people to live as they wish, would perhaps have been a more dominant factor affecting social work decision making than it is today. In the current climate, responsibility to protect vulnerable adults from harm is seen as of much greater importance. Issues such as the capacity of the individual to make an informed decision would be seen as significant. The proposed Mental Incapacity Bill advocates significant changes to expand and clarify legislation in this area. Figure 6.5 illustrates

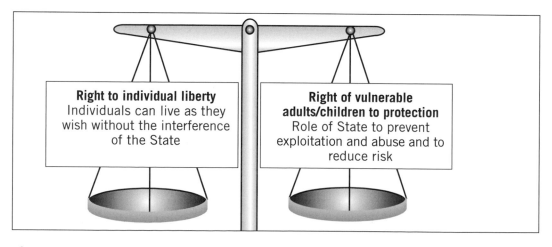

Figure 6.5 Competing tensions in the area of rights between individual liberty and protection

the competing tensions in the area of rights between individual liberty and protection.

Social care role and responsibilities

In the current social care climate the social worker working with the situation of an individual living in squalor would need to persist to try to build a relationship and to assess accurately the potential risks. A multi-disciplinary professionals' meeting would be valuable. This would comply with s 47(3) NHSCCA 90 which requires Health and Housing to be involved in an assessment where appropriate. Risk assessment and a detailed care plan to address risks would be a more likely outcome than would have been the case 30 years previously.

Achieving the right to high standards of residential or nursing care is another area in which there is likely to be a high degree of consensus about the essential importance of quality care. However, it must be recognised that there are significant tensions within the field of social care provision, which do not make the achievement of high standards of care as straightforward as it would appear on the surface. Since the introduction of community care with the NHS and Community Care Act 1990, the local authority is required to spend 85 per cent of its social care budget in the private, voluntary and independent sectors. This reflects the political commitment to market forces within the field of social care. There is also the concomitant demand on local authorities to use their ability to 'block-purchase' to keep down the costs of purchased care. Whilst this may have worked in the first few years of community care, there is now a growing problem, as increasing numbers of social care providers will not accept the rates that local authorities offer. There may be differences of £200–£300 per week between what the local authority will pay and what the social care establishment will accept. Using a resident's own savings to pay care costs under the capital limits is not seen as good practice, but there is a growing problem that there is an unfilled gap of finance that no one is legally bound to fill.

Effects of compartmentalisation of social policy

Social policy in the UK has traditionally tended to be compartmentalised, with social care seen as a separate area to education or health; the result in practice is that one area of social policy can work against another area. One example of the lack of joined-up thinking within social policy can be seen in the implementation of the Care Standards Act 2000, which led to a substantial reduction in the number of residential homes. During the 15-month period until April 2003, 745 independent care sector homes closed, with a loss of 15,100 vacancies (Laing and Buisson, 2003).

The Community Care (Delayed Discharges) Act 2003 came into force in January 2004. The aim was to reduce the long waiting period for some adults to be able to leave hospital when they are medically fit. Lack of social work staff and limited budgets are only a few of the problems that affected speedy discharge from hospital. The current legislation indicates that if a ward so wishes it can issue a Section 2

Diversity and Rights in Care

(Community Care (Delayed Discharges) Act 2003) notice to the local social services to advise that someone has been admitted (although this is not compulsory). In practice, this rarely happens. Often the first notification to be received by a local authority is a Section 5 notice, which gives social services only 72 hours in which to undertake an assessment and set up an appropriate package of care, whether this is residential, nursing, or home care. After this period, the local authority can be charged £120 per day per patient. In practice, the concerns are focused around the difficulties of responding to such tight and unrealistic deadlines when there are few staff. In many areas, there are few residential homes that will take local authority payment rates, which are seen by many homes as not financially viable. Additional difficulties may arise in obtaining home care services at Christmas and the school holidays in terms of the agencies' ability to take on additional work. It is a universal situation that local authorities struggle with the budgets they have available, given the limited amount that central government provide. To penalise a local authority that has a limited budget by fining them is an extraordinary response that has not linked up areas of legislation and social policy. The Care Standards Act 2000 has resulted in a significant closures of care homes but this has not been linked to the hospital discharge penalties for local authorities under the Community Care (Delayed Discharges) Act 2003. However, of greatest concern is the effect such tight deadlines might have on the service user.

There are serious concerns that there is the potential to rush a vulnerable adult into a major life-changing decision on the basis of one rushed assessment visit. Where risk is involved there is often pressure to 'play safe' and many local authorities have residential beds set aside. Once into that environment the opportunity to maintain independence and self-care skills is not great. Home care packages often take more time to set up, monitor and maintain. Pressures on ceiling limits for expenditure per week for older people vary from one authority to another but is additional real pressure that affects the outcome and degree of choice available for the service user.

Financial rights

In the field of financial rights, there has been a growing body of concern and anger around the denial of people's rights to free care under the NHS Continuing Care Scheme. This provision has been unfairly denied to significant numbers of the population due to restrictive and limited interpretation of the eligibility criteria. The NHS appears to have inappropriately retreated from funding health care needs. It has taken case law to redefine the appropriate responsibilities. The findings of the 1999 Royal Commission on Long-Term Care for the Elderly were not accepted by the government. Instead, the NHS Plan 2000 indicated that the NHS should take financial responsibility for nursing care. The Health and Social Care Act 2001 s 49 forbids local authorities to purchase nursing care. A three-banded scheme of financial support to meet nursing care needs was introduced in October 2001. The Registered Nursing Care Component was introduced initially for self-funding residents of nursing homes, but by 2003 it was extended to include local authority residents in nursing care. The resources required and practicalities of implementing these measures were not fully taken into consideration, resulting in massive staff work overloads in trying to reach the large numbers of older people involved. More recently, the growing body of criticism has been reflected in the Health Services Ombudsman's Report 2003, which was severely critical of the restrictive criteria around Continuing Care Funding implemented by Primary Care Trusts (PCTs) and Strategic Health Authorities. In practice, many people had been denied eligibility for Continuing Care Funding due to variations in the criteria used and inconsistency between PCTs in how they were applied in practice. The report clearly indicated that the existing processes were variable and not robust or transparent. Many PCTs and Strategic Health Authorities are revising their current procedures and reporting back the results to the Health Services Ombudsman. In terms of rights, the 'right' to continuing care funding has, therefore, been established in theory but has not always worked to the best advantage of those people it was designed to reach. This serves to highlight that in the field of social care establishing a right to an entitlement in an area such as continuing care is not always enough to ensure its smooth operation in practice.

Case law such as the Coughlan judgement, R v N & E Devon Health Authority, *ex-p.* Pamela Coughlan (July 1998) has also established clearer parameters, clarifying the ongoing financial responsibilities of Health Authorities. As funding for NHS services is free at the point of delivery, development and clarification of this area are vital in establishing people's financial rights. These are key developments in the face of growing numbers of nursing homes being unwilling to take local authority funding rates, which commonly are between £100–£300 per week less than the rate that nursing homes count as sufficient to run a business. The business objective of many social care establishments is to make a profit. Combined with budgetary pressures on local authorities, this mixture of social care and profits motive can be identified as failing to work in the interests of the service user.

Implications of the Human Rights Act 1998 for social care

Up to 5 years ago the issue about rights would have been significantly more limited than is now the case. The key change has been the adoption and implementation of the European Convention on Human Rights, enacted in the Human Rights Act 1998. Prior to this date, English courts did not have to take these principles into account. Challenging a breach of human rights was a long and expensive process. The adoption and implementation of the Act is not a static and reactive process, in that all domestic legislation has to be given a meaning in line with the key principles and articles of the Human Rights Act. Conflicts must be identified and a proactive approach adopted to ensure legislation complies with the Act. In some cases, such as the Mental Health Act 1983, a new Act is needed to ensure compatibility with the overarching requirements of the Human Rights Act 1988. In addition, any case law decisions must take account of European decisions in terms of precedent. For a fuller discussion of the Human Rights Act 1998, see Chapter 7.

Reflect on practice

What rights do your service users have? What key skills do you need to advocate for your service users? Think about the effect that written reports can play in working towards a rights-based approach.

Key skills needed
- accurate knowledge and high quality skills in communication and negotiation
- knowledge of the nature of rights and the limitations of current law
- ability to advocate and network.

Summary

○ There has been a major shift in the culture of social care over the last 20 years towards a technical-rational approach.

○ The universalist model from 'cradle to grave' has been replaced by the concept of the business objectives and market forces within social care.

○ The notion of rights within social care work has to address the tensions between the right of individual liberty versus the right of vulnerable adults and children for protection.

○ In social care, law reflects deeply rooted beliefs about how and when the State should intervene in the life of its citizens.

○ There is a plethora of guidance, legislation, regulations and local policies, requiring local authorities to provide services. However, there is much confusion about the entitlement of individuals and families to those services.

○ Problems associated with funding include the long waiting periods endured by service users for detailed financial assessment and concerns about the accuracy of assessments. People find the level of intrusion into their private finances unacceptable or anxiety provoking. There are considerable variations between authorities with regard to maximum charging.

○ Since the introduction of community care with the NHS and Community Care Act 1990, the local authority is required to spend 85 per cent of its social care budget in the private, voluntary and independent sectors.

Understanding law in relation to local authorities

Introduction

Skilled and effective social care practice needs to take into account the specifics of law and guidance. Familiarity with the key principles and provisions will enable social care workers to effectively apply law to the individual situations they encounter. This knowledge will also make gaps or mistakes in practice clear and allow the social care worker to promote the rights of the service user and carer. Partnership is the underpinning principle of effective social care practice and applies as much to working with the local authority and other agencies as to working with service users and carers. The chapter aims, initially, to identify the general responsibilities of local authorities and then to move into the specifics of social care law. Important general legal frameworks include anti-discriminatory legislation, the Data Protection Act 1998 and the Human Rights Act 1998. The second part of the chapter covers some of the law, guidance and codes of practice specific to social care. The tables contained in Appendices A.1 to A.5 cover specific principles relating to community care, child care, youth justice and housing legislation.

> ### Aims *This chapter aims to enable you to explore:*
>
> 7.1   Local authority responsibilities
>
> 7.2   The law and policy directly affecting social care provision
>
> 7.3   Bedrock law
>
> 7.4   Specific law in relation to social care provision

7.1 Local authority responsibilities

The role of the local authority in terms of social care services has changed significantly in the last 10 years. Prior to this era, the local authority was a major provider of services, whereas now the key roles for local authorities in terms of adults are:

- assessment of need
- commissioning/purchasing of services such as residential care and home care
- monitoring of services quality and value for money
- coordinating hospital discharges in line with the Community Care (Delayed Discharges) Act 2003
- protection of vulnerable adults from abuse.

Understanding the roles and responsibilities held by the local authority will greatly help to promote relationships between the two sectors and, on an individual basis, promote increased professionalism and good practice. The key issue to recognise is that as the local authority has purchased a social care service, it is ultimately responsible for the quality of care even though the provider may be independently owned and run.

The key legislation affecting local authorities in the field of community care, children and families, mental health, youth justice and housing legislation is summarised in Appendices A.1 to A.5.

Assessment of need of a disabled person

The local authority has clearly defined responsibilities and duties to promote the welfare of people who have sensory, physical or mental health difficulties, as defined by s 29 of the National Assistance Act 1948. The key way of targeting resources appropriately rests on the local authority undertaking an accurate assessment of need. The NHS and Community Care Act 1990 makes it clear that there are two situations where someone is eligible for an assessment:

- where he or she needs or appears to need community care services (NHS and CCA 1990 s 47(1))
- where he or she is disabled, he or she has an automatic right to an assessment and should be informed of this – s 47(2). This strengthens the previous legislation, Disabled Persons Act 1986 s 4, which indicated that, if a disabled person or his or her representative requested an assessment, the local authority had a duty to carry it out.

The legislation and guidance make it clear that it should not be made difficult for an assessment to be undertaken. Although a low threshold is needed, the process of obtaining one still depends on the decision of the local authority. The inference is clear that it is the responsibility of the local authorities to define what 'need or appears to need services' means in practice. Also the definition of disability is usually understood in terms of permanent and substantial effect on the activities of daily living that have been present for at least six months. The definitions of disability in practice remain heavily skewed towards physical disability. The 'right' to an assessment is therefore by no means automatic.

Clear awareness of the criteria to qualify for an assessment is also not always found and there have been significant errors made in this area. In one case a woman whose husband had a brain tumour phoned social services asking for help with her mother, who had Alzheimer's and who was also living with her. Clearly looking at the above criteria, the woman's mother and husband could have been assessed under s 47 NHSCCA 90 and the woman herself offered a carer's assessment under s 1 Carers Recognition and Services Act 1995 or under the Carers and Disabled Children Act 2000, if either the husband or mother declined an assessment. Instead the response was to ask how much money her mother had saved. No assessment was offered and the only help received was a booklet containing details of private residential accommodation. The situation came to a crisis point some months later after the woman had struggled alone to cope and had placed her mother in a residential home that was unsympathetic to her mother's needs. Correct understanding of the law is vital, not only to ensure good standards of social work practice but also to act as an advocate on behalf of a service user or carer. The importance of any frontline staff having a clear understanding of the importance of this legislation cannot be overstated.

Purpose of assessment

It is also essential to have a clear understanding of the purpose of assessment. Law and guidance make it very clear that **need, risk and services** are the three areas to be assessed and a decision made in the form of a care plan. Once an assessment has been undertaken, the resulting care plan is seen as a binding legal document and local authorities should meet the identified needs. However, there is concern that the additional phrasing 'within available resources' has been used as a get-out clause. Although a care plan is not referred to in legislation, it should record the objectives of the social services intervention. It should also cover the implementation plan and contingency arrangements and the

It is essential to have a clear understanding of the purpose of assessment

identification and feedback of unmet needs. Case law has proved useful in clarifying some of the boundaries about the rights of service users to have their identified needs met with a service provision. For example R v Essex County Council, *ex-p.*

Bucke (1977) COD66 (QBD) involved Essex seeking to transfer packages of care to cheaper home care providers. The general point made by the judge was that the local authority can take account of resources with the proviso that it never forgets that the **needs of the user are to be regarded as of greater importance than the need to save money** (Mandelstam, 1999: 575). The case of R v Cornwall County Council, *ex-p.* Goldsack (1996) threw some light on judicial interpretation of the nature of assessment of need. The judge indicated it should not be at an excessive level of detail. To record specifically that a person needed 15 hours of assistance with walking would mean that variations of provision would become too complex and therefore unworkable in practice.

The concept of need is not precise either in law or practice. The definition of need from the DoH is of necessity generalised and defines need as 'that which is needed to achieve, maintain or restore an acceptable quality of life or independence' (DoH Practitioners Guide 1991). The NHS and Community Care Act 1990 (S 4.7 C1) makes it clear that the local authority is not only required to carry out an assessment of needs, but also to make a decision regarding the provision of services to meet that need.

Key objectives

The six key objectives identified in the Policy Guidance 1990, *Community Care in the Next Decade and Beyond,* provide the direction and purpose of local authorities in the field of social and community care. These are shown in Table 7.1.

Table 7.1 Six key objectives of the Policy Guidance 1990, *Community Care in the Next Decade and Beyond*

1	Home	Keeping people within their own home wherever possible
2	Carers	Inclusion and support for carers is a high priority
3	Assessment	This is the cornerstone of good quality care
4	Mixed economy of care	85 per cent of the local authority budget to be spent in the private, independent and voluntary sectors
5	Responsibility	Clear demarcation of responsibility within the care management process
6	Better value for taxpayers' money	

The areas to be covered by an assessment were defined in the DoH Practice Guidance 1991. Assessment for older people has been clarified by the introduction of the Single

Assessment Procedure with which all local authorities were required to be compliant by April 2004. This was a key development based on the 2001 National Service Framework for Older People. The single assessment procedure is designed to avoid duplication and to ensure that the depth of the assessment matches the level of need. Assessment could, therefore, be on several levels: contact, overview, specialist and comprehensive. In addition, the use of common tools and scales within a Primary Care Trust was designed to overcome regional and local variations in assessment procedures and outcomes. The NHSCCA 90 also requires that assessments should be multi-disciplinary in nature. Section 47(3) of the NHSCCA 90 indicates that Health and Housing should be involved in the assessment as appropriate. In practice, many local authorities have an assessment format that may run into many pages. It is essential that the utmost sensitivity be used in undertaking assessments, whereby the person and his or her needs are allowed to freely indicate his or her situation. There are increasing concerns about the mechanistic way in which assessments are being carried out, which obtain much information but little of the person's real needs and wishes.

The process by which assessment is carried out was defined in the 1991 DoH Practice Guidance as the seven steps of care management (see Table 7.2).

Table 7.2 Seven steps of care management

STEP	ACTION	
1	**Publish information**	Local authorities have legal requirements to publish information about services under the Disabled Persons Act 1986 s 9, the Chronically Sick and Disabled Persons Act 1970 s 1, and NHSCCA 90 s 46.
2	**Assess the level of need**	The person's needs may be simple or complex where multiple needs are indicated. The type of assessment offered will vary according to the apparent level of complexity of the situation. Under Single Assessment, there are four levels of assessment for older people.
3	**Assessing need**	The local authority is required to assess need under s 47 NHSCCA 90 and also to make a decision about services that may be indicated. In practice need, risk and services should be taken into account also using the local authority's eligibility criteria. The assessment should cover the need for services, as defined by s 2 of the Chronically Sick and Disabled Persons Act 1970. In all cases a carer's assessment should be offered.
4	**Care planning**	This document should clearly identify the aims and objectives of the intervention, together with services and a record of unmet need and any areas of disagreement. Contingency plans should also be recorded, the care plan signed and given to the assessed person. This assessment forms the basis for the level of a direct payment.
5	**Implementing the care plan**	This will involve following each local authority's agreed funding-approval procedures with agreed start dates and clearly identified tasks.

STEP	ACTION	
6	Monitoring the care plan	It is the responsibility of the care manager to check that services have commenced on the correct date and are meeting the required tasks.
7	Reviewing	Any new package of care, whether in a social care environment or at home, must be reviewed within the first 6 weeks. Thereafter, there is flexibility to review, but there must be at least an annual review. The local authority is not required to review self-funded packages of care, although if the local authority were involved in some way, it would be good practice to offer this opportunity. There are often major backlogs in reviewing residents on a yearly basis owing to shortages of social work staff and given the current focus on hospital discharges and crisis work within locality teams for older people.

Many of the links between the social care providing sector and the local authority social workers will be in respect of providing an assessment and care plan to the social care agency and reviewing and monitoring how a placement is progressing. At times, a re-assessment of a resident may be necessary where a person's needs have significantly changed.

Feedback from many social care agencies, both in the domiciliary and residential sector, highlight:

- increasing concerns around the delays in these functions being carried out
- difficulties in accessing a social worker, and
- the tick box style of assessment, which does not promote and enhance the service user's views and wishes or the care agency's day-to-day experience.

Whilst the social work shortage is part of the difficulty, the underlying constant pressures to ensure computerisation of assessments, reviews, costings applications, budgets, and so on, place enormous time pressures on social work staff. Social workers are responding to the key pressures on local authorities imposed by the expectations of central government in that the focus is firmly on outputs, i.e., concrete measurable action that has been taken. Whilst consistency and accountability are important objectives, the outcome for service users, carers and social care agencies has not necessarily been an improvement.

Assessment of need for carers

In social care establishments considerable time is involved in working with carers. A clear understanding of their rights and the legislation affecting them is vital in providing a high standard of care.

The effective functioning of community care is heavily dependent upon the contribution of carers within the family and community. The recognition of the importance of the unpaid carers' contribution is contained in three current Acts of Parliament and is one of the core objectives of community care as defined by the White Paper, *Community Care in the Next Decade and Beyond* (DoH, 1990). The first reference in primary law to carers is in the Disabled Persons Act 1986s 8, which requires 'the willingness and ability of the carer to continue to offer that care' to be taken into account by the local authority within their assessment. The Carers (Recognition and Services) Act 1995 s 1 states that a carer is entitled to an assessment of need by the local authority on request. This should, in practice, be carried out at the same time as the disabled person is being assessed under s 47 NHSCCA 90. Best practice indicates that a separate time and place be offered for the assessment and that the carer's wishes and feelings be taken into account: carers do not actually have to offer the care in order to qualify for an assessment. A carer is defined by the 1995 Carers (Recognition and Services) Act as "someone who provides or intends to provide care on a substantial and regular basis". Good practice in a carer's assessment means that his or her social needs and emotional and physical health should be taken into account. There should be a clear identification of the tasks they are undertaking and, as s 8 Disabled Persons Act 1986, an assessment of their willingness and ability to continue. Partnership is crucial with both the carer and in working with other agencies. Reviews should be held regularly and there needs to be good knowledge of local and national resources. It is important to be aware that a carer may need an advocate. The assessment should obtain detailed knowledge of the day-to-day tasks and demands on the carer. Provision of information and knowledge of benefits is also essential. Awareness of changes such as in the Carers and Disabled Children Act 2000 is important as carers can now be offered direct payments in lieu of services.

Community care is heavily dependent on the contribution of carers within the family and community

The Carers and Disabled Children Act 2000 also closes the loophole whereby a carer's assessment was tied to that of the disabled person. A carer can have a separate assessment, even if the disabled person refuses a s 47 (NHSCCA 90) assessment. Good practice is that it should still be offered. However, the legislation carries no automatic rights to services with it. Financial benefits for unpaid carers are limited and many people are excluded. Acceptance of Carers Allowance can also take a carer out of qualification for Income Support (Pension Credit for older people). As Income Support is a 'passport benefit' to many other benefits, this can have the effect of seriously disadvantaging the carer. Consecutive governments have shied away from linking realistic payments to carers on the grounds that overall cost would be extortionate. The avoidance of payment to family members for their caring role is also reflected in the Direct Payments Act 1996, where relatives are excluded from payment for their services. The scheme is focused on an alternative pathway for the purchase of services that would otherwise be commissioned by the local authority. However, a recent change in DoH guidance in 2004 has now eased these restrictions.

Delayed discharges

Increasing pressure is likely to fall on the social care sector for immediate placements within the current demands of the Community Care (Delayed Discharges) Act 2003. It is possible that some people may be inappropriately placed due to the speed with which the law demands care provision be made. It is essential for social care workers to alert the local authority to situations where this may have occurred, particularly if it is felt that the service user could have returned home with a suitable package of care. The vigilance of social care workers in this field cannot be understated.

An additional unexpected offshoot of this stringent approach to hospital discharge is continuing to develop around palliative care. In practice, many nursing homes are stating that they are not specialised in palliative care and that this should be the role of the hospital. When a resident becomes ill, the nursing home, via its GP, will usually send the person to hospital. In practice, many hospitals state that there is nothing they can do medically for this person and immediately wish to send the person out again. The unrealistic pressures of the Community (Delayed Discharges) Act 2003 were evidenced by a recent example is of a woman in her 80s who had an advanced dementia. Her husband had cared for her at home with assistance from a specialist home care team. He became exhausted and deeply stressed. His wife developed extensive pressure sores, and after some weeks the GP sent her to hospital. Within 3 hours of admission, notification arrived for social services to refer her for an assessment for discharge. In hospital, the social worker found the woman in a foetal position and her breathing was shallow. She died within hours. It could be argued that the procedures had lost sight completely of this person and her moral right to die in peace and with dignity, without unseemly squabbling over her bed occupation. Sadly, this is not an isolated or unusual situation and it reflects the human cost of current social policy obsession with outputs, efficiency criteria and finance.

Local authorities may be subject to fines

The avoidance of adequate debate around resourcing changes in hospital discharge has resulted in conflicting pressures at a local level, which often do not work in favour of the service user or for workers employed in the social care sector. The Community Care (Delayed Discharges) Act 2003, enacted in January 2004, has resulted in local authorities being fined at a rate of £120 per person per day, where they have not been able to provide the social care resources needed. At worst, the local authority teams are given 3 days' notice by a hospital to make discharge arrangements. However, the completion of a full assessment needs to be backed by the immediate release of funding and the availability of a range of vacancies in the social care sector at the right price. None of these pre-conditions can be fully met in such time scales. Increasing numbers of social care homes have shut and a growing body of homes will not take residents at the rates the local authority pays. In many cases, there is no possibility of anyone else paying a 'top-up' fee. Hence one body of legislation such as the Care Standards Act 2000 has had the unseen effect of reducing provision, thereby adding to local authority problems. Rather than address these difficulties, another raft of social policy has the effect of fining social services and reducing their already overstretched budgets. Social policy is, therefore, not the coordinated linkage of centralised initiatives but a series of conflicting and disparate demands in terms of outcomes, processes, time-scales and targets, which do not appear to take account of the real pressures in the social care field at a local level.

Protection of vulnerable adults

The 2000 DoH document 'No Secrets' (2000) recognised the importance of adult protection and the role of the local authority. Each local authority is now required to have a borough-wide adult protection policy. The Protection of Vulnerable Adults (POVA) is a major initiative identified in the Care Standards Act 2000 and taken forward by the DoH to tackle this area. The central aim of POVA is to set up a list that identifies care workers who are unsuitable to work with a vulnerable adult. Often in the case of adult protection concerns involving nursing and residential care, there is overlap between social services and the Commission for Social Care Inspection. In practice, whilst all cases should be notified to the CSCI under Regulation 37 of the Care Home Regulations 2001, their main remit centres on the quality of care provided within that home. In cases of concern about an individual, it took a ruling from the High Court to identify that social services have the lead role. Usually, a strategy meeting (involving all parties, including the local authority and the CSCI attending) may be held in cases of concern in the social care sector. This may be widened to their involvement within the domiciliary care agencies, now that they too have to be registered. There are clearly identified procedures and regulations for residential and nursing homes in terms of notifying social services of concerns and the local CSCI. Within each social care agency, there must be clear procedures so that staff know how to proceed in cases of concern. One recent heartening trend has been the increasingly active role taken by the police in this area. In reality, it is not always easy to obtain sufficient evidence to gain a conviction (required by the Crown

Prosecution Service prior to court action being initiated). As a result, the police have been reluctant to spend time and effort in this area, though this trend is now changing. It is also of interest that more cases have been brought to court and in several cases custodial sentences have resulted.

In cases where social care workers feel they cannot raise their concerns to the management of that home, there are whistle-blowing procedures protected by law. The Public Interest Disclosure Act 1998 has stated that where a worker has 'a reasonable belief' that there has been malpractice, the Act offers protection for that worker for disclosures made in good faith to bodies such as the Health and Safety Executive (Cull and Roche, 2001: 109). There is also protection for workers who raise concerns internally. Disclosures to the media and police are also safeguarded, subject to a specific trigger being identified.

CASE STUDY — Failure to meet a service user's needs

Maisie is aged 87 years and lives in a nursing home. She is normally very quiet and does not make many demands. She was placed in the home by the local authority 9 months ago after she fell and had her hip replaced. No one from social services has ever visited Maisie. There was no care plan and, apart from a contract sent through the post, no one from the placing authority has made contact. Recently, she has become very confused and has started shouting and hitting out at staff. The unit where she is placed say they can no longer meet her needs. What do you do?

Main issues

- Maisie should have been reviewed within 6 weeks of her placement and there should have been a detailed care plan of her needs.
- Her needs have changed and now she needs a reassessment.
- Contact should be made with the placing authority and a reassessment of need requested.
- It is important to inform the local authority, as they are funding the placement. It is not good practice to transfer Maisie to another unit without full consultation and agreement with Maisie, her family and the local authority.
- You need to think about your role in ensuring Maisie's rights are upheld. An accurate report is vital, and key staff should be present on the assessment. Knowledge of systems, such as the Registered Nursing Care Contribution and Continuing Care funding should inform your approach. What about Maisie's right to be part of the process and to be fully consulted? Think about putting the exchange model into practice, where time and energy are spent with Maisie to enable her to be fully involved.

7.2 The law and policy directly affecting social care provision

The key factor is to understand how the law and social policy look in real life and how the service users and carers with whom social care workers come into contact are affected. You will also begin to understand why and how your own practice is influenced and understand the reasons for some of the tensions and conflicts that you face.

All the areas of legislation detailed below are central to social care practice. They apply to social care agencies and many voluntary and charitable agencies, as they undertake functions that would otherwise be carried out by the local authority. Hence the legislation affecting local authorities is also binding on social care agencies.

There are 5 types of law that need to be understood in the field of social care (see Table 7.3).

Table 7.3 The structure and types of law

Primary law	These are Acts of Parliament such as:
	• The NHS and Community Care Act 1990
	• The Care Standards Act 2000.
	Acts of Parliament are written like books but instead of chapters, they are called Parts (such as Part III of the National Assistance Act 1948; Acts contain the duties and powers of local authorities).
	Acts have sections not paragraphs. For example, referring to someone who has been 'sectioned' and admitted compulsorily to a psychiatric hospital refers to section 2, 3 or 4 of the Mental Health Act 1983.
	At the end of an Act you may have a Schedule. This is like an appendix or epilogue in a book and contains instructions and duties such as in Schedule 2 of the Children Act 1989.
	An essential aspect of understanding primary law is to know the difference between a 'duty' and a 'power'.
	A duty means it **must** be carried out with no exceptions. In law the word **shall** shows that a duty is present. A power is an action that **may** be carried out by the local authority if resources and the political and economic climate is favourable. The word 'may' in an Act signifies it is a power.
Secondary law regulations	This is law that goes through Parliament and often provides clearer information about how an Act of Parliament is to be carried out. Current examples are the Employment Equality (Sexual Orientation) Regulations 2003.
Directions	These are issued by the Secretary of State to local authorities under the Local Authorities and Social Services Act 1970 s 7. The local authority has a duty to follow these. One example is the Complaints Procedure Directions 1990.

Guidance from DoH	These tend to be of two types. Policy Guidance such as the 1990 White Paper: *Community Care in the Next Decade and Beyond*. The other type is Practice Guidance such as the 1991 *Practitioners' Guide to Community Care*. Policy Guidance gives details around what should be done whereas Practice Guidance gives more information around how it should be carried out.
Case law (also known as common law)	This is made by judgements from the higher courts such as the High Court, Court of Appeal and House of Lords. It is binding on lower courts. With community care there has been a mushrooming of legal challenges since the 1990 NHSCCA given that the wording was very generalised.

7.3 Bedrock law

In working in the social care field, there are both specific and general areas of law that social care workers need to be familiar with. There are three key pieces of general legislation that underpin any intervention within the social care field. These may be referred to as bedrock law since all actions and interventions of social care professionals must incorporate these underlying core legal requirements. There are three key areas of law in social care in this field.

- The Human Rights Act 1998.
- Anti-discriminatory legislation.
- The Data Protection Act 1998.

Human Rights Act 1998

The legal situation in case law regarding social care providers and the Human Rights Act remains ambivalent. On the one hand, it is clear that social care providers are undertaking functions and services that otherwise would have been provided by the local authority. On the other hand, there are two current rulings from the Court of Appeal, one finding that a social care provider was not bound by the Human Rights Act and another relating to a housing association that ruled that they were bound by the Act, as they received financial support from the local authority.

The Human Rights Act 1998 adopted the European Convention of Human Rights (ECHR). This was drawn up after the Second World War to prevent any further recurrence of the mass oppression and genocide of groups such as the Jewish community. It is based on a commitment to individual rights and freedom from State oppression. The Act came into force in October 2000 and is now part of UK law. Previously people had to apply to the European Court of Human Rights in Strasburg, but this is no longer the case, as any legal proceedings in the UK must take account of the Human Rights Act when judging whether an action is legal, rational or reasonable. The Act adopts the ECHR and contains 16 rights. Some of these are absolute rights such as Article 3 'Prohibition of torture'. Others such as

Article 8 'Right to respect for private and family life' are qualified rights so they need to be balanced with risks to and the rights of society. Limited rights cover Articles 4–12 and Protocol 1, Articles 1 and 2.

Key Articles that influence the interpretation and implementation of all the other Articles are **Article 1 'Obligation to respect human rights'**, and **Article 14 Prohibition of discrimination**.

PROHIBITION OF DISCRIMINATION

It is important for all public bodies, including social care establishments, to review and amend their policies and practices to give them a meaning that is compatible with the Human Rights Act. Only in a case of State emergency can the government pull back from some of the Articles. However, some Articles such as Article 2 (Right to life) cannot be changed, except in respect of deaths resulting from lawful acts of war.

Absolute Rights
Article 2 Right to Life
Article 3 Prohibition of Torture
Article 4 Prohibition of Slavery and Forced Labour
Article 7 No Punishment without a Crime

Limited Rights
Article 5 Right to Liberty and Security
Article 6 Right to a Fair Trial
Article 9 Freedom of Thought, Conscience and Religion
Article 10 Freedom of Expression
Article 11 Freedom of Assembly and Association
Article 12 Right to Marry
Protocol 1 Article 1 Protection of Property
Protocol 1 Article 2 Right to an Education

KEY PRINCIPLES

There are two key principles contained within the Human Rights Act 1998: proportionality and non-discrimination.

- **Proportionality** is focused around accountability for decision-making. Policymaking and implementation must take account of compatibility with human rights as well as financial control and must demonstrate that one group is not receiving less favourable treatment than another comparable group.
- **Non-discrimination** is focused around demonstrable procedural fairness and reasoned decision-making. This is to comply with Article 6, which relates to fair determination of people's civil rights.

The Human Rights Act 1998 also includes the **First Protocol**. Article 1 relates to Protection of Property and would be relevant to vulnerable adults who are subject to financial abuse relating to their property and finances whilst in a social care establishment.

Article 8 is especially relevant to working in the social care sector, as it includes reference to protection from intrusion into private and family life.

Where it has been proved in court that a violation of any of a person's human rights has occurred, a range of alternatives is available. This includes damages and declarations of incompatibility, and/or judicial reviews.

APPLICATION OF THE HUMAN RIGHTS ACT TO SOCIAL CARE

Although it is still unclear how far the Human Rights Act 1998 affects social care establishments, it is advisable for them to incorporate the principles of the Human Rights Act into policies and rules, decision-making, staffing and personnel procedures, in running the establishment and also in the manner of relating to the public. Social care is very much involved with protecting and promoting people's mental and physical health. Working in the social care field is at the overlap between private and public life. Allowing people freedom of thought and expression in terms of religion is essential in good quality care. The importance of non-discrimination is identified in Article 14.

Anti-discriminatory legislation

The vast majority of public sector bodies must comply with the equality legislation. However, these laws apply clearly to independent, private and voluntary social care provision if they are providing a service on behalf of a public authority. The local authority will require these agencies also to comply with the legislation.

Anti-discriminatory practice (ADP) is absolutely pivotal in the delivery of good quality social care. Essential skills with ADP include the ability to be proactive as well as reactive. These requirements are also reflected in current equality legislation. In many respects, the Human Rights Act 1990 clearly outlines key general principles, whereas equality legislation such as the Race Relations Act 1976/00 and Disability Discrimination Act 1995 are more specific. Legislation, however, has its drawbacks; there are still many areas of discrimination that have no specific legislation attached to them. One example is discrimination on the grounds of age. Although legislation is planned for December 2006 there is no current legal provision in this area.

Social care workers are involved with a wide diversity of people who are often disempowered and vulnerable, either by reason of the position society accords them, or by the resource limitations they encounter. Anti-discriminatory legislation covers key areas of provision of goods and services, employment, education and housing.

Knowing the law in itself is not sufficient to ensure good anti-oppressive practice. Social care workers and especially those with managerial responsibilities need to develop a critical awareness of their own value base and how this impacts on their own professional conduct.

There are three grounds covered by current discrimination law. These are shown in Table 7.4.

Table 7.4 Grounds covered by current discrimination law

Direct discrimination	This means treating a person less favourably because of his or her race or sex etc.
Indirect discrimination	This means applying a condition that disadvantages a group of people. For example, the previous height requirements for the police disadvantaged some minority groups whose average height was less than the requirements. Another example is of insurance companies charging higher premiums on the basis of post codes on the assumption that areas with higher proportions of black people should be charged more for insurance.
Victimisation	This refers to treating people less favourably once they have raised a concern about the legislation and have instigated a formal complaint or proceedings under the Employment Tribunal.

The current key legislation that covers discrimination includes:

- Equal Pay Act 1970
- Sex Discrimination Act 1975
- Race Relations Act 1976
- Disability Discrimination Act 1995
- Human Rights Act 1998
- Disability Rights Commission Act 1999
- Race Relations (Amendment) Act 2000
- Special Educational Needs and Disability Act 2001
- Employment Equality (Sexual Orientation) Regulations 2003
- Employment Equality Regulations (Religion or Belief) Regulations 2003.

All the current areas of legislation are implemented by commissions; for example, the Disability Rights Commission was established by the Disability Discrimination Act in 1999. All these agencies have codes of practice.

The majority of equality legislation covers areas such as employment, housing, access to goods and services, and education. However, the Race Relations Amendment Act 2000 has extended public authorities' responsibilities to any functions they carry out.

- Disability Discrimination Act 1995 (Amendment) Regulations 2003 (expected to be implemented in October 2004). This will remove the exemption from small employers and also end the current occupational exclusions such as police, prison officers, etc. Harassment of disabled people by employers will also be outlawed. In addition, prejudice, as a basis for discrimination, will be outlawed. The burden of proof in employment tribunals will alter so that employers have to demonstrate that their actions were not discriminatory rather than the burden of proof being placed with the disabled person to prove that discrimination took place.

● In addition, the Queen's Speech 2003 contained the government proposal to legally recognise same-sex relationships as civil partnerships. If passed as legislation the proposals mean that civil partners would be recognised in law. Couples would give notice of their intention to register and after 15 days would be able to complete the registration. There would need to be a formal court-based process to dissolve any partnership.

RACE, DIVERSITY AND EQUALITY

Race equality legislation previously covered areas such as employment, access to goods and services, and education. Under the Amendment Act 2000 any functions of a public authority are now covered. In certain clearly defined situations, positive discrimination is permitted under the Race Relations Act 1976. This covers cases where there is a genuine occupational qualification, or where a particular group has been under-represented. However, when employing an individual in his or her own home an employer is still allowed to discriminate about whom to employ without any legal redress. The essence of the 1976 Act was to establish that it is not legal to discriminate against a person on the grounds of colour, nationality, race or ethnic origin.

The Race Relations Act 1976 has been extended and reinforced by the introduction of the 2000 Amendment. This has made it easier for the Commission for Racial Equality to police and enforce the requirements of the Act by use of compliance notices. The key section is s 71, which states that every body will,, in carrying out his or her functions, have due regard to the need to:

● eliminate unlawful racial discrimination, and
● promote equality of opportunity and good relations between persons of different racial groups.

The Race Relations Amendment Act 2000 developed further the essential importance for anti-discriminatory practice to be proactive. Other agencies that must now comply with this legislation include the police and Customs and Excise. An additional section has also been added (s 19) to ensure that the Act is compliant with Article 14 of the Human Rights Act 1998. This makes it an offence to undertake any action that is discriminatory.

All agencies are required to publish a yearly race equality scheme, which identifies the areas of concern and the Action Plan to address those concerns. This includes areas such as staff training, and ensuring ethnic minorities have access to information and services. There are general and specific duties under this legislation, which relate to policy-making, service delivery, and employment issues such as promotion and training.

SEXUAL ORIENTATION, RELIGION AND BELIEF AND RIGHTS

From December 2003 new regulations came into force covering these areas. This outlaws discrimination in these fields in employment and creates a new category of harassment defined as 'unwanted conduct that violates people's dignity or creates a hostile, degrading, humiliating or offensive environment' (DTI, 2003). The previous categories of direct, indirect discrimination and victimisation also remain in force in these areas.

Data Protection Act 1998 and confidentiality

The Data Protection Act 1998 makes it a legal requirement to keep service user information confidential. This Act establishes rights to confidentiality covering both paper and electronic records. The Act provides people with a range of rights including those shown in Figure 7.1.

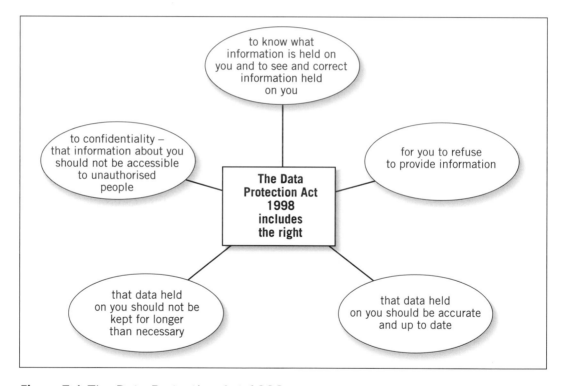

Figure 7.1 The Data Protection Act 1998

The law set out in the Data Protection Act 1998 has been incorporated into the regulations set out by the CSCI and the GSCC. For example, Standard 10 of the CSCI's National Minimum Standards for Care Homes for Younger Adults is set out in Table 7.5.

Table 7.5 Standard 10

10.1	Staff respect information given by service users in confidence, and handle information about service users, in accordance with their home's written policies and procedures and the Data Protection Act 1998, and in the best interests of the service user.
10.2	Service users and their families have access to their home's policy and procedures on confidentiality and on dealing with breaches of confidentiality, and staff explain and/or ensure service users understand the policy.
10.3	Service users' individual records are accurate, secure and confidential.
10.4	Staff know when information given them in confidence must be shared with their manager or others.
10.5	Information given in confidence is not shared with families/friends against the service user's wishes.
10.6	The home gives a statement on confidentiality to partner agencies, setting out the principles governing the sharing of information.

All services now need to have policies and procedures on the confidentiality of recorded information. This has implications for what records may be disclosed to friends and family and policies must also cover a person's right to see his or her own records.

BOUNDARIES TO CONFIDENTIALITY

Service users have a right to confidentiality but a responsibility in relation to the rights of others. Confidentiality often has to be kept within boundaries or broken where the rights of others have to balance with the service user's rights. Keeping confidentiality within boundaries is where a carer tells his or her manager something that he or she learned in confidence. The information is not made public so it is still partly confidential. Information may need to be passed to senior staff when:

- there is a significant risk of harm to a service user
- a service user might be abused
- there is a significant risk of harm to others
- there is a risk to the carer's health or well-being.

Some examples of these situations are given below.

- An old person in the community refuses to put her heating on in winter; she may be at risk of harm from the cold.
- A person who explains that his son takes his money – he might be being financially abused.
- A person who lives in a very dirty house with mice and rats may be creating a public health risk.
- A person is very aggressive, placing the carer at risk.

CASE STUDY – Confidentiality

Ethel is 88 years old and receives home care. One day she says: 'keep this confidential, but I don't take my tablets – I'm saving them so that I can take them all at once and finish my life if my pain gets worse.' Ethel manages to say this before she can be told that some things can't be kept confidential.

Does this information have to be kept confidential? Ethel has a right to confidentiality, but she has a responsibility not to involve other people in any harm she may do to herself. She doesn't have a right to involve a care worker in her actions. The information about the tablets should be shared with appropriate staff and her GP, who might discuss the matter with Ethel.

Ethel's neighbour stops her care worker as she is leaving one day. The neighbour asks: 'How is Ethel? Is she taking her tablets?'

Can the care worker tell the neighbour of his worries? Before giving any information to anyone, carers have to ask the question: 'Does this person have a need to know?' A need to know is different from wanting to know. Ethel's neighbour might just be nosy, and it would be wrong to break the confidentiality without an important reason. If the GP knows Ethel doesn't take her tablets she may be able to save her life. But the neighbour should not be told.

KEEPING INFORMATION ABOUT PEOPLE

The Data Protection Act was passed in order to protect people's rights in relation to the way information could be stored about them. The Data Protection Act 1998 replaced an earlier law from 1984. All information about people now has to be kept in accordance with the following principles.

- Information or data must be **fairly and legally** obtained. People must not be misled about the purposes for which information is gathered.
- Data must be gathered with the **permission** of the people involved and processed for limited purposes.
- Data gathered has to be **adequate**, **relevant** and **not excessive**. Data must be accurate and kept up to date.
- Data must **not be kept for longer than is necessary** for the purpose it was originally gathered for.
- People have the right to find out or **access personal data** being kept about them and certain other **rights** about the way in which data can be used.
- Data must be kept **secure**. Organisations must make sure that data is not lost or made available to unauthorised persons. The security principle means that data must be kept confidential.
- Data **must not be transferred** to a country outside the European Union unless there are guarantees of data protection.

> ### GOOD PRACTICE: INFORMATION
>
> - Keep information confidential and only pass information on to people who have a right and a need to know it.
> - Record information accurately.
> - Keep records safely so that they can't be altered or lost, or seen by people who do not have a need to use them.

ACCESS TO RECORDS

Not all care staff may have access to all the information about service users. CSCI's Minimal National Standards require services to establish written policies on confidentiality and record systems. Services will keep a record for each service user. Some homes may have personal files on residents, which all permanent staff have access to, although some sections may be restricted to senior staff.

The information available to all permanent staff might include personal details such as the person's doctor, next of kin, age and religion. Details of personal finance, action to be taken after a resident's death, and legal arrangements, may be restricted to senior staff because other staff do not have a need to know this information in order to care for residents.

CONFIDENTIALITY AND THE NEED TO KNOW

Good care practice may involve asking service users if we can let other people know things. It would be wrong to pass on even the date of a person's birthday without asking him or her first. Some people might not want others to celebrate their birthday! Jehovah's Witnesses, for example, usually believe that it is wrong to celebrate birthdays. Details should be kept confidential unless the person tells us that it is all right to share the information. The exception to this is that information can be passed on where policies establish that others have a right and a need to know it.

Some examples of people who may have a need to know about individual work with service users are shown in Table 7.6.

Table 7.6 People who may need to know about an individual service user

Managers	He or she may need help in making decisions that affect the service user
Colleagues	These people may be working with the same person
Other professionals	These people may also be working with the service user and need to be kept up to date with information

GIVING INFORMATION

When information is passed to other professionals it should be passed on with the understanding that they keep it confidential. It is important to check that other people are who they say they are. When answering the phone it will be important to be confident of the identity of a caller. Phoning a caller back provides a safeguard that you are talking to someone at a particular number or within a particular organisation. It may be important to ask for proof of identity before passing any information on to a person that you don't know.

Relatives may often say that they have a right to know about service users. Sometimes it may be possible to ask relatives to discuss issues directly with the service user rather than giving information yourself.

Relative:	Has the doctor said anything more about my mother's illness?
Care worker:	I expect your mother would like to talk to you directly. Shall I show you to her room?

It may often be important to explain that confidential information cannot be shared without a service user's consent. Another problem involves the difficulty in obtaining accurate information.

The risks of inaccurate information include:

- serious delays in meeting people's needs
- not being able to follow up enquiries
- making mistakes with arrangements for people's care
- missing meetings or important arrangements
- not providing a professional service to people
- not being able to organise services for others properly
- other professional workers not having the right information.

Many organisations use printed forms to help staff to ask important questions and check that they have taken accurate information. Service users' personal records are likely to be written on forms that use headings. When writing information down it is a good idea to check that the service user agrees with what is being written. It may be useful to check the spelling of names and repeat phone numbers back to the person in order to check that they are correct. Gathering accurate information may also be assisted by using a form or a prepared set of headings to help check relevance and focus of information.

When recording personal information it is important to be as factual and accurate as possible. It is important to describe only the facts or the events that happened, without giving interpretations.

RECORDING INFORMATION, STORING AND RETRIEVING RECORDS

Personal records and information may be kept electronically on a computer, or manually in handwritten or printed files. Whichever way records are kept, there should be a range of security measures to make sure the information stays confidential and is not lost or inappropriately altered.

Manual records

- Keep records in a locked room or a locked cupboard where only authorised staff can gain access to the files.
- Do not be take records out of a particular room or area – to avoid the risk of them being lost or left somewhere where others might see them.
- File records using a system such as an alphabetical one so that they can be found easily.
- Find out about the policy on who should update or change details.
- It may be good practice to record the initials of who made the recording and the date of any changes.

Electronic records

- Keep a 'back-up copy' in case the computer system crashes.
- Use a password security check to ensure that only appropriate staff have access.
- Find out about the policy on the printing of details (similar to manual records) so that hard copies do not get lost, or seen by others.
- Find out about the policy on who is authorised to update or change records. The recording system must prevent information being altered or lost by accident.
- Print out faxed documents in an appropriate confidential area and keep the documents in a manual system to prevent inappropriate people having access to confidential material.

If service users' records are not managed in accordance with the Data Protection Act and NCSC regulations service users might suffer a range of damaging consequences, which might include those shown in Figure 7.2.

If care workers fail to follow appropriate policies and procedures for handling service user's information, they may experience a range of negative consequences, which may include those shown in Figure 7.3.

GOVERNMENT POLICY

In the future there are plans to further increase openness and reduce unnecessary secrecy. (Freedom of Information Act 2001). The onus would be on information to be readily released unless there was evidence that harm would clearly be caused. The possible areas of exemption would be:

- aspects of national security
- internal policy discussions in government
- law enforcement
- personal privacy
- business activities/trade secrets
- safety of individuals, public and environment
- references given in confidence.

Source: Department for Constitutional Affairs

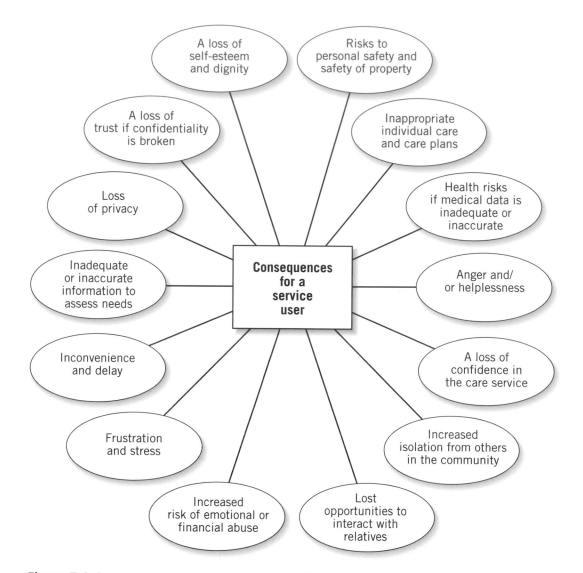

Figure 7.2 Consequences for service users if their records are not managed in accordance with the Data Protection Act and NCSC regulations

The Freedom of Information Act is being implemented in three stages and will come into force in January 2005. The key features include:

- a public right to know about information held and the procedure to access this
- exempted information unless maintaining the exemption can be justified
- rights to access information held by public bodies such as central government, NHS, schools and police. The Data Protection Act 1988 covers access to information by individuals, whereas the FOI 2000 covers information about public bodies
- the creation of an Information Commissioner and Information Tribunal
- schemes for publication of information to be adopted by public authorities. The format of the scheme to be approved by the Commissioner
- accurate and robust systems for managing information.

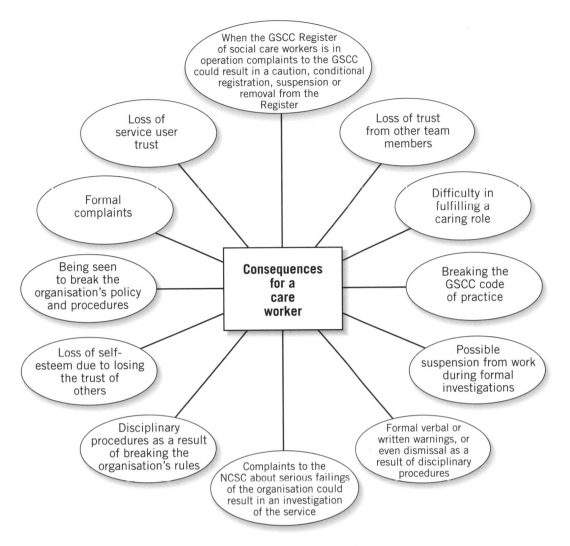

Figure 7.3 Consequences for care workers if they fail to follow appropriate policies and procedures for handling service users' information

7.4 Specific law in relation to social care provision

Care Standards Act 2000

This key piece of social care legislation established the National Care Standards Commission (renamed in 2004 as part of the Commission for Social Care Inspection) and the requirements for registration of social care establishments, including domiciliary care agencies for the first time. The importance of national minimum standards was identified, combined with the use of codes of practice. Protection of vulnerable adults was a core part of this Act and the framework for the registration and regulation of the social care workforce was also established. Independent health establishments and boarding schools were also included within the scope of the Act. The local authority social care domiciliary services and care homes were also now included and required to meet the same standards as other providers. The Act was also responsible for the establishment of the General Social Care Council and the National Care Standards Commission. The CSCI is the key body in regulating social care standards whilst the GSCC is responsible for registration and codes of practice in the social care workforce.

National Minimum Standards for Care Homes and Regulations

The power to introduce National Minimum Standards was introduced by the Care Standards Act. Currently there are fourteen sets of National Minimum Standards as implemented by the Department of Health. In addition, there are 19 sets of regulations covering health and social care. In relation to care homes for older people 38 Standards are grouped into seven clusters. These are outlined in Table 7.7.

Table 7.7 The National Minimum Care Standards for Older People

CHOICE OF HOME	STANDARDS 1–6
Health and personal care	Standards 7–11
Daily life and social activities	Standards 12–15
Complaints and protection	Standards 16–18
Environment	Standards 19–26
Staffing	Standards 27–30
Management and administration	Standards 31–38

Similar areas are identified in the 30 minimum standards for adult placements, but it is interesting to note how much more emphasis is given to individuals' needs, choices and lifestyle than is the case for older people.

National Occupational Standards

TOPSS (Training Organisation for Personal Social Services) has produced a series of occupational standards relating to social care practice, linked to NVQ qualifications. In addition, there are induction and foundation standards linked to the national standards to raise the level of qualification and professional expertise of social care workers. It is vital for all managers and deputy managers to have a copy of these. They can be obtained from **http://www.topssengland.net**

Code of Practice for Social Care Workers (TOPPS)

The six key requirements for social workers outlined in the code of practice are as follows.

1 Protect and promote the interests of service users and carers.
2 Strive to establish and maintain the trust and confidence of service users and carers.

3 Promote the independence of service users whilst protecting them as far as possible from danger or harm.

4 Respect the rights of service users while seeking to ensure their behaviour does not harm themselves or other people.

5 Uphold public trust and confidence in social services.

6 Be accountable for the quality of their work and take responsibility for maintaining and improving their knowledge and skills.

Employers of social care staff are also required to take these requirements into account when making decisions about their employees' conduct. To enhance the professional standards of social care workers there are clear expectations and time scales in terms of qualifications to be achieved by social care staff.

In addition there is also a Code of Practice for Employers of Social Care Workers where five key areas are identified. These are outlined below.

1 Ensure people are suitable to enter the workforce and understand their roles and responsibilities.

2 Written policies and procedures are required to be in place for social care workers to meet the Care Council's Code of Practice for Social Care Workers.

3 Training and development opportunities must be in place for workers to develop their skill and care knowledge.

4 Policies must be in place to deal with dangerous discriminatory or exploitative behaviour.

5 The codes of practice must be promoted to care workers, service users and carers.

Quality of care in practice is not always easy to define. A key indicator is provided by the culture of care amongst the staff. Communication is another key issue that cannot be overlooked. For example, it is common for care staff never to have seen the detailed care plan sent by the social worker. One home decided to put copies on the inside of residents' wardrobes as a prompt to all staff. One example of poor communication occurred when an 82-year-old woman with advanced Alzheimer's went into a nursing home for respite care. The social worker and daughter had spent several hours typing a very detailed care plan. In underlined capitals her severe allergy to pork was identified. The daughter visited her mother on the first day to find scrambled egg and bacon being served to her mother. The cook knew nothing about the concerns and had never seen a care plan for any resident. In many homes, only a certain grade of staff were allowed to write in the care notes, lower paid staff were not shown care plans and lines of communication of concern were very unclear. In better social care homes, the domestic and catering staff were included in training programmes.

Law in practice in social care

The increasing regulation of the social care workforce is a major change in social policy and reflects the increasing influence of central government. It is important to identify some of the factors that contribute to the problems of putting policies into practice at a local level.

The stress levels in social care work are high with significant rates of staff turnover and shortages of qualified social care workers. The factors that contribute to this ongoing lack of stability in social care include poor pay and conditions, unrealistic demands in terms of deadlines and time scales, the emphasis on paper/computer recording with concomitant moves away from administrative support, justified in terms that social care workers will become 'multi-skilled'. At an individual level many staff experience a sense of responsibility but with little power or control. Added to this, there may be a sense of backlog and being unable to meet the deadlines. This, combined with achieving the required standards, has resulted in a 'culture of blame' within social work, where fear of legal action is very real. This has created a sense that social care workers need to practise defensively and ensure that no risks are taken, which may not be in line with key objectives such as autonomy, choice and empowerment. In relation to service users, social care workers are all-powerful in terms of individual outcomes. In practice, this is not a view shared by many social care workers, who often feel unable to cope with existing demands, compounded by a constant bombardment of new initiatives.

The level of staffing in social care homes has to meet minimum standards. Many establishments are owned privately and are profit-making organisations. The staffing levels are affected by absence and many social care homes rely on agency staff. In practice, this can make planning for training very difficult, as the priority is to ensure that staffing levels are upheld. The costs of training are considerable. Negotiating with owners for suitable funding may also be problematic. There is great value in being proactive and having a clear training plan for each year with built-in reviews of progress.

What if...

A social worker contacts you to advise that a relative has made an allegation of neglect about a resident. What are your reactions likely to be? What knowledge do you have about your own adult protection procedures? How will you respond and what can you do to facilitate the investigation?

Key issues

- All care homes are required to have proper procedures under the Care Homes Regulations 2001. The National Minimum Standards (Care Homes for Older People) 16–18 cover the protection procedures.
- Regulation 37 Care Homes Regulations 2001 requires any such incident to be reported to the local Commission for Social Care Inspection.
- Record keeping is essential in good quality care. Detailed records of fluids, medication, GP visits and issues of concern should be clearly recorded. Bruise charts, weight records and skin fragility are other key areas. What routine systems are in place to communicate concerns? Are actions recorded with the time and date? Is it clear who is responsible? Forward planning is key.

- The culture of care amongst staff is critical in the delivery of good quality care. Do staff have a sense of personal responsibility and ability to use their initiative?
- Openness, honesty and a clear understanding of the role of the social worker and CSCI. Defensive attitudes do not promote confidence or a sense of being able to work in partnership with other agencies to achieve change.

Summary

○ Government policy and guidance are very clear that partnership is of the essence. They imply a power sharing equality of approach, with the service user and carer using the background knowledge to work effectively to identify and meet their needs and to advocate appropriately where the social care provision cannot meet those needs.

○ An enhanced understanding of the roles and pressures on local government will also promote good relationships with the local authority and the local links with the Commission for Social Care Inspection.

○ Being able to see the broader picture from a national policy perspective may take away elements of 'blaming' the local authority or CSCI for their roles and tasks.

○ Key pieces of social policy, such as the NHSCCA 90 and the National Service Framework for Older People 2001, are supported by the Human Rights Act 1998 Article 14.

○ The local authority has clearly defined responsibilities and duties to promote the welfare of people who have sensory, physical or mental health difficulties.

○ The key way of targeting resources appropriately rests on the local authority undertaking an accurate assessment of need.

○ Need, risk and services are the three areas to be assessed and a decision made in the form of a care plan. Once an assessment has been undertaken, the resulting care plan is seen as a binding legal document and local authorities should meet the identified needs.

○ The effective functioning of community care is dependent upon the contribution of carers within the family and community and recognition of the importance of this is contained in three current Acts of Parliament.

○ Increasing pressure is likely to fall on the social care sector for immediate placements within the current demands of the Community Care (Delayed Discharges) Act 2003.

○ The 2000 DoH document 'No Secrets' recognised the importance of adult protection and the role of the local authority. Each local authority is now required to have a borough-wide adult protection policy.

○ General areas of law that social care workers need to be familiar with include three key pieces of general legislation that underpin any intervention within the social care field. These are the Human Rights Act, Anti-discriminatory legislation and the Data Protection Act 1998.

Appendix to Chapter 7

The appendix presents key legislation relating to:
A.1 Community care
A.2 Child care
A.3 Mental health
A.4 Youth justice
A.5 Housing

Each section begins by identifying the underpinning central legislation – referred to as bedrock legislation because it is so fundamental to all social care practice. The second level identifies the key principles affecting the particular area of legislation. The third identifies specific laws, sections, guidance and knowledge relevant to that particular field of practice.

A.1 Community care: local authority responsibilities

Key

CDCA	Carers and Disabled Children Act 2000
DPA	Disabled Persons Act 1986
NHSCCA	NHS and Community Care Act 1990
C (R&S) A	Carers (Recognition and Services) Act 1995
NAA	National Assistance Act 1948
NHSA	National Health Service Act 1977
HSPHA	Health Service and Public Health Act 1968
CSDPA	Chronically Sick and Disabled Persons Act 1970
MHA	Mental Health Act 1983

Level 1: Underpinning bedrock law

1 Discrimination legislation. Examples include: Race Relations Act 1976/00, Sex Discrimination Act 1975, Disability Discrimination Act 1996.
2 Human Rights Act 1998.
3 Data Protection Act 1998.

Level 2: Principles of community care

Six key objectives in the white paper:
1 community care in next decade and beyond
2 independence at home
3 carers, assessment
4 clear responsibilities identified in care management
5 mixed economy of care
6 better value for taxpayers' money.

s 29 NAA: duty of the LA 'to promote the welfare of adults over 18-years-of-age with sensory, physical or mental health disabilities'.

DIRECT PAYMENTS

- CDCA – direct payments to parents of disabled children and powers to make direct payments to carers over 16 years of age instead of services and disabled 16–17-year-olds.
- Amendment 2000 (over 65 year) plus Health and Social Care Act 2001 require all LAs to have a direct payments scheme from April 2003.
- Direct Payments Regulations 2003 – all LAs to make direct payments to people who are eligible and who want them.
- DPA – empowers LAs to offer direct payments to those aged 18–65.

DISABLED PERSON ASSESSMENT

- s 46 NHSCCA community care plans; s 47(1) – LA must assess if in need of community care services and make a decision; s 47(2) – disabled have automatic right; s 47(3) – must involve health and housing; ss 47(5) and (6) – emergency powers
- s 4 DPA.

CARER ASSESSMENT

- s 1 CDCA – assessment of carer if the disabled person refuses a s 47 assessment.
- s 1 C (R&S) A – assessment of carer at time of s 47 assessment.
- s 8 DPA – ability of carer to continue.

GUIDANCE

- DoH 1991 *Practitioners' and Managers' Guide* – seven steps in care management.
- DoH white paper 1990 *Community Care in Next Decade and Beyond* – S4 key objectives.
- *National Service Framework for Older People* 2001 – eight key standards.
- *National Service Framework for Mental Health* – key principles plus seven standards in five areas of service delivery.

SERVICE PROVISION

- NAA: Choice Accommodation Directions Act 1998.
- s 117 MHA – free after-care services on discharge from some sections.

- s 2 CSDPA – list of services the LA is to assess for.
- s 45 HSPHA – power to promote welfare of older people.
- Schedule 8 NHSA s 21 – duty of LA to provide services to vulnerable people
- s 21 NAA – residential care for older and vulnerable people.

EXAMPLES OF RELEVANT CASE LAW

- Gloucester 1997 – LA has the right to set up eligibility criteria.
- Gloucester 1998 – must reassess before withdrawing services.
- Complaints system: 3 local stages; 4 formal remedies
- Public Disclosure Act 1998
- Complaints procedures s 50 NHSCCA s 7 LASSA 1970

CHARGING

- s 22 NAA.
- s 17 Health and Social Services Adjudication Act 1998; Community Care (Residential Accommodation) Act.
- s 49 Health and Social Care Act – LAs cannot purchase nursing care.

A.2 Child care

Key

CA   Children Act 1989

Level 1: Underpinning bedrock law

1   Discrimination legislation. Examples include: Race Relations Act 1976/00, Sex Discrimination Act 1975, Disabled Persons Act 1995.
2   Human Rights Act 1998 – Article 3, Article 8, Protocol 1 Article 2 and principles of proportionality and non-discrimination.
3   Data Protection Act 1998.

UN Convention on the Rights of the Child 1989 – participation, protection and provision. Quality Protects 1999 means additional LA funding to improve services. Artificial division of ss 47 and 17 criticised by DoH.

Level 2: Key principles

1   Welfare of the child paramount.
2   No order principle (s 1 CA).
3   Welfare checklist and reduction in delays.
4   Duties of LA under Schedule 2 CA.
5   Significant harm.
6   Consideration of racial, religious, cultural and linguistic background (s 22).
7   View of the child (s 1(3)).
8   Partnership.
9   Empowerment.

Learning difficulties (white paper, *Valuing People* (2001) – four key values:
1   rights
2   independence
3   choice
4   inclusion.

Level 3: Specific law and guidance

SPECIFIC SECTIONS

- CA s 31 (significant harm criteria) – threshold criteria to establish harm. Amended by Adoption and Children Act 2002 to include a child 'witnessing ill treatment of another', e.g., domestic violence.
- Special Educational Needs and Disability Act 2001; Disabled Persons Act 1986 ss 5–7.

PROTECTION LAW

- CA s 47 – duty to investigate; 17 – prevention of abuse and child in need. Position regarding provision of accommodation clarified by Adoption and Children Act 2002.
- CA s 36 – education order, and s 7 Education Act 1996.
- CA s 38 – interim care order; s 31 – care order – making of care plan now a statutory requirement under Adoption and Children Act 2002 as court unable to make a care order without a supervision order.
- CA s 43 – child assessment order; ss 44 and 45 – emergency protection order.
- Special Educational Needs and Disability Act 2001 – LAs must liaise with school transition plans for disabled school leavers and give advice (s 2) to parents are child's special needs and any special educational provision; s 7 – LEAs must have an independent mediator and (s 3) a Special Education and Disability Needs Tribunal has been set up.

GUIDANCE

- 2000 DoH Assessment Framework.
- DoH 1999 *Working Together*.

ACCOMMODATION

- s 22 and 23 – duties of LA to looked-after children.
- CA s 27 – power for LAs to call in other agencies to help safeguard/promote welfare.

Domestic violence

- Family Law Act 1996 – (s 7) welfare reports.
- Protection from Harrassment Act 1997.
- Family Law Act 1996 Part IV – exclusion; non-molestation orders.
- CA s 37 – court can direct the LA to investigate a child's circumstances;
- s 16 – family assistance order; s 8 residence order; contact order; prohibited steps; specific issue; ss 2–4 parental responsibility.

Changes

- Family Law Act 1996 ss 44A and 35A exclude perpetrator in child protection cases.
- Public Disclosure Act 1998.
- CA s 26 – complaints procedures.
- 1996 – children's service plans.

Recent change: Adoption and Children Act 2002

- s 6.2 – unmarried fathers can acquire PR (parental responsibility) by registering with the child's mother. Step-parents can also acquire PR by agreement.
- Creates guardianship order for children where adoption is not appropriate.
- s 8 – after 3 years, foster parents can apply for s 8 orders.

A.3 Mental health

Level 1: Underpinning bedrock law

1 Discrimination legislation. Examples include: Race Relations Act 1976/00 (s 71), Disabled Persons Act 1995, Sex and Discrimination Act 1975.
2 Human Rights Act 1998.
3 Data Protection Act 1998.

Level 2: Key principles

CURRENT PROVISION

As defined by the Mental Health Act Code of Practice 1983 (revised 1999):

- recognition of human rights
- respect for individuals and AOP practice
- needs must be assessed
- treatment must be given in least controlled/segregated way, taking into account risks to self/others.
- promotion of self-determination/personal responsibility
- discharge from compulsion as soon as possible.

PROPOSED CHANGES

The Mental Health Bill 2002 extends the scope of compulsory treatment into the community. The position of 'informal' long-stay patients is clarified in line with the Human Rights Act 1998. Compulsory detention orders to be reviewed by independent body. Extends the scope of Mental Health Review Tribunals. Approved social worker disappears; instead approved mental health professional (unclear if specialist training will be required at present). Nominated person to replace current pecking order of nearest relative.

Under the terms of the Mental Health Review Tribunal, the burden of proof in future will be for authorities to prove the patient still meets criteria for detention rather than the patient having to prove he or she is no longer mentally disordered.

Level 3: Specific law and guidance

KEY SECTIONS OF THE MENTAL HEALTH ACT 1983

- Mental Health Hospital Guardianship and Consent to Treatment Regulations 1983.
- Mental Health Patients in Community Act 1995 'Supervised discharge' builds on s 25 1983.
- Care programme approach introduced in 1990, upgraded late 1990s.
- s 1 defines mental disorder, mental impairment, psychopathic.
- s 2 – 28 day assessment order.
- s 3 – treatment order (6 months).
- s 3 (1) allows informal admissions.
- s 4 – emergency order (72 hours).
- s 5 – those informally admitted can apply for compulsory admission.
- ss 7 and 8 – guardianship.
- approved social worker (ASW) must inform nearest relative.
- s 13 – ASW assessment.
- s 14 – ASW report.
- nearest relative defined by ss 23 (2) (rights) and 26 (definition).
- ss 35–55 deal with patients involved in criminal proceedings.
- s 55–64 – consent to treatment.
- s 57 – most serious types of treatment, e.g., lobotomy, need doctor and two other appointees. Declaratory relief , i.e., where court decides the extent to which treatment can be imposed on patient.
- s 66 – right of detained to apply to MH Tribunal.
- s 114 (1) – approved social worker appointed by LA.
- s 115 – approved social worker can enter premises.
- s 117 – aftercare is mandatory for s 3 and patients transferred from prison.

- s 121 set up the Mental Health Act Commission.
- ss 127 and 128 – unlawful for staff to ill-treat patients or staff to have sex with patients.
- s 132 – hospital managers must tell detained patients their rights.
- s 135 and 136 – role of police to enter and take patient to place of safety.
- s 145 – definition of patient.

OTHER LEGISLATION AND GUIDANCE

CASE LAW

Winterwep v Netherlands (1979) – European Court defined conditions for lawful detention'

A.4 Youth justice

Key

CDA   Crime and Disorder Act 1998

CJA   Criminal Justice Act 1991

CA   Children Act 1989

Level 1: Underpinning bedrock law

1 Discrimination legislation. Examples include: Disabled Persons Act 1995, Race Relations Act 1976/00, Sex Discrimination Act 1975.

2 Human Rights Act 1998 is not compatible with the Mental Health Act 1983; hence the current revision of the law, especially Articles 3, 5, 6 and 8.

3 Data Protection Act 1998.

Level 2: Key principles

1 s 44 CYPA – welfare principle.

2 s 37 CDA – duty of youth courts to prevent re-offending.

3 Youth and Criminal Justice Act 1999 – restorative justice: restoration, reintegration, responsibility.

4 Schedule 2 CA – duty of LA to reduce the need to bring criminal proceedings and to encourage children not to commit offences.

Level 3: Specific law and guidance

KEY SECTIONS OF CDA

CASE LAW

- Local child curfews extended to 16-year-olds.
- Abolished *doli incapax* – right to silence 10–14-year-olds.
- Established Youth Offending Teams (YOTs).
- s 1 – antisocial behaviour orders (ASBOs).
- s 2 – sex offender orders.
- s 8 – parenting orders.
- s 11 – child safety orders.

- s 40 – LA must make youth justice plan.
- s 61 – treatment orders.
- s 65 – reprimands.
- s 66 – on final warning police refer to YOT.
- s 67 – reparation orders.
- s 69 – action plan orders.
- s 73 – detention and training orders.

OTHER LEGISLATION

- Youth Justice and Criminal Evidence Act 1999 ss 1–7 referral orders.
- s 38 Police and Criminal Evidence Act 1984 and s 23 CYPA 1969.
- s 11 Police and Criminal Evidence Act 1984 – appropriate adults.
- s 25 CA – secure accommodation.
- s 7 CJA – pre-sentence reports.
- s 12 CYPA – criminal supervision order.

RECENT CHANGES

- The Powers of the Criminal Courts (Sentences) Act 2000 re-classifies many sections of previous Acts.
- Referral orders (ss 1–5 Youth Justice and Criminal Evidence Act 1999) – are now nationwide as mandatory sentence for all first-time offenders 10–17 years of age.
- Secure remands nationwide since Sep 2002 under ss 130–133 Criminal Justice and Police Act 2001 Criteria: violent/sexual offence punishable by adult by 14yr + sentence + new = Recent history repeated imprisonable offences while on bail or in LA accommodation + public to be protected from serious harm/ prevent commission of imprisonable offences

A.5 Housing

Level 1: Underpinning bedrock law

1 Discrimination legislation. Examples include: Race Relations Act 1976/00, Sex Discrimination Act 1975, Disabled Persons Act 1995.
2 Human Rights Act 1998.
3 Data Protection 1998.

Level 3: Specific law and guidance

LEGISLATION

- s 1 Crime and Disorder Act – 1998 LAs can apply for an ASBO.
- Housing Act 1996 Part IV:
  - qualifying individuals
  - priority need
  - s 118 enables LA temporarily to house homeless
  - LA has statutory duty to provide accommodation
  - ss 198 and 199 – fear of violence LA can house in area of local connections.
- Housing Grants Construction Regeneration Act 1996 – disabled facilities.
- s 27 Children Act – LA can involve housing.
- Adoption and Children Act 2002 clarifies LA's power to provide accommodation under s 17 Children Act 1989.
- Housing Act 1985 s 8 – duty of LA to consider needs in area.
- s 47 Mental Health Act 1983.
- s 21 National Assistance Act 1948 – LA has statutory duty to provide accommodation for vulnerable and older people.
- Matrimonial Causes Act 1983 s 24; Schedule 7; Family Law Act 1996 – court can transfer tenancies.

RECENT LEGISLATION: HOMELESSNESS ACT 2002

- s 1 – LAs must have homelessness strategy and have a duty to provide accommodation no longer limited to two years. People subject to domestic violence to be treated as homeless if unreasonable to remain in own property.

- s 8 – right to review suitability of accommodation offered (now in force).
- s 14 abolishes the LA's duty to maintain housing register.
- s 16 amends who or what is defined as priority need (includes homelessness, insanitariness, overcrowding, medical welfare, specific locality). People subject to immigration control and/or serious unacceptable behaviour are ineligible/excluded. New LA duty to refer ineligible family to social security (e.g. if intentionally homeless) where children are under 18 years of age.

CHAPTER 8 Diversity and professional development

Introduction

This chapter uses the analysis of professional development contained in the National Occupational Standards. The issues of 'knowing yourself' and identifying barriers to interpersonal understanding are explored in relationship to personal narrative.

The chapter provides an analysis of reflection and the concept of the reflective practitioner. We argue that it is important to identify assumptions about oneself, whatever the depth of reflection involved in professional development. Theories of experiential learning involving the 'Kolb learning cycle' are explored. A brief explanation of learning styles associated with this cycle is provided. The central importance of exploring the self or 'I' is referred back to an explanation of action research. Practitioner research might best be undertaken with the support of others.

The final section of the chapter explores how diversity issues and dominant narratives may inform professional development involving interpersonal work. The role of counselling skills and ways of empowering and assisting service users to re-story themselves are identified.

Aims This chapter aims to enable you to explore:

8.1   Knowing yourself and identifying barriers

8.2   Reflection and the concept of the reflective practitioner

8.1 Knowing yourself and identifying barriers

Professional development within occupational standards for care workers

NVQ Unit CU 7 provides an analysis of professional development within the care sector. The unit requires workers to be able to reflect on and evaluate own values, priorities, interests and effectiveness and to be able to synthesise new knowledge into the development of own practice.

THE FIRST ELEMENT (NVQ UNIT CU 7.1)

This can be interpreted as involving four distinct areas of work.

1 **'Knowing oneself'** Firstly it is necessarily to identify, understand and reflect on our own values, priorities, interests and effectiveness. The first three performance criteria require workers to:

- identify own values, interests and priorities
- identify the impact that these issues have on practice
- acknowledge the factors that affect 'own values'.

Knowledge evidence includes understanding 'factors which affect health and social well-being and the ones of particular importance in your situation' (11).

2 **Reflection** Workers are required to reflect on and identify how personal beliefs and preferences influence own thinking of ways of working with others (PC4). Workers are required to evaluate own strengths and effectiveness in working with others (PC5).

Knowledge evidence includes understanding 'the meaning of the term **reflective practitioner** and how you can become more reflective' (21).

3 **Development of practice** Performance criteria 6, 7 and 8 require workers to monitor the effectiveness of their work, to identify ways in which work can be improved and to produce specific plans for tackling any problems, which may influence effectiveness with different individuals or groups. Knowledge evidence includes the purpose of structuring your own **action research** and developing and implementing these in structured ways (18). Point 30 asks workers to understand 'how you can evaluate realistically the outcomes of your own action research'. Workers are also expected to understand 'the meaning of the term "learning styles" and the worker's own learning style' (16).

4 **Using support** The two criteria on using support require workers to use systems and feedback from others to inform change and development. Knowledge evidence includes 'the support which others may give to reflecting on practice' (8).

THE SECOND ELEMENT (NVQ UNIT CU 7.2)

The second element may be interpreted as focused on the development of own knowledge and practice. Workers are required to:

- monitor advances in knowledge and practice
- identify opportunities to examine and challenge new knowledge
- evaluate others' work
- use others' work to develop own practice
- structure ideas for improving own practice so that ideas can be tested
- monitor own practice for effectiveness, and
- apply new knowledge in all relevant areas.

Knowledge evidence includes developing 'effective ways of challenging and developing yourself in relation to values and attitudes' (20); and 'how to tackle own behaviour and practice effectively when it adversely affects how you work with different people' (22).

Knowing yourself

Having insight into how you have built your own self-narrative may provide a vital basis for interaction with vulnerable service users. You will need to understand your own construction of self in order to be able to understand how you impact on other people. The way in which you interact with service users will be a key issue to analyse if you seek to develop your own practice.

We argue that your own interpretation of self will be influenced by:

- your own social group memberships – diversity with respect to issues such as ethnicity, gender, disability, religion and age group
- your own cultural context – the actual people and media that you have interacted with in the past and currently interact with
- the language community and form of language that you interact with
- your own self-narrative, which will have resulted from the influences above.

Exploring personal narrative

Making sense of your own values, interests, priorities and effectiveness in practice involves you in an act of conscious reflection. But just thinking about values and interests may not take you very far. Knowing yourself may make more sense if you use a theoretical model of self, such as the model explained in this section.

A person's values, interests and interpersonal effectiveness are likely to be embedded in his or her interpretation of life experience. So a starting point for reflection might be to identify some of the key influences on your own personal development. How would you explain your own personal life history? What influence did your parents and/or the people you grew up with exert on your life? What key events and changes have influenced you? What are your favourite films, books and music – if films, books and music are important to you? How would you define your own social group membership? How would you define your own ethnicity, your own age group and social class? Your own gender, sexuality, religion and lifestyle may make you different from some other people who live in a similar location to yourself. It will be vital to identify the context in which you grew up and the cultural assumptions you have adopted if you are to make sense of your own values.

In short, making sense of 'own values and interests' might best be achieved by exploring your own life story. The way in which you explain yourself is likely to influence how you understand others. Constructing your own personal narrative provides an efficient way for evidencing the self-evaluation, discussion, and educational experiences specified in the range statement for CU 7.

Crossley (2000) states that 'the personal narrative is a special kind of story that everyone of us constructs to bring together different parts of ourselves into a purposeful and convincing whole' (67). Personal narrative represents our imagined past, present and future integrated into a storylike construction.

Crossley recommends exploring self-story by working with an interviewer who will ask us a range of questions aimed at eliciting our understanding of self. The interviewer could ask questions that involve the following.

- Imagining your life as the book, what chapter headings would it have?
- What key events have happened to you? What high points have you experienced? What low points have you experienced? Can you identify turning points in your life? What is your earliest memory? Can you think of an important childhood memory? Can you think of an important adult memory or other memory?
- Who are the significant people in your life?
- What are your hopes for the future?
- What stresses or challenges are you facing at present?
- What religious, political and ethical beliefs do you hold?
- Is there a general theme that you could identify to summarise your life?

Undertaking an analysis of your own personal narrative might enable you to identify how and why your own beliefs and values have developed. Your own beliefs and values will influence how you present yourself, including how you dress and your non-verbal behaviour. Your self-narrative is like to influence a first meeting with a vulnerable service user.

What if...?

What if you were working as a care worker, and you were about to meet a vulnerable adult. This person is of a different age, gender and ethnicity than you. The person you are going to meet has experienced a very different life compared with the one you have led.

A wishful interpretation of the encounter might run something like this. You will approach the person using your social skills to put him or her at ease. You will smile and use a gentle tone of voice; you will make it clear that you are working

from a value base that includes displaying respect and dignity towards service users. Your caring attitude will display value for diversity. Because of your high level of interpersonal skill the vulnerable service user will be comforted and reassured and you will all live happily ever after.

A more realistic scenario might be that you would attempt to show respect and value for the vulnerable person, but that he or she will simply look at you with a detached and frozen expression. He or she may appear to respond to the information you offer but no real psychological contact has occurred.

Why aren't values and communication skills enough?

The summary section of the unit specification for CU 7 provides an answer to why effective communication involves more than a value system and behavioural skills.

The second paragraph of the summary section of CU 7 states: 'The first element is about reflecting on and evaluating one's own values, interests, priorities and effectiveness in practice, as it is only through knowing oneself that one can reflect on the effectiveness of one's interaction with others. This is particularly the case in the health and social care sector when so many areas of practice are inter-mixed with potentially conflicting values and priorities. This element is based on the belief that to be effective in practice one needs to know not only the starting point of the people with whom one works, but also one's own basis of action.'

But how is it possible to reflect on and evaluate 'one's own basis of action'? The idea that it is critical to 'know oneself' featured in ancient Greek mythology, but how this might be achieved might still seem mysterious today.

One way of understanding the idea of what it is to be a person is to explore how people function. People experience the world on an emotional and a thinking level. On a 'thinking level', people build and develop their own narrative explanation of self. This narrative explanation results in an infinite range of diversity. If you can understand how you have used different life experiences to build your own self-narrative then you may begin to gain insight into some of the processes that other people may use to develop their narratives.

Another idea for deepening an understanding of the issues that result in diversity might be to reflect on the processes involved in interpersonal work, as explored later in this chapter.

Meeting people – making contact

A lot of the time we will use an automatic processing system when we meet people. We form an outline sense of the other person's emotional state, and we engage with him or her without making psychological contact. An example might be a man who works as a receptionist at a conference centre. Each person must be greeted with a pre-organised set of non-verbal behaviours that are supposed to convey 'friendliness' and respect towards delegates. We all know that these behaviours are false in the sense that they do not represent the true emotional state of the receptionist – they are a stylised response expected in this social situation. The receptionist will answer questions and provide helpful information in a routine way, without learning anything about the many people he will meet. There is no meeting of minds; there is no psychological contact, other than the simple exchange of routine non-verbal behaviour and verbal information in response to questions.

There may be instances in care work where an automatic response is all that is needed. But where care workers are providing an individual service, it may be vital that psychological contact is established with the service user. For example, a healthcare worker could change the dressing on a person's leg ulcer, by announcing his or her intentions and setting to work. The ulcer might be dressed just as well as when the worker makes psychological contact, but the service user is unlikely to feel emotionally safe, valued and perhaps even respected if no psychological contact is established. Psychological contact may be established through conversation. The carer might enquire about the service user's feelings. The carer might communicate that he or she understands the service user's response. On an emotional level, both individuals may establish an openness that could enable them to learn about each other. This emotional level of warmth or acceptance creates the psychological contact that is needed in order to communicate respect, maintain the dignity of, and begin to understand the diverse nature of each service user.

Where a worker and service user have an appropriate level of emotional contact it may then be possible to begin to build an understanding of each other's 'lived experience'. Each person will have a range of social group memberships. Social group memberships will include an individual's gender, ethnicity, age group and perhaps religion, sexuality, relationship status, i.e., father, mother, daughter, sister, brother and so on. Social group membership might be seen as a way of explaining key standpoints on life experience. The life experience of men may be expected to differ from the life experience of women. The life experience of black people may be expected to differ from the life experience of white people. It will be important for care workers to recognise the many different standpoints that may influence the lived experience of others. Each individual will also have a vast personal store of remembered experience. Every person has the potential to build his or her life experience into a narrative explanation of his or her life.

Celebrating diversity requires that carers have the ability to establish psychological contact. Celebration of the diversity of others also requires the ability to begin to learn about the lived experience of others. For some people, this might simply involve listening to and learning about their narrative. For others, it could involve the need for a supportive relationship that might provide an opportunity to begin to organise their own interpretation of the events that have happened to them.

Reflect on practice

There is a story that many years ago an adolescent girl was interviewed about her life in order to assess her mental health. She answered a wide range of questions appropriately until she was asked about what she hoped for in the future. She answered that she hoped to get married and live in a banjo. 'But a banjo is a musical instrument,' replied the interviewer. 'But many of my friends live in banjos,' replied the girl. 'I think they're so much better than living like most people do.' The interviewer suspected that the girl was irrational and perhaps mentally ill.

What emotions do you have when you experience unexpected and unexplainable behaviour in other people?

The interviewer probably felt mildly threatened by the girl; but then the interviewer was unaware that the term 'banjo' was used within the local culture to describe a short, no-through road, which ended in a turning circle!

Barriers to contact

Diversity can cause some people to experience barriers to communication. If we accept the interpretation that people function on both an emotional and thinking level, then we can explore the possibility of barriers to communication at either level.

When a care worker works with a service user who has a very different life experience, there is likely to be a rapid and automatic emotional appraisal of the situation. Difference could create an emotional response of a desire to withdraw. Difference may create anxiety for the care worker. Before anything has been said, the care worker may begin sending non-verbal messages of tension and stress to the service user. The service user will also be making a rapid and automatic assessment of the person he or she sees. The care worker may remind the service user of powerful people who have harmed him or her in the past. This recognition may not be conscious. The service user may automatically 'take against' a worker on the basis of automatic reactions. If the care worker appears tense but smiling, a service user may automatically interpret this 'picture' as insincerity, and interpret the care worker as a dangerous or unpleasant person.

Once the interaction moves on to spoken dialogue there are extensive possibilities for misunderstanding. Where people have had very different life experience they are likely to employ very different concepts, and narratives to symbolise and interpret their experience. Both worker and service user may make false assumptions about the information that they hear, as in the short story above.

8.2 Reflection and the concept of the reflective practitioner

Reflection

NVQ Element CU 7.1 requires workers to be able to reflect on and evaluate their own values, priorities, interests and effectiveness. Performance criteria for this element include reflecting on personal beliefs and preferences, identifying and assessing the impact of own values, interests and priorities and exploring the influence of life experience, cultural and socio-economic factors.

Reflection involves images bouncing backwards and forwards. It therefore provides a metaphor for bouncing ideas about

But what is reflection and what does a worker need to be able to do in order to be able to improve his or her own practice? Reflection involves thinking things over. As a metaphor, reflection could be visualised as reflecting ideas inside the mind like light bouncing between mirrors. Reflection involves complex mental processing that discovers new ideas or new inter-relationships between ideas. Reflection is a thought process – level 5 in Greenberg and Pascual-Leone's analysis (see Chapter 2) – and this may result in answers to problems that are not clearly structured or straightforward. Reflection helps us to cope with uncertainty.

The philosopher John Locke explained the idea of reflection as long ago as 1690 (these ideas are separate from his ideas on the nature of reality). He describes reflection as understanding turning inwards upon itself – a person understanding the operation of his or her own mind: 'Hence we see the reason why it is late before most children get ideas of the operations of their own minds; and some have not any very clear or perfect ideas of the greatest part of them all their lives. Because, though they [ideas] pass there continually, yet, like floating visions they make not deep impressions enough to leave in the mind clear, distinct, lasting ideas, till the understanding turns inwards upon itself, reflects on its operations, and makes them the object of its own contemplation'; (cited in Brown, 1987: 70).

Jennifer Moon (1999) has written a comprehensive study of theories of reflection. Initially, she explains that the word 'reflection' is commonly used in different ways. Reflection might mean considering something in more detail as in the phrase 'let me reflect on what you are saying'. Or reflection might mean thinking about an issue for a purpose – perhaps because we have a problem to solve. Finally, reflection might mean a form of mental processing that is applied to relatively complicated or unstructured ideas in order to achieve a desired outcome (1999: 4). Moon (1999: 62) quotes an analysis by Van Manen, which categorises reflection in four different ways, (see Figure 8.1).

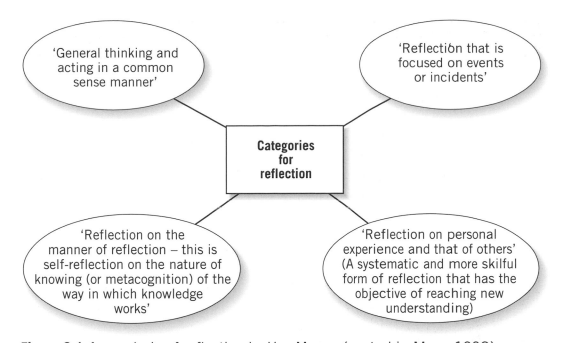

Figure 8.1 An analysis of reflection by Van Manen (quoted in Moon 1999)

Moon (1999) argues that people can use reflection in different ways and can achieve different levels of learning outcomes. She proposes a map of the types of learning that can result from reflective thinking. At the most basic level we may simply notice new things. At the most advanced level we might completely restructure our ideas of who we are and what life should be about (see Table 8.1).

Table 8.1 Moon's five levels of learning for reflection

1	Noticing	Sensory information
2	Making sense	Some links with existing understanding
3	Making meaning	Understanding that can be accessed independently of the context in which learning originally took place
4	Working with meaning	Reflection and reorganising of cognitive structures
5	Transformative learning	Creative restructuring of knowledge structures. May be accompanied with strong emotional reactions

CASE STUDY – Complaints

Every morning a resident who lives in a supported housing complex goes into the office to complain. The complaints might be about anything; sinks that don't empty quickly enough, cars that park too close to a wall, light bulbs that need changing, even though they still work! Naturally, this behaviour is annoying for the people who work in the office. But why does this resident complain?

Moon's five levels of reflection might describe the following examples of thought processes.

Level 1: noticing

Perhaps the interaction always follows a pattern. The person will wait for a short period and then launch into a verbal outburst about what is wrong. During this outburst the resident is unresponsive to the reactions of others. Having completed the outburst, the resident will look for a reaction and then storm off.

Just noticing the detail of an incident provides a start to the reflective process. It is so easy to label a service user as 'difficult' or 'challenging' and then use this label as if it were an explanation – and no further thinking is required.

Level 2: making sense

What does the resident's pattern of behaviour mean? Perhaps this confrontational exchange represents a release of tension. Perhaps the resident does not have the social and emotional skills needed to engage in more sociable conversations? Perhaps the resident is trying to create a sense of belonging within the housing complex. Confrontation is chosen because of limited social skills?

Making sense involves interpreting observation using the concepts and theories available to us.

Level 3: making meaning

What does the resident feel like when going to complain? What is the self-narrative of this resident? Like so many people, the resident may feel a little isolated – a little insecure. Perhaps – like so many people – this resident is thinking 'If I don't feel good then someone else is to blame!' Perhaps these emotions become focused on trivia such as light bulbs and the office staff are a ready focus for blame.

Naturally, real people's stories are more complicated than this, but the thought process above has created an example of thought that is more than just an explanation.

Level 4: working with meaning

A care worker thinking about the problems that service users experience might reflect on the significance of these thoughts. There are people out there who search for other people to blame whenever anything is perceived to be less than perfect. But maybe we do this too! Maybe we say things like 'they' should do something about climate change, house prices, or 'they' should do something about holes in the road? Perhaps we all retreat into a childlike state where we expect a beneficent parent to make the world comfortable and perfect for us. The service user is tapping into the same narrative that most of us adopt from time to time, the storyline that 'they' should make it better.

At level 4, reflection involves new thoughts that could, for example, impact on our assumptions about ourselves. Perhaps the difference between the service user's behaviour and our behaviour is that we are more skilled at knowing how, when and where to have a 'moan'.

Level 5: transformative learning

How far do we take responsibility for our own emotions? If you were a person who had assumed that your emotions are all caused by outside events it could be a major shock to believe that your own thinking can directly influence your feelings. Many of the assumptions we make about life are hard to change. Abandoning the belief in 'they should make my life better' and deciding that 'I' 'create my own emotions', would represent a huge shift in thinking and in the experience of living.

Learning from reflection at this level is not something that can happen on a daily basis. Level 5 identifies the kind of extreme shifts in thinking that change people's lives.

Reflect on practice

If you do not use level 1 and 2 reflective skills when working with people you might be behaving like an automaton – insensitive to the people around you. On the other hand, most people's working day involves meeting mundane deadlines and following procedures. There is rarely time for profound insights and transformation of our understanding about the world. Engaging in professional development should result in some time for reflection and this reflection might go deeper than level 2.

Thinking about levels of reflection, where are the boundaries for your own development?

The importance of both thinking and emotion

Greenberg and Pascual-Leone's (2001) model of levels of processing of meaning (explained in Chapter 2) might also be used in order to explore the idea of learning through reflection. A great deal of human experience will be processed and remembered at an emotional level. We remember sensations and feelings that we associate with people whom we have encountered. Perhaps we can recall feeling threatened in an encounter with an aggressive service user. Perhaps we can recall a feeling of joy associated with gratitude from a service user. Perhaps colleagues are somehow associated with different emotions that cause us to want to approach or avoid them? Our memories will be full of fragmented events that have emotional significance for us. When we work with people we will use feelings as a guide to how we manage an interaction. Many carers can sense how other people are receiving them. Our emotions may often act as a reliable guide to the way we are influencing, or being influenced by, people around us.

On a more conscious level (level 4 in Greenberg and Pascual-Leone's model) everyone can sense things on an intuitive level. We can often guess how a situation will turn out. We have what some people might call a sixth sense – where we know how people are likely to react towards us. At this level, our thoughts cannot be clearly expressed in words. Our understanding is tacit; we can guess things correctly but we cannot logically analyse how we know what we know. Relationships between people are perhaps largely experienced in terms of emotions, sensations and tacit or hidden understanding that cannot be completely expressed using language. Art and music exist because there is so much that we have learned and experienced about life which is only available to us at the first four levels of the 'levels of processing' model.

The fifth level of personal meaning is the level of cognitive processing that involves the mental representation of people and events using language. At this level, we can analyse and evaluate experiences. At an advanced cognitive level, we construct an interpretation of self, of other people and of the world that we live in. The interpretation of life that we build will use culturally available concepts, scripts and narratives. How do we actually do the building? One important activity will be to think things through, to bounce ideas about, or to reflect on the meaning that we attribute to our experiences.

Greenberg and Pascual-Leone's model emphasises that emotional and thinking levels of processing interact. If a care worker is to interpret an interaction with a service user it will be important to recall feelings, sensations and intuitive ideas in addition to attempting to analyse or theorise about what happened. The process of reflecting on experience might involve the creation of new ideas or a new meaning from the integration of intellectual and emotional experience.

Reflection for professional development

Reflecting on experience could involve sitting somewhere comfortable and just recalling something that happened – perhaps a conversation that created a good feeling, perhaps a conversation that created a bad feeling, or reflection on a situation such as the 'complaining resident' above. Thinking the conversation through could involve trying to find links with different levels of knowledge that we possess. A working approach to reflection might involve the following.

- Attempting to analyse the chosen incident using theory. For example, we might try to explain events in terms of concepts such as the 'communications cycle' or conversational management techniques.
- Exploring associations with previous experiences. For example, we might ask ourselves: have we ever encountered a similar situation before – if so, what happened? What emotions or expectations have we associated with the incident?
- Identifying emotional associations. What do we sense or feel about the situation we encountered? What is the significance or what meaning can we attribute to our responses?
- Identifying our own assumptions about 'self'. How did the incident influence our own narrative about 'who we are'? How might our behaviour have influenced the other person's self-narrative?

If reflection is intended to achieve the more advanced learning outcomes described in Moon's model, then it must result in new meaning or understanding. The difference between advanced reflection and 'daydreaming' is that more advanced reflection should result in new ideas or interpretations, whilst daydreaming involves the recall of experience and emotion which might then be forgotten.

NVQ Unit CU 7.1 asks care workers to identify the effects of personal beliefs and preferences on their work with others. Care workers must also evaluate their own strengths, monitor the effectiveness of their work and identify ways of improving performance. Reflection on personal experience, reflection on our own emotions and reflection on our own self-narrative may provide a way to identify these issues.

The results of reflection must be recorded if it is to provide a basis for monitoring and improving performance. Working with a supervisor and agreeing a range of questions to be explored might also help to focus reflection on practice. A person builds his or her own knowledge in the context of social interaction and interaction with media. Working with someone else might be vital to enable some people to fully engage in reflection.

Questions that might be devised to explore relationship work might for example, include:

● How far is effective psychological contact established with service users?
● How far is it possible to develop a supportive relationship and understand the personal needs of others?
● How far do the assumptions built into one's own narrative identity block or assist relationship work with others?

NVQ Unit CU 7.2 requires the ability to develop own practice and this might be done by using reflective learning skills. Donald Schön (1983) put forward the notion that professional workers achieve advanced levels of effective judgement and decision-making by developing their reflective skills. Schön's book *The Reflective Practitioner* (1983) explains how professionals develop ever-more skilled performance by an intuitive process of reflecting on problems.

'Reflection on action' requires time to think and bounce ideas about

One interpretation of Schön's theory is that a reflective practitioner is a person who can access a wide range of conscious knowledge and understanding (at least on a tacit level) and understand how his or her own emotional and cognitive systems work. This type of understanding involves 'thought turning in on itself' as the philosopher John Locke described it. If you can understand the operation of your own emotions and if you can understand the concepts and narratives you use to interpret your own experience then you are working at an advanced level of reflective skill. This level of reflection might involve 'metacognition', i.e. knowledge of your own mental processes and perhaps the ways in which you build an understanding of the world.

The reflective practitioner

Schön stressed the importance of the professional's ability to reflect on his or her actions. Thinking things over at leisure enables the practitioner to build his or her own personal store of knowledge and understanding to guide professional judgement. Schön also identified a skill of 'reflecting in action' that experienced professional workers developed. Schön's observations described how professionals could 'think on their feet' and actively connect with a wide range of personal and theoretical knowledge whilst working with clients. Schön identified the skill of reflecting in action as one of the defining attributes of a skilled, experienced professional worker.

What if…?

You walk towards a service user, who suddenly responds with aggression and threatens to attack you.

One view of the skill of reflection in action is that the care worker remembers previous experiences. Care workers can use their previous experiences to guide their response. Previous experience may be easier to remember if it has been thought through. Reflection may also help workers to discover new ideas.

Can you think of an example that might fit the situation above? Can you think of an example of a practice incident where you have had to think quickly and you have based your response on past experience?

This skill of 'reflection in action' seems to involve the ability to access a wide range of personal knowledge very rapidly. It may be possible that highly experienced carers can monitor their own thinking as they work and interact with others. Critics of Schön, i.e., Eraut (1994), argue that 'reflection in action' is simply the ability to use metacognitive knowledge in situations that require a rapid response. Whatever the exact nature of reflection in action, it is clearly useful to have the ability to be aware of your own thinking processes and personal knowledge as you work with other people. It might be reasonable to speculate that the skill of monitoring your own thinking and personal understanding can be developed by active reflection on experience in more leisurely settings.

In a nutshell, the theory of reflection explains that active thinking work is necessary if a worker is to develop his or her skills. Just memorising information, or just remembering things that have happened, does not result in new skills and abilities. Memories have to be reworked and available to guide future practice through an active process of 'bouncing ideas about'.

The development of practice

A person working within the technical-rational model might assume that effective work performance will result from learning an appropriate range of practical skills, together with sufficient information to enable him or her to perform to a prescribed standard. Continued professional development might, therefore, be reduced to continued refinement of skills and continued in-take or memorisation of information. NVQ Level 4 Standards identify the importance of reflection on personal practice. We interpret these standards as implying a focus on exploring personal systems of thinking.

We believe that the study of personal thinking is best understood from a constructivist approach. A constructivist approach to professional development would understand knowledge as something a professional person works out and builds for him or herself. The social constructivist approach would emphasise the importance of a 'knowledge community' in providing the context for personal learning.

If we adopt the assumption that knowledge has to be actively developed by each practitioner, then it becomes important to adopt some sort of process for actively reflecting on and developing our thoughts. Simply having experiences, or simply reading about theories will not be enough on their own to develop the personal knowledge needed to guide skilled performance.

The development of professional practice is usually explained using theories of experiential learning. Kurt Lewin (1890–1947) originally developed a theory of practical learning that could be used to improve problem-solving skills. Lewin's model argued that experiential learning started with the concrete, practical experience that a worker might have. If a worker carefully thought about his or her experience, he or she would be able to form ideas and generalisations that might help him or her to explain it. The next step of the process would be to test the new ideas out in practice. Experimenting with new ideas would lead to new experiences (see Figure 8.2).

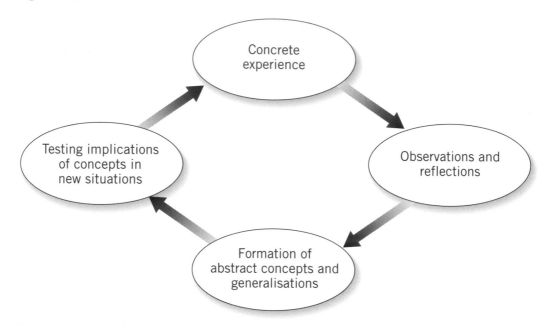

Figure 8.2 Kurt Lewin's experiential learning model as set out in Kolb (1984)

David Kolb adapted Lewin's approach to problem solving and argued that effective learning depended on a 'learning cycle' or a four-stage process, which might be summarised as in Figure 8.3.

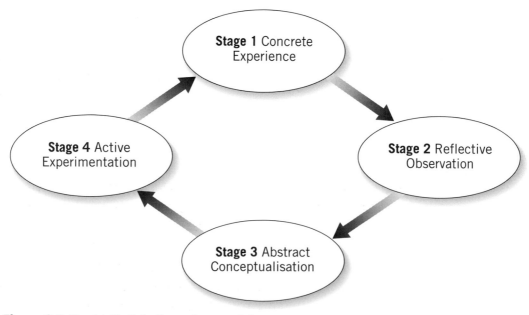

Figure 8.3 David Kolb's 'learning cycle'

An example of this learning process might work something like the study below.

CASE STUDY – A drink at lunchtime

Imagine that you are working with a man with learning difficulty. It is the first time you have met him and you offer him a drink at lunchtime. You offer the person a glass of orange squash by placing it in front of him. He immediately pushes the glass away with a facial expression that you take to express disgust.

Applying Kolb's learning cycle

Within Kolb's learning cycle you have had a concrete experience.

Stage 1

Stage 1 of the learning cycle about the individual needs of this service user is that he has rejected your provision of orange squash. But why has he reacted this way?

Stage 2

Stage 2 involves thinking through some possible reasons for the person's reaction. Perhaps he does not like orange squash? Perhaps he does not like the way you put it in front of him. Perhaps he does not like to take a drink with his meal? Could it be an issue to do with social group membership? For example, could a cold drink symbolise childhood status for this individual? Does he see adult status as defined by having a hot drink? Reflection on the non-verbal behaviour of the service user may provide a range of starting points for interpreting his actions.

Stage 3

Kolb's third stage involves trying to make sense of our reflections. What do we know about different cultural interpretations of non-verbal behaviour? What are the chances that the way we placed the drink in front of the person has been construed as an attempt to control or dominate him? We didn't intend to send this message, but the service user may have interpreted our behaviour on an emotional level as being unpleasant. The more we know about human psychology and social group membership, the more in-depth we can analyse the service user's reaction. We need to choose the most likely explanation for the service user's behaviour using everything we know about people.

Stage 4

Kolb's fourth stage involves 'experimenting' or checking out ideas and assumptions that we may have made. The worker might attempt to modify his or her non-verbal behaviour to look supportive; the worker might show the service user a china cup and saucer to indicate the question 'Is this what you would like?' If the service user responded with a positive non-verbal response then the worker would have been around the four stages of the cycle and would have solved the problem in a way which valued the individuality and diversity of the person he or she is working with.

In real life, workers might expect to have to go round this 'learning cycle' a number of times before they were able to correctly understand and interpret a service user's needs.

How fast can you work through these four stages? Would you be able to think these issues through whilst working with the service user, or would you need to go away and reflect on practice? The answer to this question might depend on the amount of experience you have had in similar situations.

What is your learning style?

Honey and Mumford (1982) developed a theory based on this idea of a four-stage process of learning from experience. They theorised that some people develop a preference for a particular part of the problem-solving process. Some people enjoy the activity of meeting new people and having new experiences but these 'activists' may not get so much pleasure from reflecting, theorising and finding answers to individual needs. Some people mainly enjoy sitting down and thinking things through. These are 'reflectors'. Some people enjoy analysing issues in terms of established theoretical principles. These people are 'theorists'. Finally, some people prefer trying out new ideas in practice. These people are 'pragmatists'. Honey and Mumford have argued that the ideal way to approach practical learning is to balance all the components of the learning cycle. Some people can achieve this more holistic approach. For other people, it might be important to recognise their own biases and to try to compensate for an over-reliance on one style.

Honey and Mumford's theory of learning styles fits the four stage learning cycle as shown in Figure 8.4.

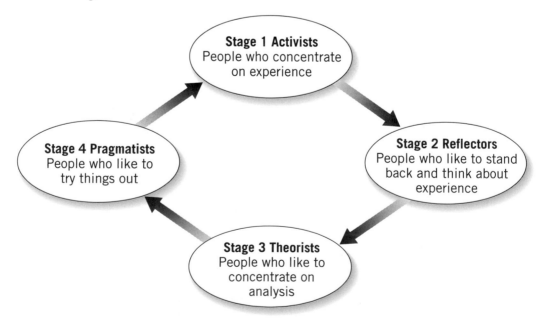

Figure 8.4 Honey and Mumford's theory of learning styles

You can test your own learning style preference or obtain further details of tests based on this theory at **www.peterhoney.com**.

One approach to action research is to adopt this four-stage model of learning from experience. You can monitor personal problem-solving at work by making records of reflection about an issue, or analysis of the issue and records of practical action taken in an attempt to meet service user needs – or solve other practical problems. It needs to be stressed that the 'four-stage' or 'cycle theory' of learning from experience is just one interpretation or model of learning from experience. This model may be useful in practice especially as a way of approaching complicated non-routine problem solving. There are many other ways in which care workers might undertake personal development.

Reflect on practice

Which of the stages of the learning cycle shown in Figure 8.5 do you enjoy most or do you enjoy each of these stages equally?

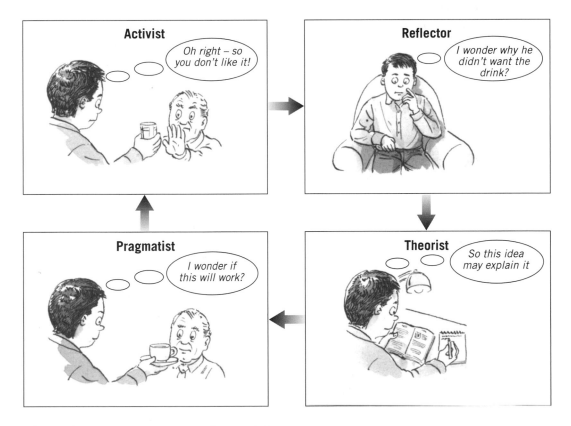

Figure 8.5 What is your learning style?

Action research

Action research is a term used to cover a wide range of different methods and approaches used to develop professional practice. Many different models and definitions of the term have been proposed – see McNiff (1988). In essence, action research represents a form of self-reflective enquiry aimed at the development of professional practice. It is 'action' because it takes the personal actions of a practitioner as the focus of study. It is 'research' because it will employ some sort of recording system in order to monitor performance. Action research will result in conclusions that can be shared with other members of a 'research community'. Results might be validated with reference to the views of other professionals or, more importantly, validated with reference to the response of service users.

McNiff, Lomax and Whitehead (2003) have produced a very useful guide to undertaking an action research project. Although their book focuses on action research within an educational context they provide clear guidance on planning, reflection, monitoring, collecting data and validating research claims within peer group and public contexts. The approach proposed by McNiff et al. (2003) places great emphasis on the need to explore our own thinking. McNiff et al. (2003) stress that the 'I' is at the centre of action research. They state that 'The personal pronoun is important in action research and must, therefore, be used with great care'.

ACTION RESEARCH

How do 'I' fit into the research?

- I am the subject and object of the research
- I take responsibility for my own actions
- I own my claims and judgements
- I am the author of my own research accounts

How do 'I' fit into the action?

- By seeing my own practice as a central focus of my research through critical reflection and self-study
- By encouraging others to participate in a negotiated definition of shared practices
- By showing respect for other ways of doing things
- By showing humility and exposing my vulnerability
- By being open to argument
- By being willing to accept that I could be wrong
- By owning my mistakes
- By standing my ground when principles are at stake

Source: McNiff et al. (1996: 17)

The model of action research as explained by McNiff et al. (2003) provides an effective methodology for systematic personal development. This model also allows great flexibility in the way in which practice can be explored. Reflection on personal narrative and 're-storying' might form the focus of an action research project. The importance of 'I' might be explored through analysis of own narrative.

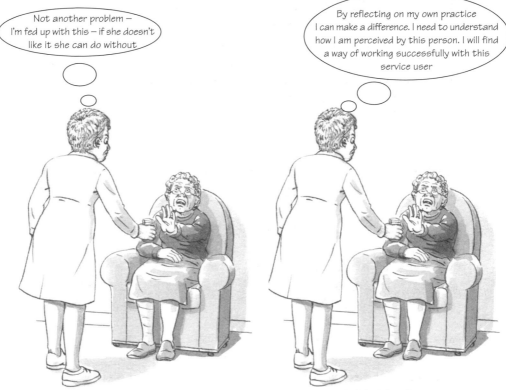

A reflective approach may enable us to go beyond our initial feelings

Developing own knowledge using reflection

Neurologists seek to explain knowledge as involving connections between nerve cells within the brain. Patterns of electrical energy flow along pathways created by our nerve cells. The more we work in set, routine patterns, the more fixed and strong the circuits in our brain become. One way of understanding reflection – at least on a metaphorical level – is that we are undertaking thinking exercises to try and make new connections. We may even attempt to restructure major patterns of routines and assumptions by participating in learning experiences that will reorganise our thinking.

Jennifer Moon (1999) points out that reflective work to develop practice will require the following resources.

● **Time and space**. Questioning assumptions and developing new connections and ideas are difficult to do if you are stressed or tired.

Reflection can help you to develop your own knowledge

- **Someone to work with**. It is possible to develop new ideas just by sitting and thinking, but most people find it very difficult to be motivated to do this unless there is an audience for their thoughts. Knowledge is usually socially constructed or, in other words, you need somebody to bounce ideas about with.
- **An emotionally supportive environment**. You have to be motivated in order to change and develop ideas. It is difficult to think if you don't have the right kind of emotions to encourage you. Many people require an emotionally safe setting in order to be creative. Effective reflection may need to take place in a setting that is free from threats.

Using support

NVQ Standards identify the importance of using support in order to reflect on practice. Support for reflection might come from a mentor, a tutor, or supervisor associated with the training programme. Within care settings many employers will provide a structured system of supervision. The GSCC Code of Practice requires care staff to undertake relevant training, and the Code of Practice for Employers requires them to provide training and developmental opportunities to strengthen and develop skills and knowledge.

Colleagues, co-workers, and service users might also provide support for reflective practice. Having an audience creates a need to clarify ideas in order to share them with other people. It can become necessary to rethink ideas so that other people can understand you. Thoughts can remain unfocused and vague if they don't really have to be explained to anyone.

In order to monitor and assess the outcomes of reflection, professional workers might choose to establish a journal or log book of events. Moon (1999) provides a review of the use of journals within the context of education. She stresses the importance of support in planning and beginning to write journal entries. Setting up a reflective journal is not always straightforward or easy. Among the issues that Moon identifies is the need to identify:

- How much of a journal's recording should be private and confidential and how much should be focused for sharing with other people.
- A system for reviewing and re-reading journal entries.
- A system for arriving at relatively brief and focused conclusions intended for discussion.

One popular method for establishing a reflective journal is to use a 'double entry' notebook (see Figure 8.6). In this model, one page or column is used for a description of events, or for private thoughts, whilst the other column or page is used for analysis or for summaries of ideas that are intended to be shared.

A reflective journal will need an agreed focus and purpose. It might be aimed at reviewing a specific area of practice or an issue or problem. A reflective journal could be used in order to explore your own communication skills. A reflective journal could be used to try to identify your own values and attitudes. Having established the

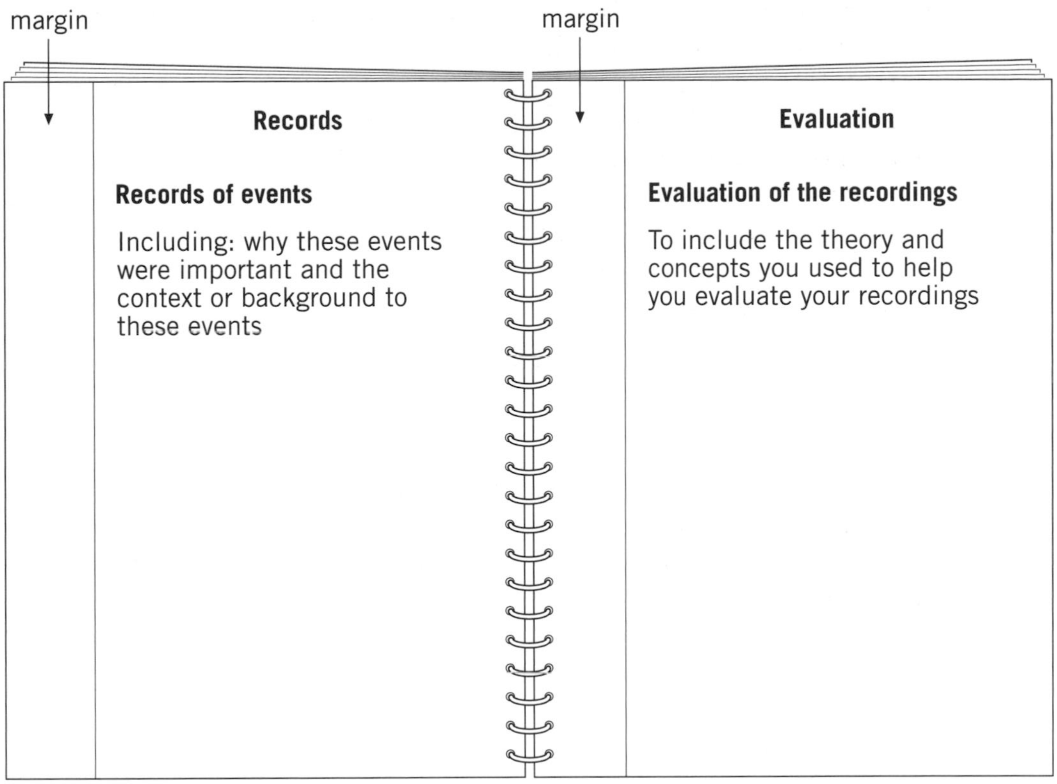

margin		margin	
Records		**Evaluation**	
Records of events		**Evaluation of the recordings**	
Including: why these events were important and the context or background to these events		To include the theory and concepts you used to help you evaluate your recordings	

Figure 8.6 One design for a reflective journal

purpose of the journal it will be important to choose a focus or a starting point for undertaking reflection.

One way to focus reflection might be to choose to record practice incidents. A practice incident is where some significant, meaningful interaction or process takes place. Practice incidents should involve the need to make a decision about what to do or how to respond. A practice incident might involve a focus on how you decided to act. Practice incidents might include working with challenging or demanding situations. They might include details of interactions with service users, colleagues, members of a service user's support network or interactions with other professionals.

In recording a practice incident it might be important to record a description of what happened. It might be useful to record an explanation of why this was significant enough to reflect on. It might be useful to record some details of the context of the incident, such as who was involved and where the action took place. The key focus for reflection might be the decisions or actions that you took and your conclusions on this issue might be focused for discussion with a supervisor.

Reflective journals need not focus on incidents. Moon (1999) describes a range of starting points that can be used as a focus for reflection. Starting points could include ideas such as:

- identifying a specific skill, or other issue to focus reflection and discussion
- identifying a theory as a focus for reflection

- structuring a series of questions associated with practice that require an answer
- designing a concept map to analyse or explain an issue
- exploring a problem through metaphor (complete the sentence 'my life has been like...')
- exploring your own narrative by focusing on a story, such as a book or a film that has made an impact on you
- exploring your own narrative by analysing significant events from your past
- exploring your own narrative by discussing imagery of symbols associated with your life.

The role of narrative in developing your own knowledge and practice

NVQ Unit CU 7.2 requires evidence of practical development work. Professional development might start by looking at practice incidents, or it might start by looking at theory. One of the most effective ways to develop skills is to observe other professionals and reflect on the significance of their actions. As the psychologist Albert Bandura's (born 1925) research suggests, one of the main ways in which humans learn is simply to copy others. A reflective journal can be designed to reflect on observed performance, reflect on own memory of performance, or reflect on a defined area of theory.

Whatever the focus, a good way to evidence the standards for CU 7 would be to design a reflective study, or a research project that explores the application of new knowledge to practice. Exploring diversity and understanding the identity and self-esteem needs of service users could produce a very worthwhile focus for professional development. Your own practice will provide examples of individual needs, but three situations are described in the case study below as a focus for discussion.

CASE STUDY – Three scenarios

- Gloria is an older woman who lives in a care home and constantly talks about the need to go to market to buy yams 'for the children to eat'. Gloria's ethnic identity is classified as black Caribbean. Gloria's behaviour is assumed by some members of staff to be associated with dementia, although there is no medical diagnosis to support this assumption.
- Kian is a young man who has a physical disability and lives in supported housing. Kian is currently working with care staff in order to plan budgets for independent living. Kian enjoys this work and generally has good relationships with the staff. Occasionally, Kian loses his temper and becomes very verbally aggressive without any obvious provocation. After this, he is usually very apologetic and upset that he cannot control his emotions.
- Harriet lives in a care setting that she has personalised with a display of soft toy cats. Harriet has good relationships with most staff. At night Harriet asks any member of staff who assists her to go to bed to name each toy cat individually and pat that cat in order to wish it good night. Some staff think that this 'cat woman' 'is daft' and they refused to engage with her in conversations about the cats.

Reflection on the scenarios in the case study

In order to begin a process of reflection – perhaps working at Moon's first levels of noticing and making sense of information – it might be useful to ask some questions.

- What social group membership issues are there?
- How might dominant narratives distort:
  - the carer's understanding?
  - the service user's understanding of self?
- What feelings or emotional reactions do we experience?
- How can we find out more?
- How can we empower the service users to be able 'to control their own story' rather than re-story their identity for them?

DIVERSITY AND SOCIAL GROUP MEMBERSHIP

Gloria's situation immediately identifies her ethnicity and her identity as a mother as key issues that are important to her. Kian's story suggests that he might have built his own interpretation of disability and living in supported housing. Harriet's story might lead us to expect that she will have built an explanation for being in care.

DOMINANT NARRATIVES

A narrative of 'senility/dementia' may threaten Gloria. Staff might assume that there is little point in listening to her and that her behaviour can be attributed to a degenerative illness. If care staff re-story her as being 'beyond communication' she is likely to experience a lack of respect, together with a lack of support for her identity needs.

Kian's behaviour might be labelled as aggressive and stereotyped assumptions about physical disability being associated with learning disability might be used to interpret his actions. If care staff re-story Kian as difficult and limited, then once again he is likely to experience a lack of respect together with a lack of support.

Harriet's behaviour might be interpreted in terms of a deficit model of learning difficulty. That is, that she treats the cats as if they were real because she lacks the intellectual ability to tell the difference! Harriet has invented her own narrative of cats with identities! The full significance of this may not be easy to understand. However, a total dismissal of her world is likely to be experienced as a lack of respect.

EMOTIONAL REACTION

If these were real people then it might be important to ask ourselves about the level of emotional response we feel. If we have no emotions and feel completely detached from the service users, then it may be that we have come to see them as objects rather than construct them as people. If we have very powerful emotions that caused us a degree of stress then it may be that we are over-involved and not maintaining appropriate boundaries in our work with service users. The five-stage model of emotional and cognitive processing developed by Greenberg and Pascual-Leone (2001) might provide a framework of theory for reflecting on our reactions.

HOW CAN WE FIND OUT MORE?

Care workers are not expected to be psychotherapists, but care workers might be expected to use counselling skills and so be able to build supportive relationships with service users. Carl Rogers (1902–1987) argued that there were six conditions that were 'necessary and sufficient' in a counselling context. Carl Rogers also argued that the humanistic approach associated with the six conditions could form the basis of 'a way of being'. The six conditions could be construed as relevant to the caring relationship and not just to therapeutic interviews. The six conditions are set out and briefly described below.

1	Two persons are in psychological contact.	This means that they can listen to and understand each other.
2	The first, whom we shall term the client, is in a state of incongruence, being vulnerable and anxious.	This means that the client's sense of self is distorted – probably by the need to live up to other people's expectations. A distorted sense of self creates vulnerability and anxiousness.
3	The second person, whom we shall term the therapist, is congruent or integrated in the relationship.	This could be interpreted as the counsellor or therapist is in touch with his or her own creative interpretation of self and is able to value and respect both him or herself and the client.
4	The therapist experiences unconditional positive regard for the client.	This means that he or she experiences a deep respect for the client.
5	The therapist experiences an empathetic understanding of the client's internal frame of reference, and endeavours to communicate this to the client.	This means that the counsellor develops a deep understanding of the ways in which the client thinks about and experiences his or her life.
6	The communication to the client of the therapist's empathetic understanding and unconditional positive regard is to a minimal extent achieved.	This means that the client believes that his or her counsellor has understood and respected him or her.

In a supportive caring context these six conditions could be paraphrased as:

1 It is necessary to make psychological contact. An understanding of emotional barriers and the complex nature of diversity may assist with this.
2 The service user may be vulnerable.
3 If a care worker has explored theories of diversity together with his or her own self-narrative, he or she may be sufficiently open to diversity so as not to feel threatened or defensive when working with people who are very different.

4 The care worker does not judge other people or evaluate them in terms of the care worker's own narrative. This non-judgmental approach conveys respect.

5 The care worker seeks to build an understanding of key aspects of the service user's identity or self-narrative.

6 The care worker uses effective listening and communication skills to maintain a relationship.

All dialogue involves the exchange of assumptions and storylines. If care workers are to build supportive relationships with vulnerable service users then listening and communication skills need to embody the principle of being non-judgemental, and seeking to understand the self-narrative of others.

EMPOWERMENT

Gloria may have stories of her life in the Caribbean; she may have stories of her friends and relatives, stories of her children. Gloria's construction of herself may be threatened in a care home where strangers surround her. The simple act of being listened to may make her feel safer. Active listening over a period of time might result in insights into Gloria's needs. Perhaps Gloria would like to visit a market in the company of friends and relatives who understand her identity? Another critical component of conversation work will be to provide a context in which Gloria can begin to make sense of the events that have resulted in her coming into care. By talking about the past, Gloria may be able to move her own story on. The care worker should not attempt to re-story Gloria's narrative, but Gloria may be able to re-story her sense of who she is if she has an audience for her conversation. If you have people's attention then you have power; powerful people always have an audience. It is in the nature of vulnerability that no one will be interested in your story!

Kian explains his angry outbursts in terms of a moral defect. He is afraid that people will reject him and yet he does not know how to control his emotions. Once again he might be able to find his own explanation for his behaviour, and negotiate a way of managing his feelings if he had a supportive listener who could work within the outline of the humanistic approach set out above. Sometimes care workers might cautiously explore different ways a person's story could be told, but it is critical that the service user has control of his or her own narrative.

Harriet has a story to tell. By learning her story of 'toy cats with a personality', care workers would be showing respect for her construction of reality. But this might feel a little scary. Harriet has broken a convention that adults are not supposed to attribute personality to inanimate objects. It is quite all right for adults to attribute unreal attributes to other people when they are in love – it is not the action of projecting personality and emotion that breaks convention. Rather, it is the unwritten rule that only children may practise this activity with objects. Care workers may feel that breaking with the convention about projecting personalities could compromise their own self-narrative.

Care workers have a right to a narrative as well as do service users. If a care worker feels threatened, then this threat might be an ideal issue for further reflection. Harriet is not behaving normally in inventing personalities. But then normality is only normal within specific communities of people. In some ways, diversity is the opposite of being 'normal'. Provided carers do not feel excessively threatened, perhaps Harriet's narrative could also be the basis for a caring conversation which might progress towards establishing the symbolic meaning of the cats for Harriet. Such a conversation might convey respect and value to Harriet.

Summary

○ A central issue for professional development is the understanding of own assumptions and thinking processes – in action research this involves a focus on 'I'.

○ Understanding our own self-narrative is necessary in order to understand our feelings and reactions towards other people.

○ Understanding and celebrating diversity should assist us in making psychological contact with people who have experienced life differently. The ability to understand others involves openness and a willingness to participate in new learning.

○ Reflection involves active work with memories of experiences and with theory. Just knowing information or remembering that events have happened will not result in skilled performance.

○ The reflective practitioner is someone who can access and think through a wide range of personal experience in order to respond effectively to situations that arise in practice.

○ One way of trying to understand learning involves a four-stage learning cycle. Some people may prefer some stages of this process to others.

○ Professional development is likely to require support.

○ Developing reflective thinking skills and engaging in practice-based research may help to develop new insights into our own and others' explanation of identity and self-narrative.

○ Basic counselling skills may provide a useful tool to assist in co-creating a story.

References and further reading

Ang-Lygate, A. (2000) 'Everywhere to go but home: on (re)(dis)(un)location', *Journal of Gender Studies*, 5 (3): 375—89.

Argyle, M. (1993) *The Psychology of Social Class*. London: Routledge.

Atkinson, D. (2000) 'Bringing lives into focus: the disabled person's perspective', in D. May (ed.) *Transition and Change in the Lives of People with Intellectual Disabilities (Research Highlights in Social Work)*. London and Philadelphia, PA: Jessica Kingsley.

Banks, S. (2001) *Ethics and Values in Social Work* (2nd edn). Basingstoke: Palgrave Macmillan.

Bems, M. (1990) *Contexts of Competence: Social and Cultural Considerations in Communicative Language Teaching (Topics in Language and Linguistics)*. New York, NY: Kluwer Academic/Plenum.

Breakwell, G. (1986) *Coping with Threatened Identities*. London and New York, NY: Methuen.

Brennan, M. (1991) 'British Sign Language: the language of the deaf community', in S. Gregory and G.M. Hartley (eds) *Constructing Deafness*. London and New York, NY: Pinter and the Open University Press, 174—87.

Brien, D. (1991) 'Is there a deaf culture?', in S. Gregory and G.M. Hartley (eds) *Constructing Deafness*. London and New York, NY: Pinter and the Open University Press, 46—52.

Carranza, I.E. (2003) 'Genre and institution: narrative temporality in final arguments', *Narrative Inquiry*, 13 (1): 41—70.

Clark, C.L. (1999) *Social Work Ethics: Politics, Principles and Practice*. Basingstoke: Palgrave Macmillan.

Croft, S.E. (1999) 'Creating locales through storytelling: an ethnography of a group home for men with mental retardation', *Western Journal of Communication*, 63 (3): 329—45.

Crossley, M. (2000) *Introducing Narrative Psychology: Self, Trauma and the Construction of Meaning*. Buckingham: Open University Press.

Crystal, D. (2003) *The Cambridge Encyclopaedia of the English Language*. Cambridge: Cambridge University Press.

Cull, L.A. and Roche, J. (2001) *The Law and Social Work*. Maidenhead: Open University Press.

De Fina, A. (2000) 'Orientation in immigrant narratives: the role of ethnicity in the identification of characters', *Discourse Studies*, 2 (2): 131—58.

DOH (2002) *Care Homes for Older People: National Minimum Standards*. London: HMSO.

DOH (2003a) *Protection of Vulnerable Adults Scheme in England and Wales. A Practical Guide*. London: HMSO.

DOH (2003b) *Regulatory Impact Assessment for the Phased Implementation of the Protection of Vulnerable Adults Scheme*. London: HMSO.

Eraut, M. (1994) *Developing Professional Knowledge and Competence*. London: RoutledgeFalmer.

Erikson, E. (1963) *Childhood and Society*. New York, NY: Norton.

Floersch, J. (2000) 'Reading the care record: the oral and written narratives of social workers', *Social Service Review*, 74 (2): 169—93.

Freedman, J. and Combs, G. (1996) *Narrative Therapy*. New York, NY, and London: Norton.

Frith, M. (2004) 'Ethnic minorities feel strong sense of identity with Britain, report reveals', *The Independent,* 8 January.

Garland, J. (1993) 'What splendour, it all coheres: life-review therapy with older people', in J. Bornat (ed.) *Reminiscence Reviewed: Perspectives, Evaluations, Achievements (Re-thinking Ageing).* Buckingham: Open University Press.

Gersie, A. (1997) *Reflections on Therapeutic Storymaking: The Use of Stories in Groups.* London and Bristol, PA: Jessica Kingsley.

Goffman, B. (1991) *Asylums.* Chicago, IL: Penguin Books.

Goldsmith, L. and Beaver, R. (1999) *Recording with Care. Inspection of Case Recording in Social Services Departments.* London: Social Services Inspectorate (Department of Health).

Goleman, D. (1996) *Emotional Intelligence: Why it Can Matter More than IQ.* London: Bloomsbury.

Graddol, D. (1993) 'Three models of language description', in D. Graddol and O. Boyd-Barrett (eds) *Media Texts. Authors and Readers (Language and Literacy in Social Context).* Clevedon, Philadelphia, PA, and Adelaide: Multilingual Matters and the Open University Press, 1–21.

Graddol, D., Cheshire, J. and Swann, J. (1994) *Describing Language.* Buckingham and Philadelphia, PA: Open University Press.

Graddol, D., Leith, D. and Swann, J. (1996) *English History, Diversity and Change.* London and New York, NY: Routledge and the Open University Press.

Greenberg, L.S. and Pascual-Leone, J. (2001) 'A dialectical constructivist view of the creation of personal meaning', *Journal of Constructivist Psychology,* 14: 164–86.

Groce, N. (1991) 'Everyone here spoke sign language', in S. Gregory and G.M. Hartley (eds) *Constructing Deafness.* London and New York, NY: Pinter and the Open University Press, 13–30.

Halliday, M.A.K. (1993) 'Language as social semiotic', in J. Maybin (ed.) *Language and Literacy in Social Practice (Language and Literacy in Social Context).* Clevedon, Philadelphia, PA, and Adelaide: Multilingual Matters and the Open University Press, 23–43.

Harre, R. (1998) *The Singular Self: An Introduction to the Psychology of Personhood.* London: Sage.

Health Services Ombudsman (2003) *NHS Funding for Long Term Care of Older and Disabled People.* London: HMSO.

Health Services Ombudsman (2004) *Ombudsman's Report on Continuing Care Update.* London: HMSO.

Holmes, J. (1992) *An Introduction to Sociolinguistics (Learning about Language).* London and New York, NY: Longman.

Holmes, J. (1996) 'The role of compliments in female–male interaction', in J. Maybin and N. Mercer (eds) *Using English: From Conversation to Canon (English Language: Past, Present and Future).* London and New York, NY: Routledge, 32–6.

Holstein, J. and Gubrium, J. (2000) *The Self We Live By: Narrative Identity in a Postmodern World.* New York, NY, and Oxford: Oxford University Press.

Honey, P. and Mumford, A. (1982) *The Manual of Learning Styles.* Berkshire: Ardingley House.

Hunter, L. and Oumaru, C.E. (1998) 'Towards a Hausa verbal aesthetic: aspects of language about using language', *Journal of African Cultural Studies,* 11(2): 157–71

Hymes, D. (1993) 'Towards ethnographies of communication', in J. Maybin (ed.) *Language and Literacy in Social Practice (Language and Literacy in Social Context).* Clevedon, Philadelphia, PA, and Adelaide: Multilingual Matters and the Open University Press, 11–22.

Iser, W. (1980) 'The reading process: a phenomenological approach', in J.P. Tompkins (ed.) *Reader-response Criticism:*

From Formalism to Post-structuralism. Baltimore: Johns Hopkins University Press.

Knight, P. (1998) 'Deafness and disability', in S. Gregory et al. (eds) *Issues in Deaf Education.* London: David Fulton, 215—24.

Kolb, D. (1984) *Experiential Learning: Experience as the Source of Learning and Development.* Englewood Cliffs, NJ: Prentice Hall.

Lambrou, M. (2003) 'Collaborative oral narratives of general experience: when an interview becomes a conversation', *Language and Literature,* 12 (2): 153—74.

MacClure, M. (1993) 'Mundane autobiography: some thoughts on self-talk in research contexts', *British Journal of the Sociology of Education,* 14 (4): 373—85.

Malinowski, B. (1993) 'The problem of meaning in primitive languages', in J. Maybin (ed.) *Language and Literacy in Social Practice (Language and Literacy in Social Context).* Clevedon, Philadelphia, PA, and Adelaide: Multilingual Matters and the Open University Press, 1—10.

Mandelstam, M. (1999) *Community Care Practice and the Law.* London: Jessica Kingsley.

Maybin, J. and Mercer, N. (1996) *Using English: From Conversation to Canon (English Language: Past, Present and Future).* London and New York, NY: Routledge and the Open University Press.

McLeod, J. (1997) *Narrative and Psychotherapy.* London: Sage.

McNiff, J. (1988) *Action Research: Principles and Practice.* London: Routledge.

McNiff, J., Lomax, P. and Whitehead, J. (2003) *You and Your Action Research Project.* London and New York, NY: RoutledgeFalmer.

Mead, G.H. (1934) *Mind, Self and Society (Works of George Herbert Mead).* Chicago, IL: University of Chicago Press.

Misselbrook, D. (1997) 'A paper that changed my thinking', *British Medical Journal,* 314 (7077): *355.*

Montgomery, G. (ed.) (1995) *Language for the Eye: An Anthology of Deaf Writing and Publication.* Edinburgh: Scottish Workshop Publications.

Moon, J.A. (1999) *Reflection in Learning and Professional Development: Theory and Practice.* London: RoutledgeFalmer.

National Institute for Social Work (NISW) (1991) *Empowerment, Assessment and Care Management and the Skilled Worker.* London: HMSO.

Ratzan, R. (1992) 'Winged words and chief complaints: medical case histories and the Parry—Lord oral formulaic tradition', *Literature and Medicine,* 11: 94—114.

Reissman, C.K. (1993) *Narrative Analysis (Qualitative Research Methods).* Newbury Park, CA, London and New Delhi: Sage.

Sacks, O. (1991) *Seeing Voices.* London, Basingstoke and Oxford: Picador.

Sanderson, H., Kennedy, J., Ritchie, P. and Goodwin, G. (1997) *People, Plans and Possibilities.* Edinburgh: SHS.

Saxena, M. (1993) 'Literacies among the Panjabis in Southall (Britain)', in J. Maybin (ed.) *Language and Literacy in Social Practice (Language and Literacy in Social Context).* Clevedon, Philadelphia, PA, and Adelaide: Multilingual Matters and the Open University Press, 96—116.

Schon, D. (1983) *The Reflective Practitioner.* San Francisco, CA: Basic Books.

Seedhouse, D. (1988) *Ethics: The Heart of Health Care.* Chichester: Wiley.

Selden, R. (1989) *Practicing Theory and Reading Literature.* Lexington, KY: University Press of Kentucky/Harvester Wheatsheaf.

Smith, L. and Griffin, J. (2002) 'Conversations with delinquents: the mingling of meagre dialogues: a pilot study', *Journal of Correctional Education,* 53 (4): 127—31

Social Exclusion Unit (1999) *Opportunity for All.* London: HMSO.

Social Trends (1997) Vol. 27. London: HMSO.

Social Trends (2000) Vol. 30. London: HMSO.

Social Trends (2001) Vol. 31. London: HMSO.

Social Trends (2002) Vol. 32. London: HMSO.

Social Trends (2004) Vol. 34. London: HMSO.

Thompson, N. (1997) *Anti-discriminatory Practice* (2nd edn 2001). Basingstoke and London: Macmillan.

Tompkins, J.P. (1981) *Reader-response Criticism; From Formalism to Poststructuralism.* Baltimore, MD: Johns Hopkins University Press.

Toukmanian, S.G. (2002) 'Perception: the core element in person-centred and experiential psychotherapies', in G. Wyatt and P. Sanders (eds) *Roger's Therapeutic Conditions (Evolution Theory and Practice). Volume 4. Contact and Perception.* Ross-on-Wye: PCCS Books.

Venkatesan, R. (2004) 'Settling in a home from home', *The Independent,* 8 January.

Whelton, W.L. and Greenberg, L.S. (2002) 'Psychological contact as dialectical construction', in G. Wyatt and P. Sanders (eds) *Roger's Therapeutic Conditions (Evolution Theory and Practice). Volume 4. Contact and Perception.* Ross-onWye: PCCS Books.

White, M. and Epston, D. (1990) *Narrative Means to Therapeutic Ends.* New York, NY, and London: Norton.

Yusun Kang, J. (2003) 'On the ability to tell good stories in another language: analysis of Korean EFL learners' oral "Frog Story" narratives', *Narrative Inquiry,* 13 (1): 127—49.

Websites

Age Positive: www.agepositive.gov.uk

Commission for Social Care Inspection: www.csci.org.uk (National Minimum Standards can now be accessed at this site)

Department for Trade and Industry: www.dti.gov.uk

Department of Health: www.doh.gov.uk

Equal Opportunities Commission: www.eoc.org.uk

General Social Care Council: www.gscc.org.uk

Laing and Buisson: www.laingbuisson.co.uk

Liberty: www.liberty-human-rights.org.uk

National Care Standards Commission: www.doh.gov.uk/ncsc/about.htm

National Census: www.statistics.gov.uk/census2001/

National Statistics: www.statistics.gov.uk

Select Committee on Health Memoranda: www.parliament.thestationery-office.co.uk/pa/cm200203/cmselect/cmhealth/1

Women's Unit: www.womens-unit.gov.uk

Glossary

action research: a form of self-reflective inquiry that researches the personal actions of a practitioner. A wide range of different methodologies have been proposed to support action research.

anti-discriminatory practice: professional practice that challenges both discrimination and the assumptions that may result in discrimination.

assessment: the process of objectively defining needs, and determining eligibility for assistance, against stated policy criteria. It is a participative process involving the applicant, his or her carers and other relevant agencies (Caring for People, DoH, 1990).

autonomy: the freedom to make individual decisions and choices within boundaries of responsibilities towards others; a degree of independence that acknowledges responsibilities towards others.

becoming need: within Maslow's theory, 'becoming needs', such as cognitive, aesthetic and self-actualisation needs, lead people to fulfil their potential and become everything they are capable of becoming.

care manager: a practitioner who undertakes most, if not all, of the core tasks of care management. The care manager may carry a budgetary responsibility but is not involved in any direct service provision (Caring for People, DoH, 1990).

care plan: systematic method, written as a formal document, for addressing needs and risks in the form of strategies, goals and service provision. A care plan is also essential for monitoring outcomes.

carer: defined in law as someone who gives, or intends to give, regular and substantial care. New

rights to an assessment and a 'willingness and ability to continue to care' also must be taken into account by the local authority.

Care Standards Act 2000: an Act of Parliament that established the National Care Standards Commission.

cognitive processing: self-awareness may involve mental processing at both an emotional and a thinking level. Cognitive processing refers to the thinking level of self knowledge.

Commission for Social Care Inspection (CSCI): the inspection authority that has taken over from the National Care Standards Commission and the Social Services Inspectorate.

communicative competence: the ability to use language that is appropriate to context, and to the participants in the conversation.

community care: the provision of services and support to enable people to live as independently as possible in their own homes or in "homely settings" within the community (Caring for People, DoH, 1990).

conscious processing: another term for cognitive processing.

consistency: a key principle in ethical reasoning. A lack of consistency might imply unfairness or discrimination.

constructivism/constructivist: the theory that people build or 'construct' their own interpretation of self. Constructivists argue that self-concept is not simply 'caused' by life experience or biology; instead, individuals actively invent a self-concept.

CU7: a unit within National Vocational Qualifications in Care entitled 'Develop one's own knowledge and practice'.

deficit needs: within Maslow's theory, deficit needs, such as physical, safety, belonging and self-esteem needs, must be resolved before a person can move on towards fulfilling his or her potential.

disability: a condition that results in a substantial effect on daily activities for at least six months.

discourse: the total rules and behaviours associated with a speech community.

discourse practices: special ways of using language that are distinctive to a speech community.

dominant narratives: ways of making sense of life that dominate a culture or a knowledge community. Assumptions and beliefs that provide a framework for individual self-stories or personal narratives.

eligibility: the conditions set by each local authority to define who may be eligible to receive a service. These conditions may change in response to the financial situation of the local authority.

emotional processing: self-awareness may involve mental processing at both an emotional and a thinking level. Emotional processing refers to the emotional level of self-knowledge.

empowerment: giving power to others. The philosophy that knowledge and power are interlinked means that the ability to take control of your personal narrative represents a form of power.

Equal Opportunities Commission: a commission that has the duty of monitoring gender equality issues in the United Kingdom.

European Union Directives: recent directives require European states to introduce legislation prohibiting discrimination at work on the grounds of age, sexual orientation, religion and disability.

experiential learning: learning that develops from practical experience. An alternative to memorising information or learning theories recounted by others.

Fair Access to Care: national system of eligibility criteria to reduce the 'postcode Lottery' of service provision.

fairer charging: national system of individual assessment care costs introduced to all local authorities. Flat rate charging schemes are strongly discouraged under the new system.

GSCC Code of Practice: a code that lays down key principles to guide the professional conduct of care workers.

hierarchy of human need: a theory put forward by Maslow that identifies different levels of human need. Deficit needs have to be resolved before an individual can progress towards fulfilling his or her potential.

human potential: a central term to humanistic theories of human nature. The purpose of life is perceived as the fulfilment of individual potential.

Human Rights Act 1998: the Act of Parliament that incorporated the European Convention on Human Rights into UK law.

human rights culture: a system of belief that identifies the importance of individual rights and associated responsibilities.

identity: how an individual person identifies him or herself. Social identity might focus on social group membership, while personal identity might focus on a wider range of concepts.

impairment narrative: a dominant narrative that explains disability with reference to defects and impairment.

inner-self: a belief in a 'real' entity within a person that is capable of being discovered and that represents a person's true nature.

Kolb learning cycle: a theory described by David Kolb that identifies four stages within a learning process.

knowledge communities: groups of people who share similar 'worldviews', assumptions and beliefs about social and physical reality.

learning style: the theory that individuals differ in the way that they prefer to learn. Honey and Mumford's theory identifies different styles of responding to the stages identified in the Kolb learning cycle.

life story work: a social care technique aimed at empowering service users to organise and explain their understanding of their life.

linguistic repertoire: the range of different ways of speaking, signing and writing that an individual person can choose from to suit the context of the situation.

metacognition: the ability to explore and to understand your own thought processes; the ability to 'know what you know' or think about your own thinking.

Multi Disciplinary Assessment Panel (MDAP): a meeting of different agencies, carers and service users to discuss complex cases involving funding.

narrative: speech, writing or signing that describes or retells an event or sequence of events. A story that is told.

National Care Standards Commission (NCSC): a body established by the Care Standards Act (2000) with responsibility for establishing national minimum standards of care.

national minimum standards: a set of requirements that forms the basis for inspection of care services. There are different sets of criteria for different services.

National Vocational Qualifications (NVQs): qualifications that focus on occupational competence.

needs: an individual's requirements in order to achieve, maintain or restore an acceptable level of social independence or quality of life, as defined by the particular care agency or authority (*Manager's Guide to Assessment and Care Management*, DoH, 1991).

O Units: a series of units from O1 to O3 found in NVQ Care qualifications. The O units establish basic principles for guiding care practice. The level of O Unit to be evidenced depends on the level of responsibility of the candidate.

PCS model: a model developed by Neil Thompson to explain the levels on which discrimination may operate and the levels on which anti-discriminatory practice needs to operate.

personal narrative: a person's own assumptions about themselves and their life. It may be regarded as another term for 'self-story' but is intended to convey the central importance of narrative and to avoid the risk of 'story' as being perceived as trivial.

phenomenology: the philosophy that our understanding of both physical and social reality is heavily influenced by perception. We do not experience the world as it really is but instead experience our distorted perception of the world.

post-modernist: a theory or work that has moved beyond the assumptions of 'modernism'. 'Modernism' is associated with the 'technical rational' idea that human experience is straightforward and can be quantified, controlled and measured.

power: in this book, power is associated with Foucault's theory that systems of understanding (knowledge) cannot be separated from issues of social control and dominance (power).

practitioner research: inquiry undertaken by members of a specific profession into issues relevant to their practice.

psychological contact: the level of engagement between people in an interaction. The term is used in this book to imply two-way communication i.e. more than a ritualised or routine one-way message.

radical social work: an approach that stresses the importance of 'structural' issues and emphasises the importance of confronting social prejudices.

reflection: a term that can mean 'to think about', but that can also refer to more complicated processes of thinking involving, for example, transformational learning.

reflection (levels of): Jennifer Moon identifies theories of reflection that specify different levels. Moon has developed her own five-stage theory of reflection.

reflection in action: a term associated with the work of Donald Schön that identifies the professional ability to problem-solve whilst engaged with a client or service user.

reflective practitioner: a professional person who is able to think about his or her own performance whilst working with others, and who can analyse this performance independently.

register: the language associated with specific contexts of situation.

re-storying / restorying: the retelling of another person's narrative. Such a retelling may often be altered or adapted by the person who is doing the re-storying.

script: a speech event that is likely to follow a predetermined pattern, and in which one person usually has greater control than the other (e.g. a consultation with a doctor, a cross-examination in a courtroom).

self-actualisation: in Maslow's theory, this term means to make progress in becoming everything a person is capable of becoming. Loosely, the term means to fulfil individual potential.

self-concept: the concept or understanding that a person has of himself or herself.

self-narrative: another term for personal narrative or self-story that avoids the risk of 'story' being interpreted as something trivial.

Sex Discrimination Act (1975) (amended 1986): an Act of Parliament designed to make discrimination on the basis of a person's gender illegal.

social constructivism: the perspective that people build or 'construct' their own interpretation of their lives. Social constructivism emphasises the importance of social context in influencing individual construction.

social group membership: broad social categories that people may identify themselves as belonging to, such as ethnic group, age group, social class, sexual orientation and gender.

speech act: a specific spoken or signed interaction between two or more people (e.g. a joke, question or statement).

speech community: people who share the same rules, behaviours and expectations about the way a language is used.

speech event: the immediate context for a speech act (e.g. a conversation or interview).

speech situation: the immediate context for a speech event (eg. a party or a courtroom trial).

story: speech, writing or signing that describes or retells an event or sequence of events.

supportive relationship: an encounter between people that conveys warmth, understanding and sincerity.

technical rational: the perspective that understanding social and physical reality is a relatively straightforward matter of definition and measurement. In this view, there is nothing inherently problematic about human experience and that definition and measurement of social issues can result in plausible technical solutions.

values: a term that identifies that something is 'valued' or 'valuable'. It becomes problematic if it results in an assumption that human behaviour is governed by an internal system of values.

worldviews: philosophical assumptions about the nature of human understanding. Worldviews may vary, ranging from the idea that human experience is straightforward through to the idea that personal experience is constructed with reference to social experience.

Index